# Don't Ask Her Name

## An Adoption Story

To Lorraine, Harith + family

With love … The family just keeps growing! We are so pleased to be a part of it.

Robyn x

# Don't Ask Her Name

## An Adoption Story

Robyn Cooper

CAPE CATLEY LTD

First published 1998
CAPE CATLEY LTD
Whatamango Bay, Queen Charlotte Sound,
New Zealand



Cover design by Don King
Cover photograph by Wendy St George
Typeset by PK Publications, Picton
Printed in Malaysia

ISBN: 0-908561-71-7

Some of the names in this book, including those of Child Welfare staff, have been changed to protect their identity.

For Ken, and for our children,
Katrina and Aaron.

## CONTENTS

# Acknowledgements

MANY PEOPLE have assisted in the making of this book. I would like to thank Heather Marshall who first taught me how to put a short story together, and Phillip Mann for giving me the encouragement and confidence to turn that short story into a book.

Chris Cole Catley, my publisher and editor, has become my friend and mentor. She has walked with me through the chapters, has become involved with my 'characters', the problems and the see-sawing emotions within the book. I thank her with love and sincerity. Also my thanks to the members of Chris's Wellington writing workshops for their support and for being an extra sounding board.

Thank you to Apii Rongo-Raea and Diane Scarrow for reading and commenting on the draft manuscript; to Alison White, Matt Tizard, Lesley Wallis, Unity Hope, Wendy St George, Kathy Staples, Deborah Bush, Sarah Carlson and Mary Newman for assisting in various ways during the preparation of the book. I thank Teava for holding on to that tape for twenty years, and my father and the Eastbourne Library staff for finding the answers to some rather odd questions.

My story as an adoptive mother is integrated with the personal stories and thoughts of many others in the family and I could not have written it without the agreement of my children, Katrina and Aaron, and their birth parents, and the agreement of other members of the family who are part of this book - my parents Mavis and Trevor, Tom, Brent and Julie, Vicki, Dianne, Lorna and Julie. I thank them all, for the talking and sharing, the help and advice, for allowing me to include personal letters, for reading the script to make sure I got it right, and for love and support and encouragement.

Finally, I thank Roger for his wisdom and understanding and for reading 'the latest page' or chapter without complaint as it was thrust at him fresh off the printer; for not complaining about losing his computer for a couple of years or about ending up as chief housekeeper, cook and gardener during the final stages of the book.

And again, for now and always, my gratitude and love to Glenis and Mary.

*Robyn Cooper*
*Days Bay, Wellington*
*June 1998*

# Chapter One

## MONDAY, 15 December 1969

SHE LIES THERE, fifteen days old. I don't see the heat rash on her face, the glued eyelashes closing an infected eye, the hips splayed out in metal casing. Not yet. I see only a baby, our baby, our daughter.

Matron bends over the cot and lifts the bundle of soft warm flesh and heavy metal into my waiting arms. "Remember, the brace for her congenital hips must stay on at all times, apart from when bathing. You'll have to wedge the napkins between her and the brace. I see you've brought a little dress to take her home in. Sorry, there's no room to tuck it in. Stick to singlets and T-shirts up top." She smiles at us. "Best of luck. She can only improve."

Is this a dream? Is it really happening, this baby? Is she really for us? She looks up at me, alert and contented. I kiss her soft warm cheek. The metal brace digs into my arm and I shift the weight down a little.

We follow Matron through the ward, past the morning tea trolleys with their stainless steel tea urns, thick china cups and saucers, and plates of Griffins vanilla wine biscuits and wholemeal digestives. Mothers sit upright in bed and babies lie beside them, cocooned in their little cribs. Mothers bend over their babies, pick them up, cuddle them, feed them. Everywhere cards and flowers. Red roses and gypsophila, pink and white frilled carnations, yellow carnations, a crimson cyclamen draped with white satin ribbon. Where is our baby's mother? Has she gone home yet?

Matron strides on. Clattering cups. Clinking spoons. Plaintive cries, gusty cries. She presses the lift button. Down to the ground floor and away from the suffocating heat of the maternity ward and into the fresh summer air. Silver beech branches are rustling in gentle differing rhythms and the sun slants twinkling patterns on the pavement. Ken smiles at me. Matron tells us to ring if we have any problems and waits on the hospital steps as we walk back to the car.

Our turquoise-blue 1952 Humber 80 refuses to start. The starter motor has jammed again. Ken lifts the bonnet and leans into the engine.

He's good at cars and knows all about distributors and carburettors and compression ratios and starter motors - I have problems with just getting the bonnet up. Matron remains on the top step, tall and erect. She likes to see her charges off safely. The engine splutters and coughs into life, and we smile at the tall figure in white and wave goodbye.

Ken drives carefully along the motorway and up the hill through suburbia. School is out. School patrol monitors stand on duty at the pedestrian crossing, holding back children from the traffic with stop signs that look like giant lollipops. We drive into the garage and carry our baby up the stairs. Should she go to sleep now? No, she is happy just lying in my arms. We sit in the lounge looking out at the city below, at the bush-covered hills and the peek of harbour. And at our daughter.

So I'm now a mother. Without feeling a developing life within me, without ante-natal classes, without parental training. Just a phone call from Miss Thomas of the Child Welfare Division of the Department of Education. "We have a baby for you."

There are some advantages to this method of family extension. I've had no toxaemia or varicose veins, no uncomfortable nights wondering which way to lie, no excruciating birth pains. I can walk from the hospital without stitches, although I will have problems contributing to the 'difficult labour' anecdotes when it is assumed that my baby has arrived the same way as everyone else's. I can avoid the rigorous stomach exercises. There are no post-natal blues, only incredible elation and pride and love. How can this happen so soon? I've known her for only two hours.

Ken mixes up the milk formula, four bottles' worth, and puts it in the fridge. I don't want to move yet. I think back to Miss Thomas's phone call of three days ago. "We have a baby for you." A call that sent my mind into frenetic twirls. I had phoned Ken. Five rings, six rings, please let him be there, a short silence as the receiver was lifted.

"She's arrived. The baby has arrived. We can go and see her this afternoon. Miss Thomas has just rung." The words had tumbled. I was squeezing the phone too tightly.

"Great. What time? I'll be ready."

"Oh." I paused. "I can't remember. She must have told me. I'll phone you back."

I hope this isn't a mark against us. I hope my intelligence rating for any subsequent baby - no, my mind is jumping ahead too fast - won't be dropped a couple of points. 'Memory poor. Can't retain facts.'

Intelligence matters. Physical features, academic and employment background, health, personal interests and hobbies all matter. They influence Child Welfare's selection of the baby. Matching babies to adoptive parents is important. I suppose that honesty on the application form is important too. Does School Certificate become University Entrance for some? Does an adoptive father with his own milk-run write managing director, or milkman? Do asthmatic birth mothers with a history of heart disease confess all to Miss Thomas and hope that someone with a compassionate heart will want their baby, or do they answer, 'Health good. No family history of insanity'?

She is still sleeping on my lap. The family are on their way to see her. The first grandchild.

# Chapter Two

I WAS THE FIRST-BORN for my parents. I was born in Wellington in the middle of the war years but was unaware of food rationing, or that my father kept a set of pyjamas at the Navy Office where he worked long hours, or of my parents' worries about how the war would end and whether Mum's younger brother would survive the German prisoner-of-war camp.

Two years earlier, in the same Bethany Hospital, another baby had been born. A baby who was to become a close part of our extended family. The baby's mother, unmarried and unable to care financially for her baby son, had worked at nurse-aiding and in the kitchen and laundry at Bethany for the three months leading up to the birth and for three months afterwards, while she also cared for her new baby and made final decisions on his future. She decided on adoption.

My mother's older sister Tresna and her husband Bill became the new parents. They had tried for many years to have children of their own but the trying had produced only miscarriages and heartbreak, and they were thrilled with this addition to their family. They asked of their siblings, family and friends that they tell no one that their new son, Bryan, was adopted. They said they didn't want him to suffer from taunts of illegitimacy. The way he arrived into the family must remain a secret.

The matron at Bethany had given Tresna the names of her new son's natural parents and told her that the father had gone to war. Each day she opened the newspaper to read the names of those listed as 'missing in action' or killed. One day she stopped looking. The baby's father was dead.

I, of course, was not yet around to know anything of this, and it was not intended that I ever find out.

A few months after my birth my parents moved to the nearby city of Lower Hutt. By the time I started school in 1947 my uncle was well back from the war, I had two younger brothers, and polio was reaching epidemic proportions. My mother heard that onion juice was a safeguard against the disease. Each morning I shuddered down a teaspoon of onion juice, a teaspoon of cod liver oil and often a teaspoon of Lane's Emulsion - just to be sure - and took off to school. I don't remember any friends from that first year. I must have reeked.

Primary school days passed with enthusiasm or boredom, depending on the teacher. We were scared into good behaviour by the headmaster who held twenty-minute school assemblies on the concrete strip outside his office every Friday afternoon where we were harangued through a megaphone about our misdemeanours of the past week. "I don't want to see any rubbish in the school grounds... Nobody moves from eating their lunch until the second bell goes... If anyone is caught around the bike sheds they will be sent straight to me." 'Straight-to-me' meant a walloping for the boys and verbal torment or the strap for the girls.

In summer the sun beat down on us on that concrete strip and in winter the cold winds whipped at our bare legs and chilled our bones but we stayed upright and faced the front, with not a whisper or a murmur. Then, "ASSEMBLY DISMISSED." We formed two straight lines waiting for our cue. The regimental march soon blared at us through loud speakers and off we marched in pairs - one, two, three, four, keeping in time to the music, marching around the concrete in a semi-circle, marching back toward the classroom, arms swinging, then knees working up and down on the spot while those in front marched single-file through the outside door and into the classroom.

Sex education was not on our headmaster's agenda and although I knew that babies grew in their mother's tummies I wasn't sure how or why. My mother decided to pass on some of the facts one evening when I was eleven. She first sent my younger brothers to bed, then looked at my father. He said he'd have a look for the leak on the roof. I heard the ladder grate against the house as Mum sat me by the fire and cut open two oranges. Oranges were a special treat. It seemed a cold night for my father to be up on the roof when he could be sitting by the fire.

Mum passed me a piece of orange and explained how girls got periods every month from the time they were thirteen or fourteen. I looked straight at the fire. My father's footsteps crunched above me.

"Every month?" I finally asked. I didn't like the sound of it and wriggled around in my chair.

"Yes, the only time you don't get them is when you're married and are having a baby. That's how you know you're expecting."

"Does it hurt?... Having a period?" The orange juice dribbled down my arm. I licked it off.

"No, not usually."

Hammerings and creaking iron sounded from above. I shoved some more coal on the fire. This monthly business didn't sound too good. I took another piece of orange and heard my mother tell how a baby got out. I still wasn't sure how it got in. My father descended after the talk finished and stood in front of the fire. He rubbed his hands together, smiled, and said, "Well, what would you like for supper?"

Several years later my mother told me not to swim or wash my hair when I had a period - something about 'being more susceptible to cold' - the advice originally passed down from her mother to her. And I discovered that all those thick white inner-soles for large feet that I'd once seen in a plain green packet were not inner-soles after all.

Our home in Hart Avenue was average-sized in an average suburban street, although we did have a corner section which gave us extra berm to play on. My mother, a devoted full-time housewife and dextrous seamstress, kept the house spotless and me in beautiful embroidered and smocked dresses. My father, an accountant and staunch public servant, was very supportive of his family and could always be relied upon to catch the 5.15pm train home from his Wellington office.

On the road outside the house we kids drew chalk lines and played tennis with the neighbours' children after school - singles and doubles and tournaments. We resented having to stop and wait if cars came around the corner, bringing fathers home for tea. When we tired of tennis it was bike rides or hopscotch, or cowboys and Indians with the girl two doors along who had a cap-gun.

From 1952, once a month on a Friday night Dad brought home three large reels of 16mm film and a projector and screen from the Justice Department. His job was to preview films to determine whether they were suitable for Her Majesty's prisoners. We kids were allowed to stay up and watch the movie after dinner, "providing it is suitable." What could adults watch that we couldn't? We didn't know the films were being checked for sex or violence.

The full-length movie was usually preceded by a cartoon or other 'shorts', and during 'permitted' movies we'd sit cosily in the lounge in our pyjamas and dressing gowns and watch Doris Day or Audrey

Hepburn, or the sailors battling it out in The Cruel Sea. The movie Salome came home one night but neither we children nor the prisoners got to see it. Something to do with its Dance of the Seven Veils. The inmates also missed out on a short called Crime Doesn't Pay. Just in case they got any ideas. The Wizard of Oz coincided with my tenth birthday and I don't know what the prisoners thought of it, but my friends and I thought it was pretty good.

One night a western arrived. My parents considered this was dubious material for young eyes. We pleaded to be allowed to stay up. After two exchanges of gun-fire my father said we'd have to go to bed, he didn't want us watching it. "Oh please, just one more shot," we said, hoping that the guns wouldn't go off again and we'd have to miss the rest of the movie. Five minutes later another 'baddie' bit the dust. "Just two more shots," we said - this one-shot business wasn't going to work. And so we progressed through the whole movie, worrying each time someone pulled the trigger that that was the finish for us, too.

We had no fridge until I was in my teens and so a special treat was to bike down to the corner dairy for a large bottle of creaming soda and a block of ice-cream. We'd sit around the kitchen table stirring ice-cream into the soda, watching it froth and foam, then sift the creamy ice-cream through our teeth and feel the fizz at the back of our throats. Sundays were a day of rest. No biking down to the corner dairy unless it was absolutely necessary, no tennis outside on the road or against the garage door, no card games. Not even any homework - it needed to be completed by Saturday night. Music practice was also exempt. Sunday mornings and evenings were spent at the Baptist church, a ten-minute walk from home.

My parents bought their first car when I was ten. A brand new Vauxhall Wyvern which in those days took two years from the time of order to delivery. I sat in the back seat as we glided down Willis Street from the car dealer's yard, breathing the boot polish smell and feeling like the new Queen. My parents believed very strongly in the family unit, in doing things together, and after the car arrived we enjoyed picnics and drives into the country. It was a secure childhood where I knew my parents would always be there.

But in growing up I sometimes wished they weren't there. They always found out what I was up to. I looked forward to the day when I would be grown-up and could do what I wanted to do, not what I was instructed or expected to do. "Being grown-up still doesn't mean that you can do what you want to do," said my father. "You'll have more worries as an adult than you do as a child." I didn't believe him.

I began secondary school in the mid-fifties - a public co-educational college of twelve hundred pupils. The principal was of the same breed as my primary school headmaster and held a tight assembly in the school hall each morning before classes. The teaching staff, dressed in black graduation gowns, processed up the aisle behind him and on to the stage, facing the pupils. The principal read from the Bible, we sang a hymn accompanied by the school pipe organ, and notices of school events were given. We were constantly reminded about the correct way to wear our uniform - "Caps and hats must be worn from the time you leave the school gates until you walk through your own front gates ... some gym frocks are too short, the hem must touch the ground when you are kneeling." The girls got told off for wearing their socks pulled up and the boys for not pulling theirs up. Anyone caught talking or sniggering visited the principal's office after assembly. We all knew that meant 'six-of-the-best' or detention. Remonstrations over, he gathered his gown around him, the staff arose as one from the stage and like sheep followed their stern unsmiling leader back down the aisle and out the door. Time for classes.

Third form general science was taken by a Canadian who didn't seem to know much about science. But the syllabus included the reproduction of the rabbit, of far greater interest to me than plant physiology or the life cycle of the honey bee. The teacher handed out drawings of rabbits and their reproductive organs and several pages of text. This was the closest the school had got to sex education. We were required to answer the written questions in our exercise books. There was no discussion.

"Do you think that's what happens with babies?" I asked a friend as we cycled down to Elbes Milk Bar after school to meet up with our 'gang' for a birthday shout of ice-cream sundaes.

"Yes, it must be," she said. I thought it a strange way to start a baby but at least I now knew how it got in.

The subject wasn't discussed again and I knew of only one girl who became pregnant while at high school. She left school suddenly, before the word was whispered around the school corridors, and I never saw her again, or knew what happened to her baby.

Most of my leisure time was taken up with tennis and music practice and youth group. And the family became involved with many of the Asian students who came to study at New Zealand universities under the Colombo Plan: students from Ceylon and India, from Indonesia, Thailand, Malaysia, Burma and Sarawak. They fascinated me - their language, their clothes, their gentleness, their *exoticness.* And we loved their food. Mum bought the requested ingredients and they cooked us wonderful curries at home and told us about life in their home countries.

One day my father said to my brothers and me, "How would you like to live in Thailand?"

"Live there? For how long?" Surely he wasn't serious. It was interesting hearing about these Asian countries from our friends but *living* there ourselves was another matter.

"Three to five years."

"I don't think so," I said. "I've got School Certificate in a few months."

"You can do it there," my mother said.

"What about my friends?"

"You'll make more over there. Dad's been offered a job in Bangkok."

"What doing?" I didn't want to go.

"Director of Finance and Administration with SEATO. It will be a good experience for us all."

And so we arrived in Bangkok, a month before my sixteenth birthday and School Certificate examinations. The heat sent rivulets of water down my face and arms and back. My clothes stuck to me and my hair turned frizzy. I breathed in jasmine scents and smells of crispy fried noodles and chillied chicken curries from road-side stalls, and fumes from the thousands of *samlors* - the tricycles powered by motorbike motors carrying twosomes in their colourful canopied rear seats. Chinese opera blasted through loud speakers from shop fronts. Markets tucked down narrow alleyways - markets with hanging dried meats and dried fish, shimmering silks and hand-woven cottons, sequinned glittering shoes, strange fruits. Golden-skinned people with almond-shaped eyes jabbered in jumbled consonants and leaned out from stilted houses on the canals to wash their clothes and clean their teeth.

I saw little of Bangkok that first month, just the hotel walls and my textbooks. My exams were held at the New Zealand Embassy and I was collected from the hotel and delivered back again by chauffeured car. The ambassador vacated his office for me, a huge room with a large desk at one end. Halfway through each exam a young Thai employee brought me a bottle of cold Pepsi on a tray with a glass of ice beside it. Yes, maybe Bangkok was a good move.

We shifted into a large, two-storeyed house after the exams. It was made of concrete with mesh screens instead of glass for windows, and shutters that we closed at night to deter the *camoys*, the burglars. On the gate-post sat a spirit house with curved Thai-style roof. The servants regularly laid food at the foot of the Buddha inside or lit candles to appease the spirits.

Mum hadn't wanted us to have servants - she said she was a good New Zealand housewife and was going to manage herself. But after polishing the teak parquet floors and trying to cope with the vagaries of a charcoal stove in the outhouse kitchen she gave in. The heat and high humidity was too much. We'd ended up with a house-girl, a washerwoman, an alcoholic cook and a part-time gardener. We children were expected to help with the dishes sometimes and make our beds in case we forgot how to do them.

I developed an unrequited passion for the Thai landlord's son who lived next door, and instead of concentrating on my sixth form New Zealand Correspondence School lessons I watched him from my bedroom window as he wandered around his garden and drank Seven-Up on his front veranda. He left after a few months for engineering studies in Europe and I decided there was no point in living in this exotic country of jasmine perfumes, gold-gilt temples, smiling people, and street-carts of aromatic foods if I was stuck inside the house all day studying the binary fission of amoeba or the effect of Bismarck on the Austro-German alliance.

My parents listened to my desires to be out of the house - to be meeting young Thai people of my own age - but they wanted me to continue studying. The Dean of Chulalongkorn University agreed to grant me the exceptional status of foreign student. Their first one. The university had been founded by the revered and respected King Chulalongkorn. The movie about his relationship with an English governess, The King and I starring Yul Brynner, was considered bad taste in Thailand and banned.

My first requirement for Chula was the compulsory uniform. "Fancy having to wear a uniform at university," I said. A seamstress sewed my black skirt and white blouse. The skirt was to be worn with a black belt, its silver buckle sporting the Chulalongkorn emblem. Emblemed buttons adorned my blouse. White socks, black shoes completed the outfit. White socks, they made me feel so juvenile. I'd progressed into nylon stockings when I was thirteen, lipstick when I was fourteen and high heels at fifteen and had thought I was very grown up. At seventeen, white ankle socks seemed like a backwards step but freshmen, first year students, had to wear white socks so white socks it was to be. As the only foreign student on a campus of five thousand full-time students - the university didn't cater for part-timers - I wanted to be as inconspicuous as possible.

The morning of my first day I was so nervous. How would I know where to go? Would anybody speak English? Would I find the classrooms? Who would be my friend? I knew no one in any of my classes. I boarded a bus at Rajacroo Lane near our home amid curious stares from passengers - this *farang*, this foreigner in *our* uniform. At five foot six inches I was taller than most Thais and had to bend low to avoid hitting my head on the bus roof. The seating was no better. Wooden seats designed for tiny people. Nowhere to hang my legs.

As we neared the university I took a deep breath and called out *jort by*, please stop. No such thing as bellpullers on these open-air buses where the conductor rides on the bonnet if the bus is so full that he can't get past passengers standing on the bottom step. More heads turned to stare at me. I probably had the tone wrong. I bundled myself together, extricating my legs and arms from those of the remaining passengers, and wound down the steps in a rush. I just wanted to get off that bus. I felt myself sink into a ditch of oozing mud and looked down at white socks dressed in grey mud. How mortifying. Crowds of black and white uniformed students near the gate were staring. Friendly, polite stares with their hands covering their mouths. I walked across the road and caught the first bus home and burst into tears as I opened the front door. My mother was sympathetic but brought me a fresh pair of socks and sent me out again.

I needn't have worried about no friends. A young woman took my hand as I re-entered the campus that first morning and introduced me to her group of girlfriends, fourth-year English students. They took me around the buildings, showed me where my classes were, arranged to meet me the next day. And remained my closest friends for the rest of my stay in Thailand. But we never talked about boys or teenage desires. That was too private to be talked about by my Thai friends.

I'd taken European foreign languages to avoid the problem of lectures in the Thai language of which I knew very little, just conversational servant-talk - "what time dinner?" or "where my skirt?" French Civilisation was taught in Thai but involved the French dictation of many Biblical stories. Not what I expected from French Civilisation. German was taught in German - a new language for me. Prince Prem, a real Thai prince and Oxford-educated, took me for fourth-year English. We studied Ibsen's *The Doll's House* and Shakespeare's *Macbeth* and I wallowed in being able to understand the language.

My social life improved dramatically at Chulalongkorn. Teenage Caucasian girls were a rarity in Bangkok. Pale skin was considered desirable in Thailand as was fluent English. I had varying degrees of each and was sometimes treated with more reverence than is good for a seventeen-year-old. The Engineering Faculty invited me on faculty excursions to beautiful remote islands, the English Faculty invited me to Somerset Maugham's eightieth birthday party when he visited the university. Many students approached me wanting to become friends and practise their English. I played lots of tennis. It was more fun on the tennis courts than trying to make sense of French civilisation. I dropped out of German as I was totally lost with the language. I'd gone to Chula for the wrong reasons - not to study but to socialise. I stayed just a year at university. There wasn't much more I could do there. I was probably their last foreign student.

Now that I had no commitments I wondered how I could occupy myself. My parents wanted me to do something 'useful' with my time. A New Zealander 'kindly' offered me their family's mending and sewing as a part-time job.

"How boring," I said to my mother. "I'm not doing that."

"If you can't find work you might have to go back to New Zealand."

But by now I wanted to stay. I asked around my friends and my parents' friends and was offered a job for twelve months as teacher of English in a Thai Buddhist school not far from our house. Help! What did that involve?

I soon found out. Two seventh form classes - comprehension and grammar, and two sixth form classes - conversation and essay writing. Each an hour long, every morning from 8am till 12 noon - Monday to Friday. Twenty hours in total for which I would be paid one pound per hour, far more than the qualified Thai teachers were paid. I was also responsible for setting their half-yearly and year-end exams.

Did they know what they were getting? A new school-leaver, a year or two younger than her students, who had never stood in front of a class and who had never learnt English grammar as it needed to be taught to 'foreign' students. I had no textbooks. Nothing. Just two weeks to prepare myself.

In the only bookshop that sold a few English textbooks I discovered a handbook published in Thailand on essay writing. It gave subject ideas, talked about the construction of an essay, then provided a model story in simple writing. I was saved. Stories such as *A Day at the Market, My Best Friend, A Good Holiday.* Hardly exciting stuff but I could expand as my confidence grew. I found a book on English grammar. Conversation would be no problem, just find a topic and take it from there. Comprehension I could manage. Give them a passage from a book and ask questions on it.

There were thirty to a class. All girls. I was surprised that discipline was no problem - Thai students were obviously there to learn. I discussed subject and predicate and extension of finite verbs like a pro with my seventh-formers. If only my high school English teacher could see me now. The conversation class was the only one where the students sneaked in some private chatter, and an occasional student got to write a short essay on 'why I should not talk in class'. The year went quickly and a Moslem school, housed in an old palace of King Chulalongkorn's, asked if I could teach English there. "And can you play the piano? We've just lost our piano teacher."

I hadn't expected the music students to speak no English. They probably wondered what had struck them that first lesson. I could converse reasonably well in basic Thai but had no knowledge of musical terms and some of these students were just beginners. We muddled through the first lesson and I went home to my English/Thai dictionary. I had bought the best I could find but it was quaint rather than erudite, *Nibondh's Thai Self-Taught* by G M B Gaudart, fourth edition, revised and enlarged. Printed in Bangkok on newsprint paper, the cover wasn't much thicker than the pages, and it came with an introduction from the author. "This book is intended for Newcombers to Thailand who wish to pick up a knowledge of words and expressions as used in general conversation. In order to speak the Thai language with perfect accuracy, students are recommended to have as much intercourse with the Thais as possible. Several alterations have been made in this edition which will materiall improve it." I flicked through the book. Lists of words and phrases in alphabetical order... Alas what grief, ashame, boa-constrictor, buffalo dunce, cocoanut leave, hypodermic needle, I cannot repress my anger, iron the flannel clothes while they are damp, quack doctor, ram the cannon... No mention of crotchets, quavers and semitones, adagio or pianissimo.

I decided to teach music terms in the English language but alter the vowel and consonant sounds to suit the Thai tongue. And I gave the words a harsh twang - that's how Thai sounded to me. It worked well and the students learnt a whole new vocabulary. I often wondered about the teacher who took over after me.

A tutor at the school asked me to be involved with English radio lessons so together with a Thai friend I wrote a weekly radio script in English, centering on the arrival of a young Englishwoman to Bangkok, and we broadcast it live at 8 o'clock each Saturday morning on the national 'English Language Lessons' radio programme. I took the role of the English woman and my friend was the Thai guide. We 'visited' markets and temples, talked about Thai customs, the Thai royal family... different subjects each week. There wasn't much time for rehearsal after the script was written, often just a quick read through and we were on air. It was great fun.

The Thais are a good-looking people, and Thai children particularly cute. My parents considered adopting a child from a Thai orphanage and 'giving it a better life' in New Zealand. They visited orphanages and talked it through with us. We weren't too enthusiastic - we were all in our teens and didn't feel the need for a young sibling. We discussed whether the child might later be pleased at her elevation in material and family comforts, or resentful at being removed from her race and homeland to live with a family of Caucasians. We didn't know. The adoption idea was eventually dropped although it seemed sad that these babies were destined to remain in institutionalised care all their childhood.

I wondered why there were so many babies in orphanages. Were they really orphaned or were their parents just unable to keep them? Were perhaps their parents unmarried? I wondered about Thai morality. I still couldn't discuss it with my Thai friends. They became embarrassed and changed the subject.

I'd become used to the fact that Thai men and women didn't show public affection towards the opposite sex. That was for the *farang*, the foreigners. But the less-educated Thai males often became bold in the presence of young foreign women who, they surmised from western movies, had a different set of rules, and they often declared their love within five minutes of meeting me. Usually followed by a little giggle or a flash of gold teeth. Street hawkers, taxi drivers, the stranger on the bus, the policeman in a sentry box at the end of our street. I soon realised that "I love you" was the only English they knew. Others, with more command of the language, sent declarations by post. One arrived from a Thai friend's cousin, a university student, who had briefly visited our house.

> Dear Sir,
> I am very glad on that day. We need to meet you again because your habit an everything useful for my mind, you are quite beautiful, I have never seen any one good as you. you may frightening and wonderful to me because you and I are not know before but I think you'll be very glad for me. You speak English quite well. And by the way you are one of pleasing too. thank you.
> Oh Miss Are you free time? I am very glad to go with me to Minburi which is my home town.
> Hoping that you arn't refuse me and for me please - thank you next time
> Sincerely yours
> Sonum
> I will not forget you to eternity and I will be your friend forever.

I found it difficult to respond to this type of letter. I should have written a nice reply and left him with a keepsake in the English language. But I avoided him and others who wrote in a similar vein. I was not comfortable with such expressiveness after a first meeting - it was foreign behaviour to me. I had several Thai male friends but was unable to think of our friendships as anything but platonic.

I was still an innocent with the opposite sex, partly due to my strong Baptist upbringing where sex, rock 'n' roll and alcohol were all danger zones. 'Total abstinence until marriage' for sex, 'total abstinence forever' for alcohol. I never knew why rock 'n' roll was on the list. Looking back, I suppose that gyrating bodies may have provoked gyrating thoughts and who knows what then might have happened to abstinence.

My parents needn't have worried. Young, single, male Caucasians were in short supply in Bangkok. Most international workers there were married with family, or just plain old. The only singles I knew between nineteen and twenty five years of age were two friendly American missionaries on motor-bikes, one overly-friendly, overly-short Scottish missionary with wandering hands, and a boring balding South African accountant with a red BMW. I didn't want to be a missionary's wife and the enticement of a red BMW wasn't enough to put up with the accountant.

So I wrote to my New Zealand friends of watching dragon-shaped royal barges on the river and paying ball-boys to run for our tennis balls and throw them back to the server. Of rings of precious stones - rubies and emeralds and diamonds - for less than a week's wages, of meeting untamed elephants on jungle roads, and saffron-robed Buddhist monks with begging bowls, of eating hundred-year-old duck eggs. They wrote back of their boy friends, Saturday night pictures, and dances at 'The Pines' and how lucky I was to be living in such an interesting country. They envied me my life style. I envied them their boy friends.

After three years the family returned to New Zealand for a couple of months before returning to Thailand for another two years. I stayed back in Wellington for my social fling, some of it with a psychology student who insisted on standing on his hands at the Willis Street bus stop. I grew tired of him and missed Bangkok so much that I gave up my job as a dental assistant - to the relief of the dentist and his patients - and returned to Thailand. My cousin, Bryan, and two friends travelled with me. From there we went on to Europe. Which is where I met Ken.

# Chapter Three

IT WAS 10 July 1963. Twelve strangers sat and talked together in a bed-sit in south-west London. Ten Kiwis, an Australian and a South African, aged between twenty and twenty-five, who had read an advertisement on an Earls Court noticeboard - 'thirteen European countries in twelve weeks for £120.00'. John, a Kiwi from Wellington and tenant of the bed-sit accommodation, had recently started up his own company, Contiki Tours, and would be organiser, driver, tour guide.

We had two hours of chat to decide whether we were all compatible. Could we survive travelling together for three months in a twelve-seater van? We thought so, paid our money and agreed to meet up in two weeks' time with a very small suitcase each.

John drove us carefully, map on knees, through Holland and Belgium to Scandinavia, and down to Germany. We became expert at erecting and dismantling tents, one for the five guys, another for the seven females. Expert at trying to convert one pound per person into a week of satisfactory meals when it was our turn to shop and cook. At staving off the haunted looks when the guys saw the pot was empty. Food had to be carefully portioned. There was never enough. Sometimes we didn't get it right and misunderstood the labels on the cans. We thought the Norwegian tomato soup disgusting, shuddering as we drank it but determined not to waste a drop. Later we discovered it was rose-hip syrup.

Ken and I had gravitated towards each other by the time we reached Heidelberg. I rather liked his looks, tall and slim, and his quiet, gentle manner. He was from Hamilton and was taking time out from his telecommunications job and joining the exodus of Kiwis to Europe, the pilgrimage that young New Zealanders like to take before being tied to regular jobs and house mortgages. We communicated easily and wandered the sights together.

The group melded reasonably well except for the Australian. We never saw him until the chore of erecting or dismantling tents was over, and we were often on board the van ready for a new day's travel before our Aussie would finally emerge from the washrooms, toilet-bag in hand. No amount of caustic comment made any difference.

The trip was without serious incident until we reached Italy. We got burgled in Milan, sideswiped in Verona and lost in Venice. In Rome we got arrested. It was Kiwi Mike's twenty-first birthday and Aussie Barry's twenty-fifth. "Let's celebrate," we'd said. "Let's become 'Ancient Romans' for the night."

So we shared one bottle of wine among the poverty-stricken twelve of us, then scrambled among our meagre clothing supplies for suitable attire. Towels substituted for togas, and men's long white shirts that shaped up at the sides for tunics. John chivalrously offered his shirt to Jocelyn, in a last-minute swap, and donned her pink frilly blouse, thinking he'd be tucked away unseen behind the wheel of the van. Elizabeth wore a tarpaulin over her swimsuit, not ideal but selection was limited. Ken and I wore leftovers. We weren't sure *what* we looked like. Aussie Barrie refused to dress-up and wore grey flannel trousers, white shirt and cravat. He was a lawyer and not prone to such frivolity.

At the Roman Forum we stood near tourists from Germany and Spain and North America and heard 'Brutus' Mike, dressed in towel-toga, deliver his impressive eulogy to Caesar. "Romans, countrymen and lovers... If, then, that friend demand why Brutus rose against Caesar, this is my answer, - not that I loved Caesar less, but that I loved Rome more..." The sun was setting, the speech delivered with all the drama that Mike could muster. The Americans seemed a little confused.

We moved to the famous 18th century Trevi fountain, and paddled among the coins, unaware of the fountain's sacred status and the fines for invading its waters. Encouraged by the crowd response - wild stares from the locals and amusement from the tourists - we dabbled in five more fountains. By now it was 10pm but the summer air was moist and warm. Our last stop was to be the Via Veneto, the street the 'stars' desire to be seen on.

Aussie Barry remained in the van. He'd been there all evening. Café drinkers on the sidewalks held cups in mid-air as our motley bunch proudly walked the promenade. Triumphant, and ready to return to the modern world, we boarded the waiting van. Seconds later, out in the darkness, a mob of excited and angry Italians began rocking, rocking the van. We couldn't move away. A door jerked open and a suited male, yelling in Italian, pulled vigorously at the tarpaulin of our front seat passenger, who wasn't willing to let it go.

Aussie Barry produced a tear gas gun and fired at the intruder. Where had he got that from? Tear gas filled the vehicle and we began coughing. Our eyes were stinging and watering. The intruder thrust his business card at us. A policeman. Plainclothed.

Through stinging streaming eyes and on police orders we followed flashing car lights to the police station.

"Just as well our parents can't see us," I said to Ken from the wooden floor of the station - criminals weren't provided with seats. I looked across the room at pink, frilly, uncomfortable John and laughed carefully. "And just as well John's parents can't see *him*." This last-minute swap distracted a little from the theme of the evening. Cross-dressing was an even more serious offence in Italy than paddling in a fountain.

By 4am we had endured six hours of individual interrogation. "Why were you dressed in men's shirts? What is your group? Why was he dressed like a woman? Why did you go into the fountain? Where are you from? What was she wearing under the towel? Give me your passport. What is your purpose in Italy?" Then we were released, except for Aussie Barry who was sent to jail for firing at a policeman.

We didn't know when or whether he would be returned to us. We drove over to the British Embassy to ask for advice. They were not amused by our situation and informed us that the authorities were holding the Australian for three days before deciding what charges and penalties would be incurred.

We recognised ourselves on the front page of a daily newspaper the next morning and asked a camper to translate the headline. He stared at us. "New Zealand Nudes on their Sordid Night Prowls." We winced. We'd never believe a newspaper report again. "Just as well my parents don't know about this," I said. Ken said his father wouldn't believe it if he read it. The newspaper gave our vehicle registration number and the name of the camping ground where we were staying. Sightseers soon began to arrive. What had we all done?

Barry had been Ken's cooking partner and their duty-week coincided with Barry's incarceration. Ken asked me to help him with the meals in Barry's absence and we peeled potatoes together in the sun. "I hope I never have nine children," I said, counting the potatoes and wondering how we could stretch one chicken to feed eleven people. At least

Barry's absence was one less to feed.

Three days later we received a curt message from the British Embassy. We were to collect the Australian from prison. Charges would not be laid but a police directive instructed us to leave Italy via the quickest route, and not to return.

At our next mail stop newspaper clippings tumbled out of letters from friends and family - clippings from New Zealand provincial papers, from Australia, from South Africa and even from England. Full names and addresses, too. We read that we had been charged with blocking traffic and disturbing the peace. Charged? This was news to us. The incident had been repeated hourly on New Zealand radio news bulletins. *The Evening Post* reported from Parliament the day after our arrest, "Prime Minister Mr Holyoake said today New Zealand had not been officially informed about the arrest of eight New Zealand students in Rome. He did not doubt we would be. He said that in Rome the British Embassy looked after the consular interests of New Zealand. From what he had heard unofficially, it did not appear that the charges would demand very serious penalties."

My grandmother said wasn't it a pity we had such an uncommon name. My parents, weary of continuous enquiries about their erring daughter, handed out copies of my version of events.

All this for a few wet ankles? We couldn't believe it.

We spent Pam's twenty-first birthday in a field in Spain away from all civilisation, and away from all water. Just the stars and a few olive trees.

After Europe Ken returned to England to work while I found work as a nurse-aide in a Home for the Aged in Denmark. Sixty-five hours a week for six pounds but meals and accommodation provided. The aged babbled in Danish at me as I tried to remove false teeth, that weren't false, for cleaning. And how much of their bodies did I need to wash? I stuck to hands and face until their bodies started to smell.

The charge nurse asked me one day if I'd ever seen a dead person. Mrs Hansen had just died and I was taken to the bed where she lay. I stared at the pale body. "You can touch her skin," said the nurse gently. The skin was cold in a very warm room.

I thought about the lifeless Mrs Hansen for many days. Where was she now? Had her spirit re-connected with dead friends and relatives or was that the end? It was my first encounter with death.

I wrote to Ken of my varied experiences. Our relationship was still fairly casual but we agreed to meet again in England and travel around the country with a friend for a few weeks before I returned to New Zealand. Three days before my ship was due to leave for New Zealand, Ken said he was coming too. I was pleased at the idea of his company as I knew no one else on board. We enjoyed the five weeks of unlimited food, and dances and swimming and socialising, but realised that our time together was always in carefree holiday situations, never in the real world.

I said goodbye to him as we sailed into Auckland. We said we'd keep in touch. I wondered if I could slot back into life in this country again.

I soon realised I had been away for too long. Everyone, it seemed, was part of a couple. My girl friends were engaged or married or 'going steady' and weren't free to socialise on a Saturday night. "We wrote and told you you'd be left on the shelf if you didn't come back home soon," said my solicitous brothers. "It looks as if you've left it a bit late."

I needed to get a job very quickly, meet new people. But I wasn't trained in anything. Perhaps I should start studying? No, I needed to earn some money and pay back travel loans to my parents. I wondered what I was going to do with my life. Why had I come home? It was great to see family and friends again but the place seemed dull. And after being independent it was hard to accept the restrictions of family life - being asked where I was going and to be home before midnight.

I scanned the Situations Vacant section of the *Evening Post.* "Position available for qualified teacher with good knowledge of classical music. Apply The Manager, National Film Library, Department of Education, Wellington." I wasn't a qualified teacher and I didn't have a detailed knowledge of classical music but I phoned for an interview.

What do people wear to job interviews? My mother suggested my best Thai-silk outfit. I trotted off in the train in my ming-blue reversible coat, and dress with co-ordinating checks of brilliant oranges, pinks, greens and ming-blue. A ming-blue hat, handbag, and high-heeled shoes all of the same silk as the coat. The shoes were decorated with little ming-blue silk rosebuds. I straightened the back seam of my nylon stockings as I walked into the manager's office.

He shook hands. I wondered if I should have worn my gloves. Mum had thought so, but I thought I had enough on.

After a few preliminaries he explained the job. "You'd be part of a panel previewing educational films and deciding if they were suitable for purchase and where they would fit into the school curriculum." His eyes flickered briefly at my hat. "You would also make film bookings and select music programmes for posting to schools. And be required to operate the movie projector."

It seemed a long way from teaching twangy Thai crotchets and when to use the 'present participle'.

I smiled at him. "I'm familiar with a Bell and Howell projector."

His eyebrows rose.

"Yes, my father used to preview films at home for the Justice Department."

"What sort of films were they?"

"Oh, things like Salome and The Wizard of Oz."

His neck moved forwards. "Salome and the Wizard of Oz? For the Justice Department?"

"Yes, actually I never got to thread the projector. My father was concerned I'd get it wrong and chew up the prisoners' films... but I watched him often enough."

"How long ago was this?"

"He stopped bringing them home about ten years ago."

"I think you'll find the model has changed since then." He didn't seem to know what to do with his mouth.

I somehow got the job. He must have liked the outfit. Twelve months later I became 'the cataloguer', wrote annotations for films screened and purchased, organised their publication into the Film Library Catalogue and worked closely with the Curriculum Unit of the Department of Education. Maybe I could last in this country a bit longer. And Ken had come down from Hamilton to look for work, and for me.

# Chapter Four

WE BECAME a couple, Ken and I. Again. He knew no one else in Wellington and we spent all our free time together. New Zealand still seemed a little dull after exotic Asia and old Europe but we sometimes booked tickets for imported stage shows that reminded us of theatre excursions in London.

Ken decided on a career change and was offered a job with Feltex Footwear, and began part-time studies for Institute of Management exams. He bought himself a push-bike so that he could get to classes, and visit me on the hills above Lower Hutt where I was still living with my parents and brothers. Group flatting was not encouraged - flatting with Ken could not even be considered. We would need to be married.

Our friends had all progressed from 'going steady' to 'engaged' to 'married'. Ken and I grew to love each other but he waited six months for an answer to his marriage proposal - his patience was remarkable. The evening following my consent we sat upright in my parents' lounge chairs and Ken asked them formally for "your daughter's hand in marriage". It was a serious occasion.

Eight months later we promised to "Love, cherish and obey so long as we both shall live," and were pronounced "man and wife" by the minister. My brothers gave Ken a sympathy card. I was almost twenty-three and Ken was twenty-four.

"Forever" seemed a long time. But I'd never heard friends, family or acquaintances talk of marriage problems. It shouldn't be too difficult. We rented a flat, in a state of bliss, and scarcely a thought of what life together would bring.

A few months after our wedding I developed crippling abdominal pains. I was nauseated and felt generally unwell. Surely this wasn't pregnancy? We weren't mentally or financially ready for a baby.

A gynaecologist with charm and gentlemanly manners pronounced that I had endometriosis, a hormonal problem that could make conception difficult, but pregnancy, he said, could give remission of symptoms. A catch 22 situation. He suggested a course on an oral contraceptive pill as the best treatment until we were ready to begin a family. I didn't doubt that I would later become pregnant.

I'd never heard of endometriosis but read that it was a condition in which the lining of the uterus is found in other areas, usually in the pelvis. Patches of uterine tissue may form cysts and lesions and grow on the ovaries, bladder, bowel, uterine surface and other pelvic organs. Endometrial tissue can even be found in other places such as the diaphragm though this is much less common. These patches can respond to cyclical hormones and swell or bleed but there is nowhere for the blood to escape to. Degeneration of the blood and tissue shed from the growths inflames the surrounding areas and scar tissue can form. It affects at least ten percent of women of childbearing age which, of course, includes teenagers and can be a debilitating condition.

The pill seemed a simple remedy for me, and within two years the pains had disappeared. "Wonderful," we said to each other. I made an appointment to see the gynaecologist again and told him of my progress and our desire to start having children. He said I could come off the pill and to come back to him if I wasn't pregnant in six months.

Five months later I was convinced I was pregnant. No period. Bodily changes. I drank lots of milk and perused dressmaking patterns in the maternity section of the Simplicity sewing catalogues. Another month of missed periods and I bought the patterns I liked and looked at fabrics. I increased my milk intake, thought of nothing but babies and made an appointment to see my GP to have the pregnancy confirmed.

He listened to my symptoms and said I was two and a half months pregnant but he declined to do a pregnancy test. I asked why I couldn't have the test. I wanted real confirmation.

"You don't need one. I'm sure you're pregnant."

I rushed home to Ken. He too was overjoyed and we celebrated with a candle-lit dinner. I bought dress materials for me, and white wool and baby patterns and number ten and twelve knitting needles. Little booties began growing. And I drank even more milk.

Three weeks later, during a rather busy weekend, I developed excruciating back pains, nausea, vomiting and bleeding. Was this normal? It couldn't be a miscarriage could it? No. Please, no.

I returned to the GP, told him of my weekend pains and demanded the test. He gave it to me.

"I'm sorry," he said. "It's negative."

I was devastated. "I must've had a miscarriage." I felt hollow as if I had lost more than a baby. I wanted to cry. Why couldn't this man have given me a pregnancy test last month? I needed to know if I had beaten the endometriosis. If I could get pregnant. And all that milk I'd been drinking - I didn't even like milk.

"You were probably not pregnant," said the doctor. Looked at me, head on the side. Didn't understand.

I went home and cried into Ken.

Two weeks later I revisited the charming, gentlemanly gynaecologist. "Where's the referral from your GP?" he asked.

"I'm sorry, I don't have one. But you told me to come back if I wasn't pregnant."

"I told you to come back within *six months* if you weren't pregnant. Why didn't you come back within six months?" His voice was clipped. Nice rounded vowels. Face reddening. Gentleman disappearing.

I looked down at my feet. "I thought I was pregnant." What was his problem? What did an extra two months matter?

"I can't see you now without a referral. You should have been back within six months. You'll need to make another appointment." He rose from behind his large desk and showed me the door.

My GP was reluctant to write the referral. "I had a run-in with him when I was a medical student," he said. "I'm not sure he's going to want to hear from me."

"I'd better stick with him. He knows my history. A GP I had in Wellington a few years ago sent me to him."

The doctor wrote his note and I re-presented myself to the gynaecologist.

He read the letter. Unsmiling. "Go through to the next room. I'll be with you shortly."

I lay on the bed wondering what was to come.

He walked to the steriliser and withdrew what looked like a very long steel needle. "I need to take samples," he said. "Determine why you are not pregnant." The pain as he thrust the spear inside me was searing. Unbearable. I screamed. He came back again. And again. Six times in all. My legs had gone into spasm with the pain. My whole body was shaking.

"You can get up now."

I couldn't move for five minutes. I could hardly stand. "Ring me next week for the results." Clipped arrogant voice.

"What's the matter?" said Ken waiting outside for me in our newly-acquired first car, our sixteen-year-old turquoise-blue Humber 80. I could hardly talk. I was still shaking. I felt violated. Bewildered. Angry with myself for lying there and taking it. At not having the courage to walk away.

Ken put his arm around me. "You're not going back there again." He thrust the gear stick into first gear. "They can't do that to you."

I phoned the nurse the following week for the results. "There's nothing showing up. You could return for more tests."

I was still in pain when I walked. "I'd rather be barren than return," I said to Ken.

A doctor later told me that those tests should have been done under anaesthetic.

I put the knitting out of sight and grieved for what I didn't have. I started taking my temperature every morning and plotting it on a chart and watching for the dips and rises. Ovulation was thought to occur around the time of a dip of several tenths of a degree for one day followed by an immediate rise of about four-tenths of a degree or more. The calendar and the dips and rises began to control our lives. We became machines. The main problem was that the best timing for pregnancy was the day before or after ovulation, and it was only after the fact that the chart told when ovulation might have occurred. Several months of charts needed to be recorded to predict the current cycle. I got tired of taking my temperature.

I was by now working for the Child Welfare Division of the Department of Education in Lower Hutt. I'd transferred within the department to alleviate the two hours of travel to the Film Library each day. Child Welfare was only a ten-minute walk from home. The job was clerical and often boring but I hoped I'd soon be pregnant and could stop working.

Then one Friday I said again to Ken, "I think I might be pregnant. My period is late." He hugged me. "But don't get your hopes up too soon."

I made an appointment for Tuesday with a local gynaecologist who didn't need referral letters. He gave me a pregnancy test. "No," he said. "You are not pregnant. You shouldn't have made an appointment for today. Tuesdays, Thursdays and Fridays are for pregnant women only." He spoke kindly, but as to a small child who has erred. "Please see the nurse for a Monday or Wednesday appointment."

I never saw him again either. Only his wife backing out of her drive twenty-two years later, and in very different circumstances.

By now I was twenty-six and Ken was twenty-seven. Four years married and no children. Every month I hoped and agonised, and every month I was disappointed. Ken went for tests. He was pronounced capable of becoming a father.

Most of our friends had children. Some of them were concerned about the non-appearance of our offspring. "You're building a house - what about some children? It's about time you gave up your job... How long have you been married now? Don't leave it too long before you start a family." I was embarrassed about my inability to reproduce but discussed it with nobody but Ken. It was a personal matter.

# Chapter Five

I CONTINUED to walk the ten minutes to work each day. Past wooden houses bordered with trimmed or untrimmed hedges or picket fences. Pohutukawa trees spaced nicely on the berms. Over the bridge - how's the river today? Past Hannahs shoe shop, Ackroyds book store, what's in the window of Peacocks Ladieswear? Past the Post Office, around the corner and there's the Child Welfare building. Up the stairs and into the reception area and office.

Child Welfare was responsible for the welfare of children up until the age of twenty-one. State wards - children made wards of the state by the court because of inadequate parents or sometimes no parents at all - foster children, young criminal offenders, and adoption placements - all came under their jurisdiction. Part of my job included helping with the accounts and keeping a record of the movements of young offenders. I sat in on meetings with the youth aid officer, a young policeman, and heard about burglaries and truanting and family violence.

Jackie, the woman at the desk next to me, had been with the department for more than ten years and was responsible for the clerical processing of adoption applications. She told me how Child Welfare were now arranging most adoptions in New Zealand. Couples who wished to adopt could also look for a child privately - perhaps through a home for unmarried mothers or their doctor - but all proposed placements, whether private or through Child Welfare, had to have Child Welfare approval.

Jackie, married for twenty years and unable to have children, had desperately wanted to adopt, but her husband was not agreeable to the idea. So she was confined to connecting desiring parents to needful babies on paper, knowing that she would never be able to become a mother. I shared my infertility secret with her; she was the only person who had told me of personal problems conceiving children. She was sympathetic to my childless state and hoped I would have better luck than she had in persuading a husband to adopt, if it was what I wanted.

What would it be like to adopt? Could I love an adopted child as much as I would love my own flesh and blood? What would Ken think about adoption?

I heard the word 'adoption' again and again at work. And watched breathless couples on their best behaviour arrive regularly at the reception desk, at the top of the stairs, to see Miss Thomas, the adoptions officer. Sometimes they reappeared several months later, a baby under one arm, the other balancing a pavlova with strawberries on top or a sponge cake with cream in the centre and sprinkled with icing sugar. A thank you for their precious baby. At morning tea in the cafeteria the Senior Child Welfare Officer, a stern erect figure, controlled who ate the 'gratitude' profferings. "The cake is just for field staff," she'd say, easing a knife into the next slice. We administration staff sat at the large shared dining table and watched the cream swirling around the mouths of the social workers, pretending we didn't care that we weren't 'qualified' enough to partake.

Yes, what would it be like to adopt? I tried to find information on the subject, a handbook for prospective adoptive parents, written for New Zealanders. I could find nothing. Nothing about processes, the questions adoptive parents might have, the trends, the statistics. Nothing either, about the effects of adoption on relinquishing mothers - unmarried mothers who were unable to keep their babies. The only publication available seemed to be *Yours by Choice* by a British author, Jane Rowe, and published by Mills and Boon. She wrote only of British laws and conditions, much of it irrelevant, confusing. Is this what happens in New Zealand?

I asked Jackie about the adoption process and learnt that the adoptive parents' first interview was with the adoption officer, Miss Thomas. She was a popular personality in the office. Although unmarried, and without children herself, she seemed caring and compassionate. After a baby was born and Miss Thomas had located a suitable couple or couples from her file she would discuss the placement with the appropriate social worker. Social workers, known as field officers, each had a geographical area for which they were responsible. They visited homes of prospective adoptive parents and worked in with the adoption officer.

"The adoptive couple is telephoned when a suitable baby arrives and is given non-identifying information about the baby and asked if they would like to see it," Jackie said. "And the birth mother is told something of the new parents. Again, no names."

"Why the secrecy?" I asked.

"It's the 1955 Adoption Act. It has made the records absolutely confidential within the department. It's considered to be in everybody's best interests.

"Sometimes babies are flown to another town if there is no suitable adoptive couple in our area, or prospective parents live too close to the child's family and might somehow be discovered. We approve the placement before the baby arrives in its new town, then a social worker collects the baby from the airport at the other end and delivers it to its new parents so that they can have the baby immediately."

"Is this the first the new parents have seen of the baby?"

"Yes, the couple just has the background information given previously by the department."

"What if the parents don't take to the baby?" The placement was already made, the delivery performed. Was there any going back?

"It doesn't usually happen."

"If you're adopting, how long do you have to wait for a child?"

"Most people want a new baby. They feel they can bond better with a new baby. It's usually about a three-to six-month wait. In the 1950s adoptive parents sometimes waited years for a baby but we don't have that problem now. It's more like a surplus. In my day couples used to get married if the woman discovered she was pregnant but they usually don't now. But it's very difficult for many of them to keep their babies with no State financial support."

So many babies available for adoption. I heard talk of matching babies of good background with parents of good background. And of difficulty placing babies of dubious background. An alcoholic parent. An unknown father. Health problems. Mother of low intelligence. What happens when a baby of less than desirable background is placed with parents of less than desirable background? What will be the result of that combination? What about couples adopting to try to save a strained, childless marriage? How would the adoption officer know of marriage problems?

And what about highly educated couples who have everything to offer in intelligence and material wealth? Are love and care and intelligence offerings enough? Does love always grow? Does adoption work?

More and more I thought about these questions.

The female field officers were young and newly married, or older and mostly never married. None of them had children of their own. I wondered how they could truly understand the feelings of birth parents giving up babies, or the feelings of infertile couples, or foster families - families who looked after children whose parents were unable to care for them, with the parents or the State remaining the legal guardians. Friends of ours, with three children of their own, heard that Child Welfare needed more short- and long-term foster homes. They became foster parents and soon had a succession of short-term foster children, for whom they were paid a food and clothing allowance from Child Welfare. Then they were asked to care for Joanne, a five-month-old baby whose unmarried mother had a history of mental illness and was unsure what to do with her baby. She couldn't bring herself to sign the adoption papers, and Joanne needed to be fostered until her future was decided.

After nine months in their foster care the baby had become a much loved member of the family and they had grown to love her as their own. "We don't know how we'll be able to give her up if the mother ever wants her back," they said to us.

One day they phoned me in tears. "We've just had a call from Mrs Curtis, our social worker. She wants us to dress up Joanne on Saturday afternoon. She's coming to collect her and show her to a prospective adoptive couple. We've just found out that Joanne's mother has decided to go ahead with an adoption. We're shattered. We told Mrs Curtis we would love to adopt her ourselves if she's available."

"What did she say?"

"That she was sorry, but they'd already spoken to adoptive applicants. And that we've never made an adoption application."

How could social workers do that? Why had nothing been said to the foster parents earlier, when the birth mother had first given her assent to the adoption? But maybe our friends had misunderstood the social worker. Maybe the adoption didn't really need to proceed as planned. Whose interests were paramount? The young child's? What did 'child welfare' mean? I was only clerical staff, and interference in the adoption process would not be welcome, but it was worth a try.

Mrs Curtis was a self-confident young woman in her mid-twenties. I told her how upset the family were, that I had seen how loved Joanne was by her foster parents and their children, and how she in turn loved them. "The prospective family have never seen Joanne. Couldn't something be done?" I was given the same response as her foster parents. "I'm sorry, but it's too late. We've already spoken to the adoptive family. The foster parents hadn't made an adoption application."

There was nothing more I could say - it wasn't my place to argue with a social worker. She saw my concern and disbelief. "Never mind," she said. "We'll find them some other children to foster."

The following Saturday afternoon the family dressed the toddler in a pink dress with embroidery smocked across the front and watched her go out the door in the arms of the social worker. Joanne cried as she was taken away. She was returned several hours later. They looked after her for a few more days while the paper work was completed, then they never saw her again. I heard a couple of years later that the adoptive parents' marriage had broken up.

A young Japanese woman and her New Zealand husband arrived to see Miss Thomas one day. They were applying to adopt a baby. Several months later they reappeared; this time the Japanese wife looked about five months pregnant. But the pregnancy was only cushions stuffed under her dress. She explained to Miss Thomas that she had to do it this way - an adopted child would never be accepted by her Japanese family or community. Her New Zealand neighbours and friends must not know that she wasn't really pregnant. The risk was too great that somehow her parents might hear of it, and they must never find out that the child was adopted.

The stuffed cushions were unorthodox and might not have produced a birth by adoption in normal circumstances, but Miss Thomas understood her Japanese fears and the cushions grew as the months progressed. I wondered how Miss Thomas would conjure up a part-Asian child on the stroke of nine months, but she did; the father was a visiting Chinese-Malaysian university student and the mother a New Zealander.

I saw the happiness on the faces of adoptive parents when they called in to the office with their new babies, and the idea of adopting grew, for me, with each period that came. I knew no adoptive parents or adopted adults with whom I could discuss adoption, but I felt sure that I could love any adopted child unreservedly. The time had come to broach the subject with my husband.

"What would you think about adoption?" I asked him one Saturday morning over breakfast. I was armed with all my information.

"Adoption? For us?" His spoon dropped back into the Weetbix bowl.

"Yes. I've been thinking about it a lot. I wonder if we'll ever have children of our own."

"It's still early days. Let's wait a bit longer. I'm sure we'll have our own. There doesn't seem to be any reason why we can't. Do you really want to adopt someone else's child?"

"It would become *our* child. And I know from work that many parents say they love their adopted children just as much as they do their biological children. Child Welfare match up the parents so that it would have the same colouring and height and they try to match the educational backgrounds as well. The child would look as if it is a natural member of our family. Oh Ken, could you think about it?"

"I'll think about it." He continued eating the Weetbix and we drank our coffee in silence. I'd better leave it for a little while before talking about it again.

What did unmarried mothers feel about giving up their babies for adoption? I knew about the social stigma. The need to go to another town to have their baby secretly to spare their families shame, to disappear for a few months so that friends and neighbours wouldn't know of their pregnant state. Society's attitude to the unmarried mother had long been based on its disapproval of women who had sex before marriage. Those who did, and became pregnant as a result, were regarded as responsible for their own predicament. An unmarried woman's pregnancy and the giving up of her baby was seen by some as a punishment for her sins. At work I heard no talk of compassion for the unmarried mother, only the pleasures of placing babies for adoption into new families.

I wondered how my friends and family would have coped had I been pregnant and unmarried. I know that because of my strict Protestant upbringing I would have felt ashamed and embarrassed. I would probably have considered adoption. It was considered the best solution for unmarried mothers without financial or family support. "You should give your baby up to a two-parent family who would have the resources to care for and love it," they were often told. Fostering was a very vague concept. I'd hardly heard the word abortion. It sounded scary and I associated it with short trips to Australia. The only other option would have been for my parents to take over the raising of the child. How would they have felt about that? How would I have coped with that? I didn't know.

Ken could see I was pre-occupied with babies. That I became upset as my married friends became pregnant. Some of them were up to their second or third child. I broached the subject of adoption with him again and he said he was unsure how he would feel as a father to someone else's baby.

I spoke with Miss Thomas about our problems - my desire to adopt, Ken's uncertainties, and how I was unsure what to do about it. She was understanding, and suggested we make an appointment to discuss the situation. Ken agreed, reluctantly, to meet with her.

Miss Thomas welcomed us into her office. It seemed strange being one of her clients. We briefly discussed our concerns and she asked whether my infertility had been fully investigated. I told her I'd had all the tests I was willing to have and that the problem originally appeared to be endometriosis which had since cleared. There seemed to be no reason why I couldn't conceive. She offered the name of a gynaecologist should we require further tests. Ken asked questions about placement of babies but didn't exude a huge enthusiasm.

"You both need to feel very sure that adoption is the answer for you," said Miss Thomas. I think you should try a foster baby first."

A foster baby? Fostering babies was not on our agenda. I knew that fostering was only a temporary arrangement. Fostered children were often moved from home to home as foster or biological family conditions changed. I wanted a baby that would remain truly ours. As if I had given birth to it.

Miss Thomas looked at each of us. "Ken can see how he feels about a baby in the house and you might become pregnant. This often happens to women looking after babies."

My mind flicked to the New World supermarket shelves. Rows of beautiful babies sitting between the Johnson's baby powder and the packets of fluffy napkins. Babies waiting to be distributed to deserving customers. To unpregnant women. To unsure husbands. "I'll have the one in the pink bonnet. Just for three months, thanks." Was it fair for us to use a baby in this way? Was it fair for Child Welfare to select babies for such a purpose or were they short of foster homes for babies and this a convenient solution? What would be the long-term effects on these shuffled babies? Wasn't a close, *continuous* relationship with their mother, or mother substitute, essential for their development? Besides, I wasn't sure how I would handle a foster baby, knowing that it was only lent to us; whether I could give it back to its mother at the end of the allocated time. I thought of my friends' experience with their foster baby.

But Miss Thomas wasn't willing for us to adopt a child if Ken harboured any doubts. Short-term fostering seemed to be my only hope for an eventual baby of our own and any altruistic thoughts towards foster babies were pushed aside as my need became greater than theirs. We signed the foster parent application form. "Just think of it as a means to an end," Miss Thomas said.

Ken seemed rather relieved that the adoption process had been delayed. I was disappointed but my consolation was that I "might become pregnant".

Ken was equally keen for a family, but the natural way. His own flesh and blood. He took solace and time-out by fishing from the wild beaches of the Palliser Bay coastline. He would get up at dawn and drive over the winding Rimutaka hills to the ocean. The continental shelf provided opportunities for a large catch. He let the wind inflate a huge plastic bag to which he'd tied a long-line with its twenty-six baited hooks. Sometimes I'd go with him if the right tides for catching fish weren't too early in the morning.

"What's that for?" I'd laughed at him the first time he wedged a barley sugar into the tied end of the blown-up plastic bag.

"When the barley sugar melts it leaves a small opening. The air escapes and the line drops down into the water.

"So that's how you caught the seagull last week? You need faster-melting barley sugars."

The system worked well in spite of my digs and while the balloon was bobbing on the waters Ken sent his surf rod spinning into the sea for fish the long-line might miss, or set up his whitebait net at the river mouth. Total relaxation for him, but I got bored and went for little walks and watched the surf smacking the rocks. Often there were several fish waiting for me when I returned.

Mrs Jane Arnold, social worker, aged twenty-two and newly married, arrived to inspect the lounge, kitchen, and two bedrooms of our rented flat to check that it was suitable accommodation for a foster baby. I wondered how suitable it really was. Our half of the house was divided from the landlord's half by a floral cotton curtain in the hallway. We had our own toilet but shared the bathroom which was "through the curtain and first room on the right". I never felt comfortable about swishing through that curtain, wondering if we might intrude on the owner's privacy. But then we'd been a bit surprised ourselves the first night we'd moved in - newly married and just returned from our honeymoon at Lake Tekapo. There'd been a knock on our bedroom door at 7am. Ken had jumped out of bed, thinking it was an emergency. "Time to get up, or you'll be late for work," the landlord had called. We'd told him we didn't need waking, we had an alarm clock. "Just trying to be helpful," he'd said. We'd thought it a little strange but now saw him only at the bathroom door, or at his back door on a Thursday night when we paid the rent.

But how would he and his wife feel about a baby in the house? One might be delivered quite soon. Sooner than we had planned for. But we could put the baby bath in the kitchen instead of using their bathroom, and perhaps the new baby wouldn't wake in the night and disturb them.

We explained to Jane Arnold that we were planning to build a house of our own; that these arrangements were only temporary. She wandered around the back garden with us and was lively and cheerful and supportive, but knew as little about bringing up children as we did.

The Senior Child Welfare Officer called me into her room the following day. "I understand you have filled in a foster parent application form and might apply later to adopt. You understand the secrecy involved in these matters. We don't wish you to have access to confidential information which may appear on your file. If you wish to proceed with the foster parent application you will need to leave this office." Stern Mrs Gribben. Why couldn't she relax a bit? "Yes,

Mrs Gribben. I'll speak with my husband about it." Darn Mrs Gribben. I could be waiting at home for six months for a child to appear and we really needed the money for our new house and for extras like doors and a washing machine and... oh the list could go on forever. Door handles and a bathroom vanity unit and what about some furniture?

"Very well," she said. "Let me know your decision." Darn Mrs Gribben and all her secrecy stuff. But I need the department. I must remain polite and smiling.

That night Ken heard my dilemma. "It's not what we planned," he said.

"Nothing is what we planned." I started to sniff.

He sat beside me. "I think you'd better hand in your notice. We'll sit on apple boxes and go without doors if we have to."

I blew my nose and nodded.

Child Welfare approved the foster parent application and within two weeks I had cleaned out my desk at work and said goodbye to the staff, who knew why I was leaving. They wished me well and presented me with an oak bonsai tree. They said they'd no doubt be seeing me again. I walked the ten minutes back to the flat, carrying my small tree, and sat home to wait for motherhood. In whatever form it should arrive.

# Chapter Six

THE PIECE OF LAND awaiting our new house was situated in a newly-created sub-division on the western hills above Lower Hutt, an area defoliated of gorse and struggling native bush as bulldozers carved and chiselled the hills to meet demands for new housing. Ken and I had wandered over these hills a couple of years after we were married, debating which patch of earth to buy. We'd chosen a section with a small view of the sea, and liked the green hills across the valley and the bush below us. It was close to shops, transport and schools for the children. We hadn't doubted that there would be children. Ours of course.

We'd drawn up plans - "How large will we make the lounge and dining room? Should we make it an open staircase from the dining room down to the garage? What sized windows do you want in the bedrooms?" - and put out tenders, for a carpenter to erect the outside shell of the house, for a bricklayer, plumber, electrician and plasterer.

It was now several months since I had left work. There were obviously not enough foster babies around to meet the demand from unsure husbands and "no reason why I'm not pregnant" wives. I collected baby clothes and bought a bassinet. I couldn't apply for another job - the baby could arrive any day.

Then came the phone call from a social worker. "We have a foster child for you."

"Wonderful." Keep calm.

My eyes spun over to the cane bassinet draped lovingly in blue. Blue could be used for either sex. I hoped they would fit in it for a few months. What do you feed babies on? I didn't have any baby formula in the house. Maybe it was on solids. I'd never changed a napkin before. Should I confess my ignorance at this stage? It was suddenly all very real.

"She's an orphan."

An orphan. How tragic.

"I'm afraid she's a little older than you expected."

If she was too big for the bassinet we might have to borrow a cot. I wondered if she would fall out of a bed. "That's all right. We'll manage."

"She's sixteen years of age."

I pushed the phone at my ear. She must mean sixteen months.

"I know you were expecting someone a little younger but Jennifer is a state ward as she has no parents or financial support, and she needs a home during the school holidays. We thought you and Ken would be very suitable."

It was a teenager! We'd never looked after a teenager before. It wasn't quite what I'd given up my job for and the disappointment must have shown in my voice, but it was important to co-operate with Child Welfare.

Jennifer arrived the next day with her large suitcase. She was tall and attractive with long, brown hair. She helped me in the kitchen and we got on well. Except for the evenings. She had lots of friends who arrived in old cars to pick her up. We asked her to be home the first evening by 11pm - it was mid-week and Ken had work the next day. And 11 o'clock seemed late enough for a sixteen-year-old. She would have laughed if I'd said 9.30pm - the time I had to be home when I was that age.

At 11.30pm there was still no sign of her and we went to bed. I couldn't sleep and looked at the clock. Midnight. Ken was making complaining noises. He needed his sleep. One o'clock. Thank goodness he's fallen asleep - the night wouldn't be doing much for his paternal instincts. A baby would have been easier. At least you know where they are. One thirty. Still not here. The baby books I'd read hadn't prepared me for this. What did Dr Spock have to say about errant teenagers? If this was what fostering was about...? But no, she was an orphan and must have had a tragic life. And what do we know about teenagers? Maybe they're all like this. At 2am I heard the back door open. She was home. I could sleep. I'd talk to her in the morning.

There were stories over breakfast about the car breaking down. She was sorry. The following nights as she went out the door I reminded her of the home-by-11pm rule. "I won't forget," she said as she gaily strode out of the house. But she did forget. Always a reason.

I contemplated how a baby would turn into one of these teenagers. Do we ever want a teenager? But for now, what do we do with a teenage orphan who is a state ward who doesn't obey instructions? We can't complain to Child Welfare - they might be concerned about our parenting skills. Maybe Child Welfare was testing us.

Jennifer spent a week with us then went to her friend's house in the country. I was exhausted from lack of sleep and reported back to Child Welfare at the end of the stay. "A nice girl, but she wouldn't come home in the evenings."

"She told us she'd had a ball," Jane Arnold said. "And that you didn't mind when she got home."

"Get one a bit younger next time," Ken said to me.

Not a good start.

The builder began erecting the framework of our new house. Within six weeks he had closed the house in. The roof was on, the timber cladding nailed to the frame, the windows installed and the bricklayer was finishing off a fancy brick alcove at the front entrance. It was time for the hard work to begin.

In the evenings after work, and in weekends, Ken drove the five kilometres from our rented accommodation in the valley to our intended hillside home. He lined walls, attached architraves and skirting boards and fitted a staircase from the dining room to the basement below. He'd never built a house before but seemed to just know where to hammer in nails. I felt a little helpless in the face of such industry. He was working all day, and working much of the night and I was just washing, cleaning, cooking meals, shopping and waiting for motherhood. I decided to enrol in painting and paperhanging classes at night school. I could at least paint and paper when the walls were ready.

Then Kirsty arrived. She was four months old and adorable. A real baby. It seemed like a dream. She fitted nicely into the bassinet and came with her own clothes, milk formula, list of feeding times and Plunket book. The rest was up to us. I was suddenly aware of the enormous responsibility of looking after someone else's child. Everything had sounded simple on paper but I knew nothing about babies. I'd never minded one before, for even a short time. I read the instructions on the milk formula can and mixed up some milk.

Kirsty's mother, Debbie, called in to meet us the first evening. She was warm and smiling, nineteen and unmarried, and had rejected the idea of adoption for her baby. Her only alternative was having the baby fostered as she needed to work to support them both. She was to collect Kirsty each Friday night for the weekend and return her on Sunday nights. I told her how well the first day had gone - Kirsty had drunk her milk and slept at the prescribed times and what a lovely baby she was. I didn't tell her how long it had taken me to get a napkin on her. Debbie said she'd been surprised to hear that we had no other children and asked if this was the first baby we'd looked after.

We were lucky, and so was the landlord, that Kirsty was a placid baby. She slept through the night and was gurgly and responsive in the day, but I still found myself getting really tired. There didn't seem to be time to do anything except look after Kirsty. It was a full-time job. How could it take so much time when she just had to be fed and changed? But I loved having her and missed her in the weekends. She cried when she left us on Friday nights, and she usually came back on Sunday nights with a nappy rash which I'd cleared again by the following Friday.

Kirsty had been in three foster homes by the time she reached us. Child Welfare requested that we have her for four months. Long enough to get pregnant but not long enough to get attached?

But I harboured thoughts of keeping her, of adopting her, and was proud of her progress. She was sitting at five months and doing press-ups at six months. I took her to Plunket and practised baby care on her. I proudly walked her down the street. She reached out for us and cried if anyone else picked her up. Ken made a fuss of her, but tried not to become involved emotionally. After two months I knew I had become emotionally attached. How could I not? I was just wanting a baby and here she was, depending on me for everything and responding and returning my love. I constantly reminded myself that this was only a temporary arrangement, she wasn't mine, she was only helping to get me pregnant. But the heart, not the head was ruling the relationship. I spoke to a Child Welfare officer about my difficulties. I was told again, "Just think of her as a means to an end."

Ken was spending all his spare time at the new house and I rarely saw him. We decided we would see more of each other and could work on the house more easily if we were living in it. The doors still needed hanging, the kitchen bench was a piece of plywood, the gib board was waiting for its wallpaper, the shower for a shower box, and the particle board floors for carpet. We bought a bed and chest of drawers, said goodbye to the landlord and transferred ourselves and

Kirsty to the new abode.

We seemed more of a family in our own house, and Kirsty was a central part of it. "We'd better get the balustrade around the staircase before she starts crawling," I said to Ken.

One day I bumped into an acquaintance while out shopping. Kirsty lay gurgling in the pram, her dark expressive eyes gazing at us. "I didn't know you had a baby," the woman said. "Isn't she cute."

"We're just fostering her," I said. "For a few months." It seemed hard to say.

She looked down at Kirsty. "You should be having your own children before you start looking after other people's." I felt the hot prick of tears and nodded and walked on. I couldn't tell her we desperately wanted our own children. Tell her the reason we were fostering. Only the family now knew that, and only recently. It was all too difficult to talk about.

After four months Debbie asked if we could keep Kirsty until she was two years old. Ken didn't want us to. He could see how attached I had become to this baby. *I* wondered how I could look after her for another sixteen months then let her go. I wanted to keep her forever.

"I can't keep her," I said to a Child Welfare officer, when she called in a few days later on a home visit and we discussed Debbie's request. "We really love her. I'll never be able to give her back after two years."

"When do you want us to take her?" Miss Simpson was sympathetic.

"As soon as possible," said Ken.

Debbie called in to see us that evening after work. Child Welfare had contacted her about the intended move. She seemed puzzled as to why we didn't want to keep this baby of hers whom we loved. "I've become too attached." I couldn't say any more for a few minutes - my throat was too thick. And the tears were waiting, scarcely held back. Then I said how I worried for Kirsty, all the care changes she was having. Debbie said she'd be all right, she had continuity with her every weekend.

Miss Simpson came for Kirsty the following day. Her little bag of belongings and clothes and favourite toys was ready in the lounge. I hoped she wasn't going to another temporary situation like ours. She needed some stability in her little life. I understood how Debbie didn't want to give her up and how the only way she could keep Kirsty was to continue this arrangement of foster homes and weekend visits, but how was her baby going to fare with all these temporary homes and mothers? How many more times could she be given a new five-day-a-week mother before serious bonding problems would arise?

Did Child Welfare talk about this with young mothers who wanted their babies fostered? I felt guilty and sad for not providing the stability that Kirsty needed. I knew she would grieve for us as we would for her. She was as much a part of us as we were of her.

"Where is she going? Could we see her sometimes?" I asked Miss Simpson as I slowly put Kirsty into her arms. Ken stood beside me. Kirsty reached back for us and cried.

"I'm sorry," she said. "She has new foster parents now."

It was like a death as we closed the door on her.

I kept wondering how she was doing without us. Where had she gone? Was she happy? Did she miss us? Child Welfare would tell us nothing. For many years I looked at babies in prams and pushchairs, hoping to find her again. As time went on, I looked at toddlers and pre-schoolers of Kirsty's age and then at older children. I looked at women in the street, searching for Debbie, her mother - I just wanted to know how Kirsty was. We never saw either of them again.

What now? I still wasn't pregnant, and Ken, although much closer to the idea of adoption, still hadn't fully decided. We directed our energies into the house and Ken sometimes went back to Palliser Bay to fish.

One day the phone rang. It was Child Welfare. "We're wondering if you would mind fostering a couple of boys for two weeks. We know you don't want another baby and the teenager was a bit of a handful but these children are aged ten and eight and we're having problems finding somewhere for them to go. Their mother is sick and their father needs to put them somewhere for the school holidays. We wondered if you and Ken could possibly help out."

So we were still on the foster parent list. "I'll check with Ken and let you know," I said. A ten- and eight-year-old didn't sound wildly exciting, but if their mother was sick and Child Welfare really needed us... maybe it was good insurance policy to keep in with them, for the day when Ken agreed to adopt.

Ken wasn't too enthusiastic about the proposal, but said it was up to me, that I'd be the one at home with them all day.

Tony and James were lively and only semi-controllable. They loved the stairs and raced down them, out the back door, around the side of the house and in again through the front door. I asked them not to, but by the next day they had forgotten all instructions. They drew pen lines directly on to the new dining-room table that my parents had given us and picked the few flowers I had in the garden. I warned them not to go near the beehive at the bottom of the section.

An amateur beekeeper friend in Hamilton had offered us a nucleus hive when we'd holidayed up north at Christmas. He knew Ken had kept hives before he met me.

"It will be great to have our own honey," Ken had beamed at me.

"But how do we get them home?" Not with us, surely.

"We'll pop them in the boot."

"The boot? How can we carry them in the boot? It's an eight-hour trip home."

But Ken had nailed flyscreen mesh on to a large wooden box and I'd watched from the safety of a lounge window in Hamilton as he puffed smoke into the friend's hive and transferred four frames of honeycomb and hundreds of bees and their queen into the box. It only just fitted into the boot of the car.

It had been a stifling hot summer's day as we drove south and I'd sweated and stuck to the vinyl car seat, while the Humber's cooling fan blew in hot air. I could hear the frantic fanning of bees' wings above the droning of the engine as they tried to create a circulation of air within the hive. Bees soon began appearing on the back window ledge - sticky overheated bees crawling back and forth along the ledge. How long would they remain on the ledge? I watched one attempting to divert over the back seat.

"The bees are escaping," I'd said to Ken, my voice a shrill panic.

"Oh. They'll be all right."

"They'll sting us." I was agitated by his calmness. I'd never wanted to bring the bees in the car boot.

"They won't hurt you. They're too overheated to fly." He flicked the right indicator and began passing a truck laden with sheep for the slaughter.

"They're still coming out of the boot. There are dozens of them back there." I daren't take my eyes off the ledge. My neck was getting stiff.

"Don't worry. They're Italian bees. They're more gentle than German bees."

The jostling sheep had stared down at us as we slowly gained on them, our old Humber straining at the steep hill.

"What if they start flying?"

Plaintive cries reverberated from the sheep, still staring.

"Don't keep looking at them."

"But they're still crawling up and down the back window ledge. Some of them are dropping on to the back seat."

He concentrated on getting past the sheep truck and I gave up on the bee commentary and rubbed my neck.

The bees and I had arrived home in an equally stressed state but now, six months later, the hive was increasing in size. I didn't want it disturbed by two young boys looking for excitement and I knew Ken would be annoyed if they interfered with the hive.

I'd tried to keep the boys amused most days - out to the zoo, the Trade Fair, the shops - but today we were home. I sent them outside to play. All was quiet. Suddenly, there were screams and yellings and scramblings back inside the house. Hostile yellow and black objects began dive bombing the lounge windows at speed, and making erratic swoops and spins. I yelled at James and Tony to shut all the windows, then, "What did you do to them?"

"Tony threw a rock."

"You did too." Tony glared at James.

They sensed my anger and retreated to the bedroom. I searched for Ken's beekeeping book. Found it. Chapter Ten, page 86. Swarming. Well no... not exactly a swarming. Chapter Six, Hive Management. "Avoid agitating the bees. Puff smoke gently into the entrance. This pacifies the guard bees and helps to disorganise the colony's defence system." Mine were hostile rather than agitated. Closer to warlike. How to light the smoker? And what about the bees that were dive-bombing the windows? I'd need to wear Ken's safety equipment - hat and veil, overalls, boots and gloves - they were about four sizes too big for me. It might be safer staying inside.

I checked the windows and phoned the neighbours with an apology and told them to stay indoors and I'd bring them some honey when things had quietened down. Tony and James were instructed to remain inside for the rest of the day. The two weeks' holiday shortly came to an end and they didn't want to leave. They thought they'd had a marvellous time.

They'd done nothing for my maternal instincts.

# Chapter Seven

SIGNS OF SPRING were appearing. Newly-born lambs huddled against their mothers in the paddocks, and daffodils and jonquils and scented freesias were poking up in the garden. It was three months since James and Tony had left us and eight months since our initial adoption enquiries with Miss Thomas. I was still not pregnant in spite of our four foster children. Or maybe *because* of our four foster children.

Dinner was over and I was reading the front section of the evening paper. "How would you feel about adopting a child?" Ken asked from the other end of the couch as he flicked through the left-overs of the paper. I looked at him in surprise.

"What do you mean? Are you saying you're happy to adopt?"

"Yes, I think I'm ready for it."

Maybe the fostering experience *had* worked in a strange sort of way - he couldn't face any more foster children? Maybe he was concerned we'd still be looking after other people's children in twenty years' time and still with none of our own. Now wasn't the time to ask him. But I knew he missed Kirsty almost as much as I did. I was overjoyed and hugged him and danced around the room and hugged him again.

My parents were delighted and very supportive when I phoned with news of our plans. It would be their first grandchild. "You and Ken are related by love and choice but not blood," said Mum. "Your baby will be the same." Vicki, my seventeen-year-old cousin, arrived for a short holiday. I told her we were applying to adopt a baby and she too was delighted. I phoned Miss Thomas who sounded pleased for us and said to call in any time for the application form.

"I'll pop in to Mum and Dad on the way to Child Welfare," I said to Ken as he was leaving for work the next morning. "They'll want to see Vicki."

"Don't forget to top up the water in the radiator before you go. It's leaking." Ken gulped down the last of his coffee and picked up his briefcase. He kissed me on the cheek. "See you tonight."

He'd agreed to adopt, I could manage a radiator top-up. I could manage anything. And topping up a bit of water was easier than groping around the engine for a starter motor solenoid that still jammed.

In the garage I lifted the Humber bonnet and was presented with a confusing array of inner workings. I should remember where the radiator is.

"Which one do you think it is?" I asked Vicki. She had no idea. I unscrewed the most likely looking cap and gave the opening two pints of water. It gulped it down greedily. I gave it another three. And another three. After twenty pints I suspected the radiator hole was larger than Ken had imagined, and we drove the three kilometres to my parents' hillside house and up on to their driveway. The temperature gauge was almost at bursting point.

"It shouldn't be boiling after all that water," I said to Vicki as we got out of the car. A stream of yellowish oily liquid was pouring out of the vehicle and on to the clean concrete drive beneath.

My father came out to greet us.

"Hi," I said. "What do you think the yellow stuff is on the concrete?"

He bent down and examined the mixture. "Have you done anything to the car recently?"

"No, but I've just given the radiator twenty pints of water."

"Twenty pints?" His eyes widened. He felt the engine. It was still really hot. "Where did you put it?"

"Just there. In the radiator."

"Just there! Are you sure?... You can't have." He shook his head. "That's where the oil goes!"

"Oh no! Is that easy to fix? I'm meant to be picking up our adoption forms this afternoon. Can I drive it into town?"

He shook his head again. He opened his mouth and shut it.

I got my mother to phone Ken. My mother got on well with Ken. "Tell him it's still driveable," I whispered at her as she struggled to convey the news in a serious tone of voice. I looked out the window. My father was still up at the car, staring at the oil filler and his stained concrete drive. Vicki was having convulsions on the front lawn. I got a fit of the giggles and wondered what damage I'd done.

Ken was admirably restrained at the news. He organised a tow truck to deliver the Humber to the nearest garage for a full flush out, suggested a Car Maintenance for Women course for me, and said I wouldn't think it all quite so funny when the bill arrived.

The tow truck arrived half an hour later and the driver hitched up the car. "Gawd, if my girlfriend did this she'd be history. Do you have the keys?"

"Er... actually we just use a screw driver or the end of a comb if you've got one. It doesn't need keys. The screwdriver is in the glove box." I watched it leave the driveway, half hanging from the tow truck, and felt something strangely akin to compassion.

The man at the State Insurance office said they'd never had a claim like it, and Ken said he hoped that my knowledge of the internal workings of babies was greater than that of our motor vehicle.

We duly completed the adoption application forms, detailing our age, place of birth, marital status, occupation, race, religion, physical features, state of health, employer, value of current assets, weekly income and outgoings, source of income, debts and estimated amount owed, family composition, reasons for wanting to adopt and a declaration that we had no previous criminal convictions. I wondered about Rome. No, that was an arrest, not a conviction.

We were interviewed by Miss Thomas who asked why we wanted to adopt. We said that we hadn't been able to have children of our own. She asked us about the colour of our eyes and hair and other physical features, about our health and educational qualifications, and wrote the answers on to a form. We were asked if we had a preference for a girl or a boy. We asked for a girl - we both wanted one. I suspect that Ken was a little uncertain about the male heir issue, although he hadn't spoken about it. We were asked to provide two personal references - commenting on our suitability to be adoptive parents. As we'd never been adoptive parents before, this task may have been difficult for the assignees. I don't remember any questions about our attitude to unmarried mothers.

The police report supplied to Child Welfare was clear of convictions. A field officer would be sent to our new house to make a report on the home situation, and our suitability to be adoptive parents.

The house was becoming more inhabitable but there was still a lot of work to do and we knew that once a baby arrived we would have much less time. Ken's father drove down from Hamilton to help us for a few weeks. He was retired and had been widowed since Ken was eighteen. Ken's mother had contracted a mysterious disease they'd called creeping paralysis and which Ken said he'd been told wasn't hereditary.

We were pleased to see his father arrive but he stood at the front door looking embarrassed as he explained that he had put his foot on the accelerator instead of the brake and hit our car which had been parked out in the street.

The push had sent the Humber down the road and on to the boot of our new neighbours' late-model station-wagon. It was our turn to be embarrassed as we stood at the neighbours' front door and explained the situation - just when the Humber had been working so well, too, after its recent flush-out. The insurance company were less receptive than the neighbours.

Ken's father worked really hard at finishing off architraves and planting shrubs at the front of the house. Ken hung doors and fitted kitchen cupboards. I painted and wallpapered the nursery, then graduated to the hall and living areas.

I had procured some black Thai cotton material, hand screen-printed with fine gold patterning, to use instead of wallpaper on the dining room wall above the open staircase, and persuaded Ken to do the pasting and hanging. "It will remind me of my Bangkok days," I said as he perched and balanced on trestles mounted at a precarious angle on the stairs.

The wall reached above the staircase for eight feet and I gave instructions from ten feet back as to horizontal and diagonal pattern matching, while Ken wrestled with yards of sticky, floppy material that stretched further every time he removed it to improve the alignment, trying to keep his balance on the tottering trestles. Trying, not always successfully, to control his tongue as well as the material. "It might have been easier if you'd lived in a mud hut in your teenage years," he muttered as the black cotton draped itself over his head and shoulders and stuck to the trestles.

I went for a walk while he completed the job and we hung a large round llama rug over the worst of the stretching and bubbling. We put a wrought iron balustrade around the staircase and I painted it black and added fine lines of gold paint to its curves to match the Thai material behind it. We hoped that the social worker would consider it a suitable home in which to bring up a child.

The Child Welfare officer for the Western Hills inspected the house and property. We advised her that we were still working on the bathroom, and the kitchen bench top was due any day. We discussed babies. I told her I felt more confident about handling a new baby after our experience with Kirsty and I wondered how other new adoptive parents coped, with no ante-natal classes and no training in child care easily available to them. How glad I was she had come to us as a four-month-old baby and not a fragile newly-born.

We told friends and remaining family that we had applied to adopt a baby, and discovered that friends from our Contiki trip in Europe were in the same situation - unable to have children and preparing to adopt. We joked that it must have been the water in France. A friend who had worked with me at Child Welfare, and who was also five years married and no children, confessed that she and her husband were also thinking of adoption: "We might have had more success if we'd tried the back seat of the car before marriage." My grandmother thought we were doing a wonderful social service, providing a home for a child who didn't have one. My Aunty Tresna said, "As far as I'm concerned they'll always be your natural children."

Child Welfare shortly advised that approval of the house and its occupants was given. We waited only another three months for the phone call to say that our baby had arrived. Then, would we like to go to the hospital to see her?

# Chapter Eight

WE ENTERED the heavy swing doors of the hospital maternity wing, the linoleum floors a polished brown, the central heating oppressive. My stomach was tight and fluttering. What would she look like? "She's a lovely baby," Miss Thomas had said. Did she say that to all prospective parents? What if the baby didn't appeal? We probably wouldn't be offered another baby for a long time. Ken squeezed my hand.

Matron was welcoming and we followed her through the ward. Past mothers and babies, four of each to a room, floral arrangements and admiring visitors. We were led into a single room, the only furniture a table and a white cot with the name Rachel Susan pinned above it. We approached the cot.

A beautiful fair-skinned baby with delicate features looked back at us through one opening blue eye, the other closed with conjunctivitis. We gazed at her, we memorised her features, we touched her tiny fingers. Ken and I looked at each other through misty eyes. There were no doubts. She was for us. "She's lovely," I whispered, the only sound that would emerge from my throat.

The matron stood proudly beside the cot. "Yes, she's a dear little baby and her mother was a very nice girl. She went home a few days ago. If you'd like to come back tomorrow we'll show you how to manoeuvre her out of the brace and you can bath her. We've had eight children born this year with congenital hips, all girls. She will need the brace on for at least six weeks. Thereafter it will be regular checks for three years to make sure the hip bones are remaining in the sockets."

We wondered if there was a family history of congenital hips. No one could tell us.

Her first mother. I wanted to know more about her. Not just that she was unmarried, aged seventeen, University Entrance, height 5'6", slim build, eyes greyish-green, intelligent girl, lived with a gynaecologist and his family for some of the pregnancy, came from Invercargill; the information hastily scribbled on to a scrap of paper after Miss Thomas had phoned the good news through. I wanted to know how this mother felt about leaving her tiny baby behind. What about the father, aged nineteen, height 5'8", eyes brown, very good looking, technician, likes sport, music? Did the mother have his support? Did she have the support of her family? What was she going to do with her life? What were her hopes for her child? What did she know about us, the parents dealt out for her baby? But most of all I wanted to thank her for this baby, to reassure her that she would be cared for and loved.

I phoned Miss Thomas.

"Oh, hello Robyn. Matron tells me you're delighted with the baby you have just visited. I'm so pleased. Yes, that's a good idea having a session or two at the hospital to learn how to manage the brace. No, sorry, we just can't pass any messages on to the mother. She has gone back home and will be starting a new life for herself. She is putting all this behind her. I'll arrange for the interim order of adoption to be prepared. We'll try and arrange it for tomorrow." Miss Thomas was gentle but firm.

I wasn't reassured. I needed to communicate with this mother. I would love to have met her. It was such an extraordinary gift, giving your baby to a stranger. We had no option but to accept Child Welfare's ruling.

"She's a cute little baby. We've grown quite fond of her here. What are you calling her?"

"Katrina Maree." I grinned at the maternity nurse. "I need a lesson on brace extraction." I followed the nurse to where our baby lay. She picked her up by the brace and put her on the table. I gazed affectionately at Katrina who seemed to accept her shell without complaint.

"Now if you can bend this lower part of the brace back out of the way - where it curves up between her legs - you'll get her left leg out. That's right. Now the same with the right. Good. Now just try and lift her up at an angle and slide her body downwards and away from this section of the brace that runs up her back and over her shoulders. No, it's not easy but I think you'll get used to it. Good. Now just slide her into the water. Oh, she likes that. She can kick her legs and move again. When do you take her home?"

"On Monday." I sloshed the water around my beautiful new baby. She seemed so tiny after Kirsty. I dried and dressed her, and sneaked a cuddle before putting her back into her metal casing.

When Ken and I walked up the long flight of stairs to the lawyer's office, to sign the interim adoption order, it was a short informal happening. The birth mother had signed the consent form ten days after Katrina was born. We knew she had to wait ten days after the birth for the consent to be valid. Miss Thomas had told us that we would have to wait for a minimum of six months before the final adoption order could be made effective. During that interim period the birth mother could change her mind if it was proven that she had signed the interim consent against her will. We had been told not to worry about the mother changing her mind. "It's a very unusual event, and the mother has to prove that she was of unfit mind at the time of consent. The interim order has never been revoked in my experience."

The lawyer produced the form, part of which was covered with a piece of white paper. He looked at us and pointed to the bottom of the form. "Don't ask her name. Just sign here, please." The birth mother's identity - the key to our child's genetic history - lay underneath that scrap of white paper. It would have been a simple matter to have knocked the paper off. We didn't dare. We might be reported to Child Welfare. Child Welfare might not offer us a further child.

*To Robyn and Ken, a daughter,*
*Katrina Maree. 8lb 3oz*

No birth date, no place of birth at the request of Miss Thomas. "Birth mothers have been known to trace their children through the birth notice in the newspaper." It looked a bit stark, as if we weren't overjoyed about the arrival, but the 8lb 3oz did expand it slightly. We decided against printing `chosen daughter'. We wanted Katrina's arrival to appear 'normal' to those who didn't know of our adoption plans. Besides, we hadn't chosen her, Child Welfare had, although we totally approved of the choice.

We registered Katrina's birth and were asked if we wanted 'adopted' written on the birth certificate. We said no. Births, Deaths and Marriages advised that if Katrina needed a copy of her birth certificate our names would be listed as her parents. Details of the original birth registration with her birth mother's name could not be disclosed.

We felt quite comfortable and composed with this new baby and could thank our experiences with Kirsty for that. Katrina slept through the night from three weeks of age and was an easy baby to care for. We commented to friends that we would love to be able to meet her mother. She had given us her baby and we knew we would want to tell Katrina all we could of her mother as she grew older. Well-meaning advice came back to us, "It would be unwise to consider any contact... You don't know what sort of person she is, whether she'll try and take her daughter back... It's better this way, she can't trace you... Children can only have one mother... You never know what emotions she may be going through, whether she might want her child back... Why do you want to? She's yours now..."

But for us the desire to communicate with Katrina's mother at the time of her birth was greater than the fear of a mother returning to claim her child. There was a general assumption by society that some mothers giving up babies for adoption didn't care about their babies and they would just be happy for someone to give their baby a home. But they must care, I thought. It must be the most terrible, difficult and painful decision to give your baby away. Wouldn't the mother be reassured by some sort of communication, through Child Welfare as third party, from the new parents? "Child Welfare don't do that," we were told by the visiting social worker.

They did conduct regular home assessment visits and told us to tell Katrina of her adoption while she was still very young. The officer was unobtrusive and encouraging. But we were strongly advised against contact with the birth parents, not to try and look for them. "It would only confuse Katrina, and the mother's life would be disrupted. You're her parents now. It's in everybody's interests to forget the past." Similarly we should avoid contact if the natural parents managed to locate the child.

The hospital paediatrician advised us, when Katrina was two months old, that she could be removed from her brace, but would require regular check-ups on her hips until she was three years of age. We'd got used to picking her up by the brace which supported her neck, back, and limbs, and she seemed so light and floppy after it was discarded. But we could now put dresses on her and plastic pants over her napkins and, most importantly, cuddle her without a metal frame dividing us. We loved her so much and she felt truly ours.

Child Welfare reports were in favour of the adoption process being completed and, eight months after the interim adoption order, we put a pretty pink dress on Katrina and presented ourselves at the Family

Court. We wore our best smile for the judge. He smiled benevolently back at us, asked us if we were enjoying parenthood, then stamped the final adoption order. Katrina, now a bright, healthy baby, was legally ours.

*Effects of the Final Adoption Order*
*"In New Zealand law, adoption involves a once-and-for-all substitution of new parents for the existing parents of a child. This substitution is total. The existing birthparents cease in law to be the parents of the child, and the adopters become the parents for all purposes, with the child being deemed to have been born to them in lawful wedlock."[1]*

# Chapter Nine

*Not flesh of my flesh, nor bone of my bone*
*But still miraculously, my own*
*Ne'er forget, for even a minute*
*You grew not under my heart*
*But in it*

A FRIEND gave us the poem. It expressed our sentiments as adoptive parents. Sometimes we repeated it for Katrina. We started telling her of her adoption at about nine months of age. Practice runs, really. We knew she couldn't understand but each time we found it easier to say. "You are our darling adopted daughter." "You are our wonderful adopted daughter." Warm words so that Katrina would learn to associate adoption with warm, loving feelings. With happiness. We hoped that by the time she was old enough to understand, adoption would feel a natural part of her upbringing. We bought her a book called *Mr Fairweather and His Family*. "One day Mrs Fairweather said, 'I know we are very happy but there is something missing.'

'What can it be?' said Mr Fairweather. 'We have a dog and we have a cat. Perhaps we need a budgerigar.'

'No, not a budgerigar,' said Mrs Fairweather, shaking her head.

'What about a baby elephant?' said Mr Fairweather.

'I know just what we want,' said Mrs Fairweather. 'We want a baby boy or a baby girl.' But although they waited a long time, no..." It became a much loved bedtime story.

We often wondered about Katrina's mother. What was she doing? How was she feeling about the loss of her child? Was it affecting her life? Where did she live? Had she got married? Did Katrina have brothers and sisters? Her mother became a fantasy figure. We knew so little about her.

Ken continued working on the interior of the house and I finished the painting and wallpapering to our mutual satisfaction. We turned our attention to the section outside and Ken constructed wooden moulds, two foot six inches long and six inches high, in which to make crib wall blocks. Each evening after work he hand-mixed concrete and poured it into the moulds, after extricating the previous night's work. Six months later he considered he had enough blocks to begin the Great Wall Project. A wall sixty feet long - the width of our section - and twenty feet in height. We would need a massive amount of clay fill to build up the area and create a flat back garden.

Truckloads of clay regularly passed our house on their way to the tip as more hillside continued to be carved up in the area for home building sites, and we diverted them down to the bottom of our driveway, in reverse gear, where they off-loaded their spoil. They were happy to oblige. Our back garden was a lot closer than the tip.

By the time Katrina was two we decided we would like a sibling for her. I still hadn't become pregnant. We made an appointment with Mrs Nolan, Miss Thomas's successor. She was middle-aged but, as with all the female field workers at the office, had no children of her own. Applying to adopt seemed so much easier the second time around. We asked for a boy; Ken's doubts about an adopted male heir had disappeared with the arrival of Katrina, and 'flesh and blood' was no longer important to him. We couldn't imagine that any child born naturally to us could be more loved than our adopted child. We didn't expect to wait too long for our next baby. There were more baby boys than baby girls available.

Mrs Nolan phoned us two months after our application. "We have a little boy we think would be suitable for you. Unfortunately he has some minor medical problems - a hernia and an undescended testicle. He is also a little underweight. He is just 6lb."

Ken and I visited the baby at the hospital. Matron made a fuss of Katrina, one of 'her' babies, and led us to the cot. He was a nice-looking little baby. We asked about the health problems.

"The testicles should descend by the time he is five, "she said, "but you won't be able to let him cry for long. The hernia might rupture."

How do you stop a newly-born baby from crying?

The baby had deep brown eyes and olive skin. We wondered why a brown-eyed dark-skinned baby would be chosen for a fair-skinned blue-eyed family. Should adoptive parents expect that they be matched with babies of the same colouring as themselves, when natural children often have different colouring from their parents? Perhaps colouring is the only similarity we are able to have. But somehow the baby didn't feel right for us. We should have been enthusiastic about this new baby, but we weren't.

What would Mrs Nolan think if we expressed doubts about a baby that she had chosen for us? Can adoptive parents reject babies? How long would we have to wait for another baby? Would they *give* us another baby? We'd had no doubts about Katrina. Why did we feel unsure about this little boy?

I phoned Mrs Nolan the following morning, still uncertain of what to say. She'd be wondering why she hadn't heard from us. After five rings I hung up, hung up on the insistent ringing in my ears. I walked around the garden pulling out the weeds, and breathed in the warm smell of newly mown grass - the next door neighbour's grass. I walked inside again and fiddled around on the piano, then realised I couldn't delay ringing any longer.

"We've been to see the baby," I said to Mrs Nolan. My voice sounded lifeless.

"Oh, I was just about to phone you, Robyn. We have some sad news. We've just been contacted by the mother's lawyer. She has changed her mind. I'm very sorry."

She had changed her mind! I felt an enormous relief. I didn't know what to say.

"This is most unusual and you must be very disappointed, but we'll find you another little boy."

"Thank you," I said. His mother had changed her mind. We didn't have to make the decision. Wasn't it fortunate I'd delayed phoning.

The following week I checked out the records on our physical features. I was listed as brown-eyed, and Mrs Nolan corrected the file.

In Whitcombe and Tombs bookshop I noticed *A Guide To Adoption in New Zealand* by Eileen Saunders, an ex-Child Welfare officer who had been responsible for making adoption placements. I bought a copy of this new publication and was able to read, for the first time, a book written for adoptive parents in New Zealand.

Lewis Anderson, Superintendent of Child Welfare in New Zealand wrote as part of his foreword in the book, "New Zealand's first Adoption Act was passed in 1881, and the one currently in force was passed in 1955. The latter is, in my opinion, a good Act embodying the best of overseas provisions. Adoptions are big business, in that currently nearly

4,000 adoptions a year are made in this small country with a population of under 3,000,000. All the indications are that the numbers of orders will increase." He sounded like the manager of a giant baby factory. What would mothers giving up their babies feel about these comments?

The author, Eileen Saunders, wrote in her introduction, "On the whole adoption is very much 'in'. Indeed it is almost fashionable and it is certainly very much an accepted custom. Adoption is for many children their only chance of a normal life."

I learnt that in 1968 when I began thinking about adoption there were 3780 adoption orders made, and seventy-five percent of these children, mainly under a year in age, were adopted by strangers. In the same year, 8094 illegitimate births were registered, which was thirteen percent of all live births. About thirty-five percent of these babies were adopted, twenty-four percent remained with their mothers, and about twenty-three percent with parents not legally married.

Then I read the section, 'Can the Mother Take the Baby Back?'

"The mother cannot simply 'change her mind' once she has signed her consent. If, before an interim order is made she really does change her mind she must inform the court. You must, however, have opportunity to make your application, and the court will decide. Once an interim order is made the magistrate would be unlikely to upset an order without grave cause. A final order cannot (except in some cases so rare as not to concern you) be upset. The reason this rarely happens is that no good social worker ever pushes a girl into a decision about adoption, not only because it is unfair to the girl but also because she would have legal grounds for a sympathetic hearing in such a case if she could prove she had given her consent under pressure."

Had the mother of the baby boy offered to us already signed her consent before she changed her mind? It didn't matter. I just wondered.

Were all Child Welfare's social workers good?

Friday, 21 April 1972

We have no doubts when we see Aaron. He is only five days old, too new for his birth mother to have signed the consent form but Mrs Nolan says we can see him early to make up for the previous disappointment. It is a different hospital from where Katrina was born. She is excited about her new brother and sits on a little chair in the hospital room and helps me feed him. He drinks the milk down happily.

He has blond hair and blue eyes and looks like Katrina. I notice a dent in each temple and ask Matron about it.

"He was a forceps delivery. The dents will disappear." She walks over to a table and brings me a large bundle. "His mother is a lovely girl. And she has left these for you." Smocked night gowns, a shawl, a tiny cream crocheted jacket, helmet and booties. A pile of napkins. I feel a lump in my throat. I must let her know that her son will be precious to us too. I am unaware, then, that she is in the same building, only a few doors away from us. Grieving.

We ask about circumcision.

"Are you Jewish?"

"No, we're not."

"You don't chop off your ears just because you don't want to wash behind them."

We feel suitably chastised and drop the subject. I vaguely remember circumcision being something you do because of the war and the sand in the desert.

I finish feeding him and marvel at our new son. He is so beautiful. We return home and I phone Mrs Nolan. No delays this time, just an urgent desire to say how wonderful he is and to ask her if she will pass on a letter of thanks to his mother for her son and for the clothes she made and left for him.

"Yes, he is a lovely baby. We'll arrange for the forms to be signed in five days' time and you'll be able to take him home. No, I'm sorry we can't pass on any letters. The mother has left the district now and we can't get in touch with her. In any event there must be no communication with her. We can't give you her name, and your names can't be divulged to her."

"I'd leave my surname and address off the letter, of course."

"No, we can't. But don't think of this crocheting as being done for you or the baby. She'd have had a lot of time to fill in while she was pregnant. Anyway she's putting it all behind her now and starting a new life."

Why can't I leave a letter? Anonymously. His mother will be wondering so much.

And I don't believe she just crocheted those garments for something to do.

*"I could not believe I had created this little person. It seemed as if I was the only one who had given birth. I was absolutely elated. I told him how wonderful I thought he was. I must have kissed him at least a hundred times, his little face, his eyes, his nose, his fingers, his ears. He never cried. Babies supposedly know the sound of their mother's voice so maybe he felt some sort of comfort with me talking. His face was so soft. Every time from then on, whenever I touched a new baby's face, I thought of him and that very special hour we had together." [2]*

# Chapter Ten

AARON slotted into our family as if born to it. We loved him from the start and marvelled at our great fortune in having these two wonderful children. And I loved being a full-time mother. None of the mothers in our part of the street had paid employment and our children grew up with a variety of neighbourhood friends and in a variety of neighbourhood backyards. Their pre-school days revolved around playdough and Lego, sand-pits and swings, make-believe libraries and schools, dress-ups, tea-parties and swimming. Most backyards had some sort of pool, even if it was only a collapsible one that was put away for the winter. Aaron developed a passion for tractors and bulldozers and quivered with excitement from the age of eighteen months whenever he saw one. *Farmer Small and his Tractor* became his favourite book.

Passing trucks continued to disgorge their fill into the back of the section, and Ken's crib wall finally reached its desired twenty feet in height. He ordered truckloads of topsoil to cover the clay fill. The newly-created flat land enabled him to plant fruit trees and a vegetable garden, with a large area of lawn for the children to play on. He terraced the garden with mini crib walls and put up extra fences in the children's play area, and from split quarry-rocks and cement he built stone walls each side of the driveway.

It was time to tarseal the drive. Ready-mixed hot tar was delivered to the house and a fifteen-year-old lad from the tarsealing company was assigned the task of compressing the hot mix. He drove a small yellow roller, slowly up and down the driveway, consolidating the hot black sticky stuff.

Halfway way through the operation something went wrong between the driver and the gear stick on the roller. The yellow machine shot down the drive at speed and the fifteen-year-old lad jumped off and rolled down to the right of it. Unhurt. Through the newly erected wooden fence on the top terrace went the yellow roller, over the mini crib wall - just a six foot drop - past the para pool on the left, and into the carrots and lettuces. A large mound of rhubarb finally halted its progression, six inches from the Great Wall. Ken arrived home from work to find a man from the tar company wound up in a profusion of apologies with promises to rectify the damage, a crane on the sticky tar trying to reach over into the lower terrace to extricate the roller, and the children in a state of great excitement. Farmer Small and his tractor had come to life in their own backyard.

Our children enjoyed the neighbourhood. They were not regarded as 'different' by their friends because of their adoption: it was not as issue. Some neighbours had even forgotten they were adopted. We talked about it on occasions with Katrina and Aaron as they were growing up. We told them that their mothers had loved them very much and didn't want to part with them, but were unable to look after them; that their mothers wanted the best for them with both a mother and father to care for them. The children accepted their adoption as being as natural and normal as any other form of family extension.

One day I overheard Katrina and a young friend talking in her bedroom.

"Is this a photo of your mother?"

"Yes. And my father," Katrina said.

"Where are you?"

"Oh, I wasn't born then."

"Were you just a seed in your mummy's tummy?"

"I didn't grow in my mummy's tummy. I grew in another lady's tummy."

"Oh, did you? Have you got any more clothes for this doll?"

I increasingly suspected that there would never be any 'babies growing in my tummy'. My endometriosis had worsened again over the years and medication for the problem was no longer effective. The nausea and pain were relentless. Then I missed three periods in a row. Was this pregnancy?

I visited the gynaecologist that Miss Thomas had previously recommended. He was kind, compassionate and interested in me as a person - not just as a gynaecological abnormality. He had a photograph of his wife and children on his desk. I suspected that was a statement, in case any of his patients wanted to fall in love with him. He listened to my story, the endometriosis problems, the treatment for it, the infertility, and our adopted children. He asked if I would mind waiting in the waiting room for about twenty minutes - he had just one patient left for the day, and would like to spend more time with me.

I soon returned to his room for an examination. "You have a lump in the uterus, about the size of an orange. It may be the endometriosis or some other abnormality. Or it may be that you are pregnant. We should do a test now. How would you feel about pregnancy?"

"I'd be thrilled. But if I'm not, I won't be too disappointed. If you'd asked me that question four years ago I would have given you a different answer from today. But our two adopted children are all I need. They feel just as much ours as if I'd given birth to them."

He took the urine sample. It was negative. The small surge of hope died.

"We need to do something about this problem - it has been going on for too long. I would initially use a laparoscope, a tube with a light in it, to see what is going on. This is done under anaesthetic and involves just a tiny incision in the abdomen. If possible I would cauterise any growths. If this is not possible we may have to remove your uterus. How do you feel about all this?"

"Just do whatever has to be done," I said. "I just want to get rid of this pain."

Ten days later the uterus was removed. Thirty-one was still quite young to have a hysterectomy and I suppose I should have been extremely upset at my loss, that there was now no hope of ever producing our own children. But I wasn't. It had never performed well for me and I felt much fitter physically without it.

But eighteen months later I felt unwell again, and noticed blood in the toilet. It scared me. I visited my 'You don't need a pregnancy test I'm sure you're pregnant' GP who told me it was probably just a stomach flu. But the bleeding didn't stop and I revisited my gynaecologist. The endometriosis had spread to the bowel. He was reluctant to operate again so soon, but removed the right ovary - hopefully to reduce the hormonal activity, and took out my scarred appendix for good measure. It worked.

I wondered how I would feel later on about all this extraction of reproductive parts, those supposedly vital parts of my womanhood, but it never caused me any problems, nor did I ever agonise about it.

Katrina turned five. It was time to enrol her in school. She didn't want to go without Aaron - they were the best of friends. I completed the school enrolment form - Name, Address, Date of Birth, the usual questions. Inoculations. Then, Pregnancy Normal? This was tricky. It was normal for Katrina's mother, but not for me. I hesitated, then wrote 'yes'. I supposed they were looking for behavioural problems that could be birth-related. But I didn't want the school to know at this stage that she was adopted. If there were any problems I didn't want adoption being blamed for them.

By the time she was six, Katrina had become an avid reader. We made frequent trips down to the well-stocked public library. One day she spied a book with a paper sculpture illustration on the front cover of a mother and father gazing at a baby in a crib. "*How Babies Are Made*. I think I'll have this one," she said, and added it to her little pile of borrowings. Aaron's selected reading material was confined to tractors, planes and fire engines.

In the bedroom that night Katrina got out *How Babies Are Made* and asked me to read it to them. I saw it was aimed at three- to ten-year-olds and opened the first page. "This is a story about you. Have you ever thought about how babies grow? Have you ever wondered how you were born? In this book we shall talk about how new plants and animals and human beings are created."

We read about the eggs in a plant ovary, and bees and pollen. We looked at giraffes and rabbits. At a rooster astride a hen and then the hen laying an egg and the egg "coming out of the same opening as the sperm went in". We read about dogs mating and finally about mothers and fathers and human babies.

The text and paper sculpture illustrations were explicit and the children sat enthralled. Aaron became engrossed with the paper sculptures and *Farmer Small and His Tractor* were soon discarded in favour of this real life stuff. He took the book to bed with him each night, and sat it on top of his bedside cabinet in the day time.

We had a week's spell of warm fine weather and Aaron was playing outside with Mark, the three-year-old from next door. I was busy trying to make date scones. My mother made wonderful date scones but mine never seemed to rise the same way. Aaron interrupted his play with frequent trips into the house, rushing down to his bedroom and rushing out the front door again. He stopped by at the kitchen on his fifth trip and said, "Have we got any more dolls or animals?" He was holding his favourite red rabbit and Katrina's crocheted doll with the pink dress and long woollen plaits.

"Yes, there are lots in the toy box, love."

"I got those before," and he rushed out the door with the doll and the rabbit.

I poked some extra dates into the scone dough and peered out the window to see what games they were playing. Mark was standing on the lawn, his hand-knitted woollen jumper bulging out in front of him. "Put your legs apart. Now just stand there while it's born," said Aaron as he plunged his arm up inside the bulging jumper and slowly drew down the red rabbit. "Now give it a drink," as he lifted Mark's woollen garment and thrust the rabbit's head at his chest. The ground was covered with dolls and stuffed animals of all description. There had obviously been a multiple birth. The 'doctor' bent down and picked up Katrina's china doll, the one with the curled blonde locks. The session wasn't over yet.

I walked outside to the lawn, dusting my floured hands on my jeans. Mark's mother, eight months pregnant, wasn't in sight. I wondered what she would think of my son's activities. It was only the previous week that he had donned his batman cape and mask and flown from the window of his bedroom to the lawn three feet below, solely for Mark's benefit.

"Time to pack up and come in for lunch," I called and put the book on the floor of the car ready for returning to the library.

At the kitchen table Aaron sat the red rabbit beside him while we ate peanut butter and marmite sandwiches, and carrot sticks and the date scones. Well-browned squat scones with bits of date sticking out of them.

We drove down to the library that afternoon, stopping to pick up a neighbour at the bus stop. "Hello there," she said as she twisted around to greet Aaron strapped into his car seat in the back. "Are you reading a book? That's nice. What's the name of it?"

"*How Babies Are Made*," and he held up a picture of a baby emerging from its mother. I groaned. How had he reached it?

"That's a good book for the back seat of the car," said the neighbour.

That night it was back to *Farmer Small* and *The Penguin Who Hated The Cold* and *Boris The Whale.*

Our old Humber made only three more trips to the library. Its brakes failed one afternoon while it was parked on my parents' sloping driveway. We heard the crash as it hit the neighbours' concrete wall at the bottom. The wall was unmarked but the car's boot was crumpled out of recognition. The vehicle was towed away from the same address for the second time, this time not to return. It was written off, an ignominious ending for our old turquoise-blue Humber 80.

We bought ourselves a slightly newer car and Ken suggested we try it out on the hills and visit his old fishing haunts in the Wairarapa. We came home with twenty kahawai. A school of them had moved through the long-line attached to the balloon. They weren't my favourite fish but Ken had bled them immediately after removing them from the hooks and said that would improve the flavour.

"What are we going to do with twenty dead kahawai?" I asked as they sprawled all over the kitchen bench, mouths ajar, glassy eyes staring at me.

"I think I'll smoke them. But it'll take three days to dry them before they're ready to be smoked."

"Are you going to hang them on the line?" Feeble attempt at a joke. He'd never smoked fish before. I hoped he knew what he was doing.

"No, the birds would get them. They'll have to go on the lounge floor."

"The lounge floor?"

"Yes. Best place. Lots of sun. They'll dry well."

The carpet hadn't been down very long and there wasn't a lot of spare room for twenty bled kahawai but Ken put lots of newspaper underneath them and salted them well.

"That's to preserve them," he said. "Stops them going off." The children gazed in wonder through the closed lounge glass door at all the fish on the floor.

Two days later a neighbour called in to borrow some butter. She wondered about the strange smell in the hallway. "It's the fish," I said. "They're in the lounge. Come and have a look at them. Just one more day and they'll be ready."

Judith held her nose as the door opened and the smell hit us. The sun was streaming into the room. Fish lay in front of the sofa, beside the piano stool, under the coffee table, in front of the window.

She stared around the room. "What are you doing with these?"

"We're going to eat them. It's how fish are prepared for smoking."

Judith left in a hurry, without the butter.

By day three we could smell the fish from the bathroom at the other end of the house. Ken lit a fire of manuka chips in a metal box, inserted two oven racks, and put the fish on the racks. They lay there for an hour absorbing the manuka smoke. He tenderly removed them, sealed them in plastic bags and put them in the freezer. Except for two fillets that we were to have for dinner.

I might just try a bit for lunch, I thought. See if the smoking has improved the flavour.

I ate most of the smaller fillet. It wasn't bad, just a slightly unusual flavour which I attributed to the manuka chips. I washed my lunch plate and noticed my hands were red. They began to itch and my face felt hot and flushed. My knees were burning and felt fiery. Bright red knees. How strange. I felt all right but peered at my face in the mirror. A bright red face and two bloodshot eyes stared back at me. I watched the redness move slowly down my body. It has to be Ken's fish, I thought. But does a fish make you itch? Turn you red? I phoned the "You don't need a pregnancy test I'm sure you're pregnant" doctor.

"Come down to the surgery if the symptoms still persist in half an hour," he said.

I drove down the hill half an hour later. "The colour's reached my chest," I said to the doctor. "Can fish do that?"

"It's unusual," he said, and jabbed my right arm with a needle. Within minutes the colour had drained away, leaving me pale and wan.

I phoned Ken. He told me not to touch any more of the fish. I phoned Paulette, my sister-in-law. She asked me to bring the fish up for her cat. It was a black cat. "It can hardly turn red, can it," she said.

I took six fillets to her house. "See how Whiskers goes on these. There's more in the freezer if you'd like them."

She phoned me the next day. "The cat's fine," she said, "and we're improving. I made fish cakes for us last night. I was getting a bit low on the housekeeping money and Lindsay likes fish. My hands started itching just mixing up the fish and potato. Lindsay went bright red in the face and got bloodshot eyes within minutes of eating it. We both did. I confessed about the origins of our meal and he wasn't too thrilled. But there wasn't much point in going for an injection - it would have used up the savings I'd made on the housekeeping money." She laughed. "Only problem was, we had our first meeting of the Caged Bird Society last night. There were twelve of us in this huge hall. You should have heard the noises our stomachs were making and our faces and eyes were still bright red. We looked like a couple of parrots. My hands are still itching."

I rang the Health Department for information the following morning. They advised me to contact the DSIR. A scientist arrived and removed all our remaining kawahai from the freezer. He said he was currently researching toxic reactions to fish that swim in shoals but normally samples were irretrievable, having been already eaten. He went through Paulette's rubbish bin for her contribution to marine science. One month later he sent us a letter. "We thank you for the use of samples made available to us in the research of toxic substances in pelagic fish. It has been determined that the condition is caused by a bacterium which is found in pelagic fish and which becomes toxic if fish is left in warm conditions for a period of time before eating."

Ken had his fishing and I decided to pursue an interest in organ music. With Katrina at school and Aaron at kindergarten most mornings, I took organ lessons, and spent hours at a church in the valley practising exercises from the *Bach Technique of Organ Pedalling* and *Trevor's Book of Organ Voluntaries.* Working two hands on two manuals was not difficult, but learning to play with two feet as well took some severe concentration. Katrina and Aaron liked to come down with me after school and play ministers and churches while I practised.

"I'll be Prime Minister," said Aaron leaning over the pulpit at the congregation of one. "We'll now sing *Bananas in Pyjamas.*"

"You can't sing that. It has to be a church song."

"What about *Magon the Dragon*?" Aaron waved a hymn book around and almost lost his footing on the chair in the pulpit.

"You can be the congregation and I'll be the Prime Minister."

"Shall I take up the collection? Who's got some money?" A question Aaron was still asking twenty years later.

The Reverend Howan stopped by at the organ for a quick chat. "What did God say?" called Katrina from the pulpit as the Reverend disappeared into his study.

"He's not God, he's the minister," I said as I started practising the next prelude on my list.

The children spent many hours playing crawling games under the pews but Katrina recently confessed that their favourite pastime was picking off the little rubber bits from under the floor mats at the front door and feeding them into the grille vents on the church front wall.

I was sensitive to comments from well-meaning people who looked at the children playing and said, "Wasn't it good of you to take such children into your home... Aren't they lucky children." Why should children be considered lucky to have love and a normal upbringing? If anyone was lucky we parents were, who had our 'own' children in spite of our infertility. How many biological parents are told that their children are lucky? Perhaps I was too sensitive. Families 'born' by adoption were still considered unusual by some people, and not as good as traditional families.

Others were unaware that our children were adopted and I cringed inwardly at comments they made about adopted children. "How could people love someone else's child as much as their own biological child?" or "They have two children plus an adopted daughter." Was an adopted daughter not a proper child? We were aware that natural parenting was regarded as a superior form of parenting. We'd thought so ourselves until we became adoptive parents.

But for the most part our children were regarded by our friends as a normal part of the family, and Katrina and Aaron were lovingly embraced into our extended family. They were much-loved grandchildren and spent many happy hours and days in my parents' care.

The organ lessons continued, now on a pipe organ, and I loved the sounds it produced. My tutor asked me if I was interested in playing for a local funeral director. The organ was a tinny electronic Yamaha situated at the rear of the chapel. It had a loose swell pedal and the slightest pressure on the pedal sent surges of increased volume on to the backs of the assembled mourners. I had about four funerals a week and friends wondered how I survived such a morbid existence. I learnt which ministers tried to make the service meaningful and which ones just intoned on through the formal funeral service, regardless of the religious beliefs or non-beliefs of the deceased.

I was never sure what musical requests I might have. *The Lord's My Shepherd* and *Abide with Me* were top favourites. Safe hymns, most people knew them. It would be embarrassing to farewell loved ones with scrambled singing and thin unsure sounds. As I strung the chords together I often thought of the *Titanic* sinking and those aboard bravely singing the first verse of *Abide with Me* before descending into their watery grave. Or was it *Nearer my God to Thee*? I really should check it out.

One day I played for a Spiritualist funeral. I'd never played for a Spiritualist funeral before and was a little startled when tappings and scratchings sounded along the chapel windows. The mourners were also distracted. Was this Margery trying to reconnect with Henry? Tap, tap, they weren't going away. Cyril, the funeral director, sidled up to me in the back of the chapel. "Is that you making all those noises?"

"Definitely not," I said. "They're coming through the windows."

He went outside to investigate earthly reasons for the disruptions. I heard a shrieking and a running of feet. The tappings ceased. Cyril slipped back into the chapel, and stood beside me at the organ. I looked questioningly at him. "The pupils from the alternative school for college drop-outs," he whispered. "It's next door." The mourners concentrated again on the eulogies and words of comfort, unaware of the source of their discomfort.

The phone rang one Tuesday morning in July. "Two o'clock on Thursday afternoon and they want *Silent Night* as the coffin goes out."

I laughed. "You're having me on. You're not? Just make sure the vicar explains that this was a favourite song and not the organist gone loopy." But the vicar didn't, and I received strange looks from mourners' heads as they turned backwards to stare. *All is calm, all is bright.* The notes drifted reluctantly from the organ. Cyril wished me Happy Christmas as I left the chapel.

I enjoyed relating these stories to the family. Ken and the children grew accustomed to my tales of the unexpected.

# Chapter Eleven

LIFE WAS GOOD. And then Ken came home from work one wintry day and said that the company he worked for had sold out to its parent Australian company. His position as production manager no longer existed but he would be transferred to another company within the group, on the same level. He was unhappy about the transfer.

"Let's go to England for a while instead," I said. It was fifteen years since we'd first met there and I was ready to travel again. "We'll use your superannuation savings for fares, buy a Mercedes Benz in Germany, stay away the required twenty-one months to bring it back duty-free, and with the profit when we sell it we'll recoup the superannuation money."

Ken was immediately enthusiastic. It sounded like an adventure and the proposed financial arrangements encouraged him to consider it seriously. Aaron and Katrina at just seven and nine thought a plane trip to a foreign country sounded fun. With little further prompting Ken resigned from work, collected the necessary superannuation booty, and three months' salary. We made plans to leave in three months' time. Christmas in London!

Friends were surprised and reactions were mixed at our proposed venture. "Do you think you'll be able to get a job over there... What about the children's interrupted schooling?... Go for it, I wish I could... Where will you live?... I love England, you're so lucky... Is it wise giving up your job - do you think you'll be able to get another one when you get back?... I wish my husband would be willing to do that."

My cousin Vicki was now working as a social worker with the Department of Social Welfare in the South Island. Child Welfare had amalgamated with Social Security in 1972, the year that Aaron was born, and had become the new Department of Social Welfare. Vicki suggested I bring the children down for a holiday before we left for England.

We loved her wee cottage in the country. An old wooden cottage surrounded by meadows and fields. She was growing her own vegetables but we usually forgot to gather them for dinner before dark. She had no torch so we'd drag her push bike out of the shed and into the garden. I'd try and hold the back wheel up and the kids turned the pedals as fast as they could, trying to produce light from the dynamo while Vicki dug potatoes and pulled carrots.

Teava, her boss, was interested in my adoption experiences and asked if he could interview me for a staff training tape he was making of discussions with adoptive parents, birth parents and adopted persons. We sat in Vicki's lounge, and she entertained the children in another room while I talked of our reasons for adopting, the selection and approval process, foster parenting, telling our children of their adoption. The secrecy issues.

"Did you know that the natural mother has the right to know, at the time of placement, the identity of the adopting parents?" Teava asked.

I was very surprised. "No, I didn't. It was stressed on us that we must not know the natural mother's name."

"Who told you that?"

"Child Welfare. And we were told that our names would not be given to her. How long has this right been enforced?"

"It has never been enforced, because of the traditions of secrecy surrounding adoption. Adoptive parents usually don't want the natural mother to know where her child has gone because of worries about interference, and so on... Have your children asked you anything yet about their mother?"

"Our eight-year-old asked me her name just a few weeks ago and I had to say, 'I'm sorry, I don't know'. I could tell her only of her interests and physical features as I remembered them from Child Welfare's initial phone call. I didn't even have a first name to give her."

"Would you like to know her name?"

"Yes, I would." Of course I would.

"I suggest you approach Social Welfare in Lower Hutt, telling them that you have just found out there is a legal right for the natural parents to know where their child is, and that you would like to have the names of your children's parents in case they ever want to find them."

"Are they likely to give them to me? They wouldn't pass on a letter to their mothers for me. I can't imagine them giving me their names."

"You'd have to push for it. You would need to convince them that you don't want to use the names now, and that any future contact would be made only through Social Welfare. They could also give you written details about the parents' backgrounds. I think it's important to have that information to hold on to in case the records are destroyed.

"I'm sure the search thing is made more intense because the information is not there. I think that the development of adoption in this country will follow that of England and Scotland and elsewhere, where Social Welfare or some other Social Welfare agency will be used as an intermediary between the parties, and arrange a meeting. But, until then, it's very handy to have the names of the natural parents."

Teava asked me what my hopes were for my children and I said something about them being happy, well-adjusted and reaching their potential - he thanked me for the interview and switched off the tape recorder. I probably learnt more than he did. I wondered how Teava's views sat with a government department obsessed with secrecy.

Later I read in *Adoption Today*, by Jenny Rockel and Murray Ryburn, "Until 1955, birth parents could discover the names of the adopters by exercising their right to inspect the court records of the adoption. Since that time, those wishing to know the identity of their child's adoptive parents have had the right to insist on signing the General Consent F (number 2), which must include the names of the applicants. Only a tiny percentage of birth parents have been aware that they were entitled to this information. Not only birth parents but most social workers, and lawyers too, seem to have been ignorant of these provisions. Many social workers acknowledge that even if they had known this information, the prevailing climate of secrecy would have made them hesitant in offering the choice to their clients."

I suppose that social conditions and accepted protocols within Social Welfare might also have made social workers hesitant to offer General Consent F (number 2) form to their clients. As Teava said recently to me, "Adoption removed the stigma of children born out of wedlock and legitimised them. It also legitimised the position of unmarried pregnant women. They were able to go to another town, have their babies adopted and return home to be 'normal' again. It was the job of the department to legitimise everything. We all accepted that was what society wanted and the legislation fitted within that. We weren't there to question that these young mothers might have a brain, might have different plans and desires for their babies."

Vicki and I discussed my interview with Teava when the children were in bed in her little cottage. Then she said, "There's something that's been bothering me for a long time. I'm feeling terribly guilty because I'm aware of an adoption within our family and I don't know if the person involved knows he is adopted."

I looked at her. Questioningly.

She hesitated. "Did you know that Bryan is adopted?"

"No!" I was shocked. Bryan adopted! "I had no idea. How do you know? Bryan has never mentioned it to me." All this time we'd spent together as children, and the time together in Europe, and he'd never talked about it. He was now aged thirty-seven and was married with three children. He would surely know. But why hadn't he mentioned it when we adopted our children? Why hadn't his mother, my Aunty Tresna, mentioned it when we adopted our children? Why had my parents never talked about it? I couldn't believe it.

"I can't remember when I was told," Vicki said. "But Mum and Dad told me not to mention it to Bryan as they don't know if he knows. I thought you would have known. I've been wanting to talk about it with you for some time and thought you would understand, because of your own situation."

I couldn't think of anything to say.

"Social Welfare's attitude that adoptive parents tell their children of the adoption while they are very young is the antithesis of what has happened in our family. It's not my place to reveal it to Bryan if he doesn't know but I just wish I'd never been told. I don't want to know about it if Bryan doesn't know."

Bryan adopted. If I'd grown up with the knowledge I wouldn't have thought anything about it. But why the secret? I knew he was the love of his mother's life. And he had built a house next door to hers so that he and his wife and daughters could be there for her, and she for them. She was still widowed and living alone.

I was suddenly angry that I had not been told. That other members of the family knew, and not me. But how would Bryan feel if he had not been told and ever found out? How much worse it would be for him. Anger would not be a strong enough word. Did his wife and children know?

I visited my mother on my return to Lower Hutt and asked her if it was true about Bryan.

"Yes, it is true," she said. "We were always worried you might hear it from someone else. Tresna asked all the family to keep Bryan's adoption a secret and I've kept my promise to her until now. At the time Bryan was adopted, the words 'bastard' and 'illegitimate' were still associated with babies 'born out of wedlock', and Tresna was trying to protect him. She wanted to tell him of his adoption when he was seven, but couldn't. Later, when Bill was dying, he made her promise that she would never tell Bryan that Bill wasn't his natural father. Bryan was fourteen then. Tresna did ask Bryan as he was growing up how he would feel if he was adopted and he said he wouldn't want to know. From his remark she thinks he knows, but nobody is really sure and Tresna can't talk about it."

Why can't my aunt talk to me about it? We're both adoptive mothers. I'll have to be careful what I say. She doesn't know I know her secret.

I found short-term employment with the Electoral Office Division of the Department of Justice in Lower Hutt, checking actual votes against the master electoral roll, and reluctantly said goodbye to Cyril and the funerals. The increased income would help with travel costs. Ken worked at home on renovations, preparing for our exodus.

My job gave me access to electoral records and I spent many hours amongst rows of shelving, checking voting lists against names and birth dates, looking for duplications. The shelf records were not available for public scrutiny and I wondered again about our children's mothers. I hadn't yet plucked up courage to contact Social Welfare but if only I knew their names, I could investigate their whereabouts and occupations right here.

A colleague from my Child Welfare days was working in the Births, Deaths and Marriages division on the ground floor of the building. She asked after the children and I told her that one day when the children were ready we would love to meet their natural parents.

"Now that I'm working in the building can I find their names?"

"You won't find them," she said. "They're inaccessible to the public." She lowered her voice. "What are their birth dates?"

I gave them to her. The following day she handed me a data-entry card with holes punched all through it. Lines of numbers streaked across the card. Down the side it read, Registrar General's Office. Along the top, Surname of Groom, Christian Names, Surname of Bride. The bride and groom's names were printed faintly above. Who were they? I was puzzled.

"Turn it over," she whispered. There, among the punched-out holes, were the names, date and place of birth of our children's mothers. Written in red biro pen, and in her neat handwriting.

"Don't tell anyone I've given them to you."

I stared at the card. They were real people with real names. I couldn't believe that this forbidden knowledge was in my hands. "Who are the bride and groom? Are they related?"

"No. It's just an old card."

Her boss wandered over to the counter. "What time do you close today?" I asked my friend in a loudish voice.

"We're open Mondays to Fridays, 9.30am to 4pm."

"Thank you very much. I'll come back tomorrow when I've got more time." I clutched the card and left the room.

I wasted no time in going upstairs to the electoral records. I had twenty minutes left for my lunch break. Twenty minutes to find the information before I needed to be back at work, checking those endless, mainly boring, electoral lists.

There was only one listing for a person with Katrina's mother's name. She was described as a kindergarten teacher, living in Whakatane. She'd now be twenty-six. And she hadn't married. I wondered again if Katrina was her only child. How was she dealing with her loss? Why hadn't she married? Was she still sad?

Finding Aaron's mother was more difficult. She had a fairly common Christian name and surname. There were four people of her name who were born in 1950, and two of them were clerks - the occupation originally given to us by Child Welfare. Was she the clerk living in Auckland? If so, she hadn't married either. Was Aaron her only child? Did she think of him or had she put it all behind her and forgotten, as Child Welfare told her to? How had her loss affected her life?

The twenty minutes were up. I sat down again at my desk. Name - Mr John Targett, Birth Date - 17 March 1937, Address - 23 Secombe Road, Occupation - physiologist. What's a physiologist? I looked at the clock. Still two hours to go. But what if the birth mothers' names are wrong? Concentrate on your work, Robyn.

Ken was pleased with my findings. We told the children that we now knew their mothers' names.

"What are they?" Katrina said. We told them.

"What does mine look like?" Aaron asked.

I took an envelope from the writing desk and removed the scrap of paper from inside it - the original scribblings of details of their parents' statistics and interests.

"She has brown hair and greyish-green eyes and is 5'6". That's about the same height as me. She liked ballet and tennis and was twenty-one when you were born." We knew very little else except that she was from the South Island, was unmarried, and had spent four years at secondary school. We knew nothing about their personal lives, but told the children again how much their mothers had loved them and hadn't wanted to part with them. They knew how much we loved them, too. We told them often.

Aaron asked about his father. He was twenty-four, had dark blonde hair, blue-grey eyes, University Entrance and was a policeman who had gone to the United States.

The children listened as if it was another bed-time story. They said nothing about wanting to meet their parents.

"Your father might be one of the cops in Chips on TV," Katrina said to Aaron.

We let our house to a Japanese couple with three children. The wife spoke no English and Ken and I joked with each other that she would have nothing to do except keep the house clean while we were away. We hadn't reckoned on Japanese cooking methods that would leave coatings of oil on the kitchen walls, floor and ceiling. And Japanese bathing methods where the bathroom would become a sauna and the wallpaper fall off the walls.

At Wellington airport we said goodbye to friends and family and checked in our baggage - our weight limit of forty-four pounds each was spread over five suitcases. We wore our heaviest clothes, including two coats each, and carried aboard four cabin bags filled with linen and household items, and car tools. The straps of Ken's cabin bag strained under the weight of the tools as he heaved it on to his shoulder, declining the flight attendant's offer of assistance. At Auckland International Airport Ken's father gave us a woollen 'Made in New Zealand' tartan rug, which got added in to the cabin baggage.

The plane began rocking violently as we approached Singapore, and Air New Zealand's captain advised that we were moving through a tropical storm. The children vomited over their clothes and the rug, and as we were about to hit the tarmac at Singapore airport the plane was propelled sharply back into the air. "We apologise for the aborted landing," said the captain. "The tarmac was under two feet of water. We plan to land at Kuala Lumpur. We don't have landing rights but we'll need to refuel."

The Malaysian airport authorities didn't want to know about three hundred and fifty unscheduled passengers without visas, and we sat on the plane for three hours. The food had run out before Singapore and there was nothing to drink except alcohol. Finally the captain announced, "We're going to illegally disembark from the aircraft. Please take all your cabin luggage with you. You should wait in the transit lounge until further announcements are made."

Ken and I looked grimly at each other. It had been such a struggle getting everything aboard. How could we possibly cart it all around a steaming Asian city? We hauled ourselves and the cabin bags and winter coats down the aisle, the red tartan rug draped defiantly over my shoulder.

A blast of tropical heat hit us at the top of the gangway. "Do I have to wear all these clothes?" said Aaron, his face smothered in perspiration. The Air New Zealand crew appeared to be in abnormally high spirits at the bottom of the steps and promptly disappeared as soon as the last passenger had disembarked. We felt abandoned.

Six hours and numerous complaints later a convoy of windowless wooden buses turned up at the airport. It was 6am Malaysian time and the heat was still unbearable. Katrina was sick again, on the steps of the bus, before we were whisked away by kamikaze drivers who raced each other for the forty-minute trip to the Merlin Hotel, a rather grand establishment with musty padded-vinyl hallways, and curtains that operated by remote control from the bed.

We waited another eleven hours for a new flight crew to arrive from Hong Kong and deliver us to Singapore in time to board our Singapore Airlines flight to London. So much for an over-nighter in Singapore. At Athens we stopped to pick up passengers and were informed that we would remain in the Athens airport terminal until fog over London had cleared. No food was available at the airport, the city was still asleep. Four hours later we were still in Greece. We were called back on to the plane in the hope that the skies would be clear by the time we reached England.

England, France, Belgium, England, France, Belgium, England. We presumed they were underneath; we could see only blue sky and cumulus clouds as we flew around in circles for another three hours, waiting for the stubborn fog to dissipate. I was exhausted from hunger and lack of sleep. We'd had nothing to eat for ten hours; only the few passengers who'd boarded in Athens had been supplied with breakfast. How much longer would we be imprisoned in this flying machine?

"I hope we don't try to land," said the Singapore Airlines hostess sitting in friendly fashion beside me. "We don't have fog-landing equipment on these planes."

"We're going to have to divert to Amsterdam to refuel," said the captain. "You'll each be supplied with a meal voucher."

Katrina and Aaron fell asleep on the floor of the aircraft. I wasn't sure if I'd have the energy to get to the food counter.

In London we discovered that the 'Made in New Zealand' red tartan rug was missing.

We stayed with my brother Lindsay in London for a few weeks until we found accommodation; a semi-detached house in Frimley, thirty kilometres south-west of London. Frimley was once a small village - the White Hart pub in the High Street is mentioned in the *Doomsday Book* - but was now streets of post-war, detached, semi-detached and terraced brick housing.

I worked part-time as a food caterer for the staff of Marconi Space and Defence Systems in Frimley and learnt how to arrange two lettuce leaves, three slices of cucumber and a dollop of watercress on a hundred plates each morning and serve beef stroganoff and mushy peas and spotted dick from a bain marie at lunch times. Scientists from Marconi kept disappearing or dying of 'unnatural causes' and the family joked about my cooking.

I never quite coped with the British class system. The cafeteria was divided into three sections; the workers in a barn-like room with their paper napkins, plastic cups and bain marie; middle management in a smaller room with real glasses, cotton table napkins, and beer and waitress service; and upper management in their private carpeted room with its special waitress service, crystal glasses, linen table napkins, bar service, fresh flowers and a small British flag flying on the table. As a server to the workers I was on the bottom rung.

Ken took on contract work with several of the electronic industries in the area and was able to name his work schedules. He took time off for all the school holidays so that we could travel around Britain and Europe together. The children sang in unintelligible Latin in a children's choir, learnt about the Magna Carta and Hadrian's Wall, about glassblowing in Venice and salt mines in Berchtesgaden. They learned how to speak English with a British accent and groaned at my obsession with thatched cottages and 'quaint villages with cobblestone streets'.

We ordered and paid a large deposit on a Mercedes Benz to be picked up from the factory in Germany. Back home in New Zealand, a month before collection date, Prime Minister Robert Muldoon's June budget altered the rules for importation of duty-free vehicles to New Zealand. We would now have to pay the one hundred percent duty and sales tax administered on European cars. Too late to cancel the order, Ken picked up the car in Germany, drove the family once around the block in Frimley, then locked the hunk of shining dark green metal in the garage. We put a 'for sale' notice in *The Times* newspaper and two months later sold it for a very slight profit to a car dealer. Oh well, the idea was good. And what a way to spend the superannuation!

We stayed in Britain for three years instead of the intended twenty-one months. We liked the gypsy life. On the way home we bought a ten-year-old Chevy Chinook campervan in Washington DC and motored down to Florida where the Chevy kept stalling then blew up; across to New Orleans in our restored vehicle, up to Nebraska and Colorado, down to Mexico where we spent five days by campervan and train trying to find the Copper Canyon but missed it, up and across to Los Angeles, and north to Vancouver where we sold the Chevy - our home for three months - and boarded a plane for New Zealand. Back to a structured life again. It was December 1981.

# Chapter Twelve

KATRINA AND AARON slotted happily back into life with their friends in Lower Hutt. Ken and I found the transition back to antipodean suburban life more difficult. We asked the neighbours what they had been up to. One had bought a new car and new lounge and dining room furniture. There was now a Chinese takeaway at the shopping centre and the bookshop had changed hands. Nothing much else seemed to have happened except for a lessening of employment opportunities. Ken took several months to find a satisfactory job, but never regretted our decision to live in Britain.

In Aaron's first term back at school the class had to write a project entitled *All About Me*. He brought his home for us to read. "My name is Aaron. I am ten years old. I was born at Upper Hutt on 16 April 1972 and adopted ten days later. My sister was called Katrina." So much for my efforts to keep the adoption out of the school records. "When I was five I went into Room Six. The teacher there was strict. She used to tell us to crawl around the floor and pick the rubbish up. We spent most of the time looking up her skirt. When I was seven we went to England. Everything looked really old. One time we hired a narrowboat and went on some canals with another New Zealand family. We had to wear our lifejackets all the time because I fell in the canal before we left the boatyard."

What would the teacher think of his exploits in Room Six?

The following term Aaron auditioned for the school production of *Oliver* and came home with the news that he was Fagin. We were amazed, as apart from his brief foray into the English choir, he hadn't shown much interest in singing, preferring to be out on the cricket pitch or football field. He had several songs and copious words to learn for the part, and as proud parents we thought he was the star of the show. He never sang publicly again but instead took up the trumpet and at twelve became the youngest member of the Lower Hutt Municipal Brass Band. They couldn't find a uniform small enough to fit him and in his oversized jacket and trousers we laughed that he looked like the incredible hulk.

Katrina meanwhile was into piano and clarinet and drama and still enjoyed dressing up sessions with Aaron and their friends - sarongs from Thailand and Chinese pyjamas from Hong Kong and recently discarded clothes of mine, that Katrina later wore to bad-taste parties. We wondered if their birth parents had musical ability. Are talents inherited or are they a result of a child's environment?

A few months after our return to New Zealand I began getting strange unrelated health problems. Aching muscles, rashes, a lump which stuck out from my throat, and fatigue. I'd noticed city council workers spraying the gorse which backed on to our property and that of our neighbours, and spraying the fields across the road from our house but I'd thought nothing of it.

I expected the symptoms to soon dissipate, and slowly began developing a small craft business at home; glass terrariums in a variety of shapes and sizes into which I put granulated bark and small house plants and brightly coloured clay animals or feathery butterflies. Ken cut the glass after work for me, as my energy levels weren't improving, and we sold them at craft markets and through florist shops. We didn't have enough floor space in the basement to store several hundred terrariums at Christmas, and terrariums and boxes of purple and pink African violets took over the whole house. "Does your mother like these?" asked a friend of Aaron's, staring at the dozens of small glassed gardens on the lounge floor.

The council workers continued spraying the fields and our street berms and council land at the back of the section. Eighteen months after the initial symptoms I suddenly worsened considerably. I couldn't walk the few metres to the letter box without feeling faint, my heart racing and thumping, and wondering if I'd have the energy to get back to the house. My muscles ached, I had diarrhoea, nausea, burning skin, swollen lymph glands. The hard lump still stuck out from my throat. I couldn't read for long - the words became distorted. I felt generally unwell and became allergic to most foods, often with rashes after eating and an accelerated pulse which sometimes stayed at a hundred and fifty beats per minute for a couple of hours. Other symptoms came and went. Small tender lumps appeared in various parts of my body, remained about two weeks and disappeared. I sometimes had stabbing pains in my fingers and toes. I slept well but was so tired. Always tired.

I was given numerous blood tests. Everything was normal. I was sent to numerous specialists who couldn't label the problem. A physician said it had been a long grey winter but summer was coming, a heart specialist said he had seen a few cases like mine and wondered if it was viral. I was reduced to staying in bed for most of the day, and friends and family helped with housework and meals. A specially caring friend, Robyn, called in several days a week. Ken became the mother and father, often coming home from work early.

I had severe allergic reactions to any drugs prescribed, and was finally written off and put in the too-hard basket. The 'I'm sure you're pregnant you don't need a test' doctor had moved overseas and my new female doctor, who practised in our neighbourhood, told me that my immune system had collapsed, she could do nothing for me, and not to go out in a car as she'd had another patient with the same problems who had died after just a small whiff of fumes. We were left to fend for ourselves. There was no hope of recovery through orthodox medicine

Ken gave up his job and took over the terrarium business. It had grown considerably with his assistance and was now able to support us financially. I was relieved to have him permanently at home and he enjoyed being able to walk down the stairs and be immediately at work. Two years went by, of chronic fatigue. Two years of struggle. My parents still lived very close and I often went there for days at a time to give Ken a break. I was now down to six stone in weight and the family were seriously worried. I had no energy to worry, I woke up each morning feeling fine and well-rested and thinking that this was the beginning of my recovery, but within half an hour I was lying down again. I sometimes wondered if I was going to die. It felt as if just a small breath of wind would blow me away forever. Unbeknown to me, my brother Brent said to my parents, "Do you think we're going to lose her?"

A doctor friend from out of town said it could be Myalgic Encephalomyelitis, known as M.E. or Tapanui flu, and suggested I went for treatment to a doctor in Auckland who specialises in biological medicine and who was having success with cases such as mine. But I didn't think I'd have the energy to get to Wellington airport, and what about that patient who had died going out in a car? It was also quite a drive from Auckland airport to Remuera. I didn't want my children to be without a mother, even though I'd hardly been a mother for some time. Friends and family continued helping with meals and household chores.

Ken, still desperate to find help for me, visited a social worker at the hospital who suggested contacting a Catholic nun trained in NLP - Neuro Linguistic Programming. The nun came to our house and taught me a technique for dealing with the food allergies and aching muscles, and gradually I was able to increase my food intake and feel my energy levels lifting.

We decided to pursue natural remedies. A naturopath with homeopathic leanings gave me bottles of homeopathic drops for various conditions. Homeopathy was a foreign concept to me - the naturopath explained that a homeopathic remedy is one which produces the same symptoms as those the sick person complains of, and in doing so sharply provokes the body into throwing them off. 'Like may be cured by like.' Whatever it was, it produced no unwanted side-effects as the drugs had, and seemed to be working.

I was told to eat only whole foods - preferably organic, nothing with preservatives and other additives, and drink pure water. Poor Ken, in between attending to everything else, had to line up with empty sherry flagons at a tap on the Petone foreshore that delivered unadulterated artesian water, and find a source of mung beans and organic lentils and pumpkin seeds and tofu and lettuces with bug holes and other new foods that we didn't know what to do with.

"Don't think we're going to eat any of that stuff," said Katrina and Aaron, as they peered at the strange and motley mixtures in the cupboards and fridge, and the brown bottles of homeopathic preparations in the bathroom cabinet. But the NLP and strange foods and brown homeopathic bottles were having a positive effect and I thought I was well enough to fly to Auckland.

The Auckland doctor listened to my symptoms and tested me for chemical poisoning. The tests detected large amounts of paraquat throughout my system. I learnt that paraquat was potentially one of the world's deadliest toxins and had been banned in Germany for some years. "How could I have got paraquat in my system?" I asked him.

"People are poisoned from inhaling spray drift. Aerated micro-droplets of chemical pass through the alveola membrane of the lung directly into the bloodstream and are delivered from there to all parts of the body. Wherever there is a weakness, that part will collect more spray," he explained

My treatment was Vitamin C administered intravenously for forty minutes, followed by an hour breathing pure oxygen in a decompression chamber at the equivalent pressure of eight feet underwater. This combination stimulates an enzyme system in all cells of the body and enables the body to eventually oxidise the pesticide residues, which are broken down into smaller molecular fragments that the body's own eliminative mechanisms can handle.

After one week's treatment I began to feel alive again. I needed two more weeks of treatment and came home with a seventy-five percent improvement. The lump at my throat had disappeared, the aches and pains had disappeared, my skin had stopped burning. Most importantly, the fatigue and feelings of general unwellness had greatly improved. I could run and jump and shout again. Back home in Lower Hutt I read the Fire Service Assistant Commissioner's comment that this doctor's treatment of more than one hundred firemen poisoned in the ICI chemical fire of December 1984 was the only one giving his men any benefit.

But Ken and Katrina had also become unwell over the past years. For two years Ken had had severe pains in his wrist, hands and fingers, often with tingling and numbness. His arms ached, and he was unable to grip anything without pain. Even peeling potatoes and driving the car had became difficult. He was often reduced to working twenty minutes on, twenty minutes off.

A neurologist diagnosed repetitive strain injury and told him to take six months off work. "But I'm not doing repetitive work," Ken said to the neurologist, "and I can't afford to take time off work. It's our only income."

Katrina, a bright student in her sixth form year, had developed chest pains and shortness of breath, dizziness and memory losses, and was unable to concentrate at school. She'd had intermittent rashes and joint pains for four years, and an orthopaedic surgeon had diagnosed bursitis, a swelling in the ligaments, but said that an operation was unlikely to cure the problem. Aaron was suffering from hay fever symptoms. What was happening to us all?

I suggested to the family that they visit the doctor I had seen two months previously in Auckland. Ken was diagnosed as having 245T poisoning, Katrina with mild paraquat and 245T poisoning and Aaron had traces of malathion. It all seemed a nightmare.

Katrina went through the vitamin C/hyperbaric chamber regime for a week and lost the chest pains, the dizziness and the shortness of breath, and the bursitis disappeared. Ken was given ten weekly homeopathic injections and within three weeks had lost most of the pains. Within the ten weeks he was back to a full day's work with all disability gone. Aaron was given injections for his hayfever but had no improvement and declined to be jabbed with any more needles.

In February 1986, while the family had been in Auckland for a diagnosis, I had written to the mayor of Lower Hutt. "What," I asked, "have they been spraying on the gorse adjacent to the back of our section and around the streets of our neighbourhood? How often do they spray? What control do council have of sprays used by the contracting firms?" I wrote of our concerns at an ongoing spraying programme for the area and the debilitating effect that pesticides can have on people who have developed chemical sensitivities as a result of exposure to pesticide sprayings. Of the Auckland doctor's comments that he had seen three hundred cases of poisoning from pesticide spraying in 1985 and believed it was just the tip of the iceberg.

Two months later the mayor replied that they had been using 245T in our suburb and paraquat in other areas, but had withdrawn them in 1984 "because of public concern over side-effects within the community". He gave dates of past sprayings and listed sprays now being used: "Weedazol, Diacambone, TBA, SDA, Daupon and Roundup." Spraying was done only on still days. The children's playing field across the road from us had been sprayed a couple of weeks ago at the request of residents. What residents? I asked myself. The mayor added that the council would continue to do two complete sprays a year. He was very concerned that some residents might be suffering from the effects of chemical spray poisonings.

What did a few weeds outside someone's property really matter in comparison with the residents' health? What about children walking barefoot on the newly-sprayed grass berms outside their houses or on the playing fields? And what about Ken's bees? The gorse flowers on the hills around us were the predominant source of pollen for them. Was even our honey tainted?

I thanked the mayor for his letter and told him of a GP's comments that there are no 'safe' pesticide sprays - they are all designed to kill living growth and are therefore harmful to humans, that the body is unable to expel many chemical toxins naturally, and they remain in the body, causing serious health problems.

I sent a copy of my letter to the Member of Parliament for Western Hutt who was also a Lower Hutt city councillor. He immediately wrote to the council saying he believed there was a case for the removal of gorse by mechanical means in areas where spraying might otherwise prove to be a hazard to humans, and he would be grateful if this alternative could be given consideration in future.

A reply came back from the city engineer: "The Director of Parks and Recreation advises that his Department will investigate placing signs in children's playgrounds with a warning to keep off for an appropriate length of time after any spraying has been carried out. While I appreciate your concern over this matter I consider it would be an over-reaction if Council were to ban all spraying as a means of vegetation control. Some of the sprays used by Council, such as Roundup, are advertised on prime time television and if you dispute the manufacturer's claims about its safety you should take the matter up with the appropriate authority."

I didn't have the energy to fight the council, and Ken didn't have the time. Was it just coincidence that at the time I became ill we had a very high incidence of ill health develop within the six houses closest to us? Bowel cancer, severe arthritis, chronic fatigue - later diagnosed like mine as pesticide poisoning - extensive persistent rashes, cancer of the kidney, and a cot death. Three other neighbours with chronic fatigue symptoms had been diagnosed as having M.E.

A friend who owned a market garden in Otaki told us he wouldn't let his family eat the food he sends to the market for auction because of the toxicity of the sprays used, and all the stuff added to make the fruit and vegetables bigger and brighter. "I have a separate covered patch of garden for the family," he said. "There's so little control of what we spray on our food for New Zealand consumption. The public end up eating poison." Nothing, it seemed, was immune.

In 1994 Lower Hutt and Wellington City Councils trialled the patented Waipuna hot water system for controlling weeds. I wrote to the mayor and requested they adopt the Waipuna system. We received no reply.

Wellington City Council adopted the hot water system. Lower Hutt rejected it on financial grounds. Changing to the Waipuna system would cost an extra $100,000 per year, or $2.69 extra per ratepayer per year. About the same as a chocolate-dipped ice-cream. The following year a new mayor was elected. It was the Member for Western Hutt who'd suggested to Lower Hutt City Council, in 1986, that consideration be given to alternative methods of dealing with weeds.

Now, as I write this in 1998, how much has really changed in council attitudes? They are still spraying pesticides on playgrounds and berms and beside people's backyards, although we now have warning signs. They are still claiming pesticides are safe - they must still be watching the ads on prime time television. Maybe, some day, they'll be persuaded to take notice of the effects of glyphosate, the active ingredient in Roundup - council's 'safe' pesticide - on laboratory rats and rabbits. Scientific tests have shown decreased sperm concentration, increased abnormal or dead sperm, and decreased number of viable foetuses.[3] And maybe, pesticide manufacturers will take note of the 1989 FAO International Code of Conduct on the Distribution and Use of Pesticides, of which New Zealand is a signatory, and which says the pesticide industry should ensure that their product is not advertised as being safe, even with phrases like 'when used as directed'.

My children sometimes groan that their mother has become a 'greenie'.

The teenage years had arrived while I was mainly incapacitated. The age, we read, when adolescents struggle to know who they are in a very basic sense. How much would our children struggle, we had wondered? We'd also read that teenagers who are adopted may have extra problems coping as they have more questionings about their identity. But life continued as normally as it could, with me out of action. There were no great dramas, no "I wish I'd never been adopted" rages. Adoption was mentioned on odd occasions; we didn't want to put too much emphasis on their adoption but wanted them to be able to talk about it if they wanted to.

I often wondered about their mothers. What are they doing now? How often do they think about their children? Would they be happy about their children contacting them later if they wanted to? We asked Katrina and Aaron if they would like to look for their parents later. We would be happy for them to do so, and to help them in any search, we said. We knew that searching for birth parents could be traumatic, that the birth parents would have new lives and might not want to be found. What effect would the intrusion of a son or daughter have on established relationships? Katrina said she might look for her parents one day. Aaron just grunted.

Then everything changed, from Monday 1 September 1986. The Adult Adoption Information Act 1985 came into effect. There had been growing support, in recent years, for adopted people and birth mothers to have more information about each other. The social climate had been changing and the stigma attached to illegitimacy had greatly diminished. In the late 1970s, Labour MP Jonathan Hunt had first introduced a Private Members Bill which was designed to allow adopted adults and their birth parents to have official access to each other's identity. But despite repeated attempts, his Bill had failed to make progress. There had been a great deal of opposition to the proposed legislation from the National Government, particularly from then Prime Minister Robert Muldoon.

But not only from the National Government. Labour MP Dr Gerald Wall had stated in the House in 1979:

"My experience in this field goes back now for thirty-five years, and I have never known a balanced, serious woman who wanted to know what had happened to her child after it had been given in adoption. An emotionally stable woman who has given a child in adoption would have come to terms with her decision many years before, in its legality and irrevocable finality."[3]

There had been strong support for the Bill from most Labour MPs, however, and after Labour came into power in 1984 Jonathan Hunt passed it over to MP Fran Wilde, herself an adoptive mother. It was passed on a conscience vote of fifty-one to twenty-five on 11 September 1985, and ended a seven-year legislative battle.

The new Act marked an end to the thirty years of keeping the members of the adoption triangle hidden from each other, as decreed by law in the 1955 Adoption Act: 'This almost obsessive concern for secrecy was intended to protect single mothers (and their families) from the shame of unmarried parenthood, to allow the child to escape from the legal and social disadvantages of illegitimacy and to relieve adoptive couples from the embarrassment arising from public knowledge of their infertility.' [4]

Birth parents, and adults aged twenty and over who had been adopted as children, would now be able to request information about each other, and, if the information was available and the other party agreed, it would be released. Adopted persons could now obtain their original birth certificate providing there was no veto from the birth parents on the birth registration. A veto from either party would last ten years and would ensure that all identifying information was kept confidential, but might be renewed or removed at any time. For adoption orders granted after 1 March 1986 the adopted child would have unrestricted access to information once they reached the age of twenty.

Radio talk back shows, panel discussions on television, interviews with adoptive parents, adopted children and birth parents, and newspaper articles all heralded the arrival of the new legislation. Concern was expressed by some adoptive parents that contracts they had signed with the state which had guaranteed them absolute confidentiality were now invalid. Family life, they said, might be profoundly disturbed by the reappearance of their child's mother, or they might lose their children to a newly-met birth mother, or their children might be hurt by a second 'rejection'. Adoptive parents who were in favour of change talked about the fundamental human right to know the truth about origins, and the birth mother's right to knowledge and contact with the child she had entrusted to them.

With every discussion I was reminded of our children's parents and wondered whether they would be placing a veto on the birth registration or whether they wanted to meet their children again. How would we fit into one another's lives? How would our children handle the emotion of a reunion? Katrina would be twenty in just over three years.

I wondered about my cousin Bryan. Nothing had been said about his adoption, by him or my aunt, while our children were growing up. What difference would this new adoption Act make? If Bryan didn't know he was adopted, my aunt must be going through agony, wondering whether his birth mother would try to contact him. As an adoptive mother she couldn't put a veto on his birth registration details. But if Bryan was aware of his adoption, would he want to find his mother?

I tried to bring up the subject with Aunty Tresna by telling her that it was unlikely that our children would put vetoes on their birth details when they reached twenty, that it was important for adopted children to know they could find their roots. She seemed a little agitated but wouldn't talk about the subject. She didn't even want to acknowledge that our children were adopted.

Katrina rushed home from high school one day, shortly after the new legislation was enacted.

"Hey Mum, guess what? Elizabeth Brooks from my class wants to interview me for a *Youth Focus* article in the *Evening Post.* She's doing an article on adoption, and someone told her I was adopted. She's already found a mother who gave up her baby for adoption and she needs an adopted person as well. Shall I?"

"It might be interesting, but it's up to you," I said. "Have a think about it."

"She said she'd call me by my second name to protect my privacy. Hardly anyone at High School knows I'm adopted."

Katrina went ahead with the interview. She told us that she found it difficult, that she hadn't thought much about her adoption before, that she was forced to confront it and think more deeply about the issues involved. And about her first mother. She seemed a little quiet over the next few weeks.

The article was published on 2 March 1987. Katrina was slightly nervous about opening the newspaper. On page twenty-four we read the headlines, *Would Like To Know About Past*, and read on:

*"I want to know where I got this fuzzy hair from" was seventeen-year-old Maree's reason why she wanted to meet her birth mother.*

*"Although I'd love to meet my birth mother I don't want to find her now - probably when I'm twenty or so. I want to meet her out of curiosity. For a start I'd just see her briefly and then maybe I'd get to know her. Mum and Dad don't mind, they feel that it's the right thing to do."*

*Maree can't remember not knowing she was adopted.*

*"Mum and Dad used to tell me this story of how they went into the hospital to see me. I was covered in a heat rash because the hospital was so hot and my hips were in a brace." Maree grins. "The nurse said I could only improve. Mum and Dad liked the look of me and enquired about taking me home."*

*Maree thinks of her adopted mother as her mother.*

*"She has brought me up and she's had me for all but two weeks but my birth mother gave birth to me so I feel something for her and I hope she thinks I've grown into a nice sort of person."*

*Maree has no idea about what sort of person her mother is and would have liked to have known a bit more.*

*"Her personality, what hobbies she had, anything like that. Mum got some information from Social Welfare. I went over it a couple of months ago. She was seventeen or eighteen when I was born."*

*Adoption is not really a part of Maree's life.*

*"I don't really think about it very much. Only my closest friends know. I've hardly told anyone. It's never given me any trouble."*

*Maree has never felt that her birth mother gave her up because she didn't want her.*

*"It's partly because I know that birth parents don't give up their children because they don't want them, also it's the way my parents handled it."*

*Maree was taught from an early age that adoption wasn't bad.*

*"When I first understood I was adopted Mum and Dad used to say, 'Oh, here comes our darling adopted little girl,' and they put darling in front of it to make adopted sound lovely and warm - not bad."*

*I asked Maree if she looked much like her adoptive family.*

*"People say I look like Dad. I've been told that I look like my brother too (also adopted). I suppose you grow to look like the people you live with.*

*"I sometimes think that I've got half-brothers and sisters out there somewhere - which is quite cool really. I think that it would be good to see them as well, then I'd see more or less what I would have turned out like if I'd stayed with her."*

A week later it was Aaron's turn to rush through the door after school. "What were you doing at the letter box at half-past three?"

"Just collecting the mail." I was surprised, I thought it was fairly obvious.

"You were there as the school bus went by," he said, "and some of my friends saw you."

I looked down at my clothes. Yes they were all on, and my hair wasn't in rollers.

"And they said, 'There's your mother.'"

"Yes," I said. "I saw Blaik at the window and waved to him."

He groaned. "Please don't be at the letter box again at half-past three. It's embarrassing. They all know you're my mother."

I smiled. Fourteen-year-old boys.

At fifteen Aaron decided he wanted flying as a career. I suggested he look at the Air Force. Aaron, who preferred to leave his bed unmade and his shoes uncleaned, seemed a little concerned at how regimented it might be. *I* thought the Air Force might succeed where I had failed. "But they only have a very small intake," he said. "I probably won't get in. And you need really high grades in physics and maths."

"You might have to work a little harder at school and play a little less," said Ken.

Katrina was unsure of her plans. She loved Spanish and travel but wasn't enjoying her seventh-form year. So she took a job with an accountant who gave her time off for Spanish classes at high school, and saved hard for programme fees for a student exchange programme to Argentina. By the end of the year she had sufficient funds.

We waved goodbye to her at Auckland airport, with some misgivings. She was YFU's (Youth for Understanding) first New Zealand exchange student to Argentina and she had only a temporary family to live with. We had no idea of where she would live or how she would fare. We would miss her bubbly personality, her detailed sharing of daily experiences. Perky, a budgie that Ken had bred for her, would also miss her. He wanted only Katrina and flew on to her shoulder whenever he was out of his cage.

It was January 1988, and the year that Ken was diagnosed as having motor neurone disease.

# Chapter Thirteen

KEN'S SPEECH had become slightly slurred a few weeks before Katrina left for South America. We wondered if it was a slight stroke but he said he felt very well, and refused to visit a doctor. I hoped it was nothing serious. I was not long recovered from some of the effects of the pesticide poisonings and was looking forward to some normality in our family life.

Katrina contacted us soon after her arrival in Argentina. "How's Dad?" "He's fine," we said. "Just the same." She told us she was living in a town called Esperanza and how much she was enjoying her host family for the year - Mami, Papi, and their four children. Mami and the three younger children didn't speak English and Papi was vice-president of the agricultural university and an authority on cows. The Post Office was on strike and there'd be no mail for a while. "The family are enrolling me in the French section of the school as they say that the students who are doing French this year are a nicer group than those studying English. I'm not too happy about learning French in Spanish, but the schools are on strike over teachers' wages and likely to be so for a couple of months. My Spanish should be a bit better by the time school finally opens."

Aaron heard about the education strikes and wondered about Argentina for his seventh form year.

I started learning Spanish through the New Zealand Correspondence School so that I could communicate with Mami. In May we sent Katrina a tape of our activties, and spoken messages for her new family. Ken had several tries at recording a message but kept tripping over his words, or slurring them. He sounded as if he'd been over-indulging in his home-made wines. I wondered if Katrina would notice a deterioration, and what the Argentinian family would think. Ken was still refusing to accept that he might have a problem.

Katrina did notice and I finally persuaded Ken to visit the doctor. We'd found one who seemed to really care about his patients and who prescribed homeopathic medicines when appropriate. He sent Ken immediately to a neurologist who spent an hour probing and testing and questioning, before delivering his verdict. We'd never heard of motor neurone disease.

"But I feel perfectly well, apart from the speech and an uncomfortable feeling with my throat muscles," Ken said. "I've just been mixing concrete this morning. Putting in the foundations for an aviary."

"It's a very serious condition that you have. A motor neurone is a nerve cell that carries messages from the brain to the muscles of the body. When a person develops motor neurone disease there is damage to these motor neurones and the nerve supply to the voluntary muscles is impaired. With no nerves to control them the muscles gradually weaken and waste away, affecting speech, swallowing, and movement of the body and limbs." The neurologist was solemn. Unsmiling. "Unfortunately there is no treatment and no cure. I should tell you it's probably not worth your while continuing to build the aviary."

We couldn't believe it. He was feeling fine. We'd beat it. Why should it be terminal? And how could a neurologist be so negative? By the time he got home again, Ken was angry at the neurologist.

He resumed the building of the large outdoor aviary and stocked it with canaries. He'd already been breeding budgies, with varying success, for some time in our basement. "I'll take him a baby canary next year," he said. "Just to prove him wrong." We still didn't accept that it had to be terminal.

We read up on the disease. Approximately one in every 50,000 people develop MND each year. In five to ten percent of cases there is a familial pattern to the disease. Is this what Ken's mother died of, thirty years ago? In the latter stages the patient may not even be able to scratch an itch. In some cases there is difficulty controlling the expression of feelings, and inappropriate laughing or crying can occur. Research recently undertaken in Britain shows that people who have worked in the leather industry, and been in contact with the solvents used, have the highest incidence of motor neurone disease. Ken had worked in the leather industry for fourteen years. Life expectancy from onset of the disease is between six months and three years. But Stephen Hawking, the brilliant Cambridge physicist, was still alive twenty-six years after being diagnosed as having motor neurone disease.

Ken was referred to the Physically Disabled Service at the Hutt Hospital and his articulation tested by a speech language therapist. He went reluctantly. He wasn't yet accepting the label 'disabled'.

Katrina returned from Argentina at the end of the year, a confident young woman, widely travelled in Argentina, and fluent in Spanish. Although we had gently warned her of Ken's condition, she was shocked at the deterioration in his speech since her absence.

There must be something we could do.

We tried homeopathic medicines. And we visited a Maori medicine healer, a tohunga, in Rotorua who told us how to gather mawe and kawakawa leaves, and gave us bottles of tawhero and matipou preparations. We told the caretaker at Percy's Reserve, near home, of Ken's problem and how we had discovered that the trees we needed were in his domain. Could we pick some leaves off them? He gave his consent and according to instructions we picked the leaves or bark from the side of the tree which faced the sun, and boiled them in glass containers that were to be used for no other foods. Ken drank the brown bitter liquids. His condition stabilised for several months.

Then his left ankle and foot weakened and he leaned a little as he walked. He had physiotherapy at the hospital's rehabilitation gym, and the Physically Disabled Service suggested a splint but he didn't want one. We noticed that his leg muscles were wasting. I told him it was dangerous to continue cutting the glass for the terrariums - we'd sell the business. But he insisted on going down to the workshop. While he had the use of his hands and arms he'd keep working and looking after his birds, he said.

His speech had become very slurred and he wrote us notes if we couldn't understand him; swallowing was difficult and he was losing weight. Kay, the community health speech therapist, visited us at home and monitored his speech. She advised him on breathing techniques and how to deal with choking. We liked her gentle professional manner.

Our income from the business had been insufficient to support us financially for several months now, and we were living on our savings - I couldn't work, I needed to be near Ken. He reluctantly agreed to apply for an Invalid's Benefit. Katrina contributed to the budget from her wages. Aaron was still a student.

My Aunty Tresna also became ill. She was now eighty-one years old and had suffered from rheumatoid and osteo-arthritis for thirty-five years. Drugs to treat the arthritis had caused stomach ulcers, and she now had a fading heart and was not expected to live much longer. She was hospitalised for an infection and given massive doses of antibiotic that cost one hundred dollars per swallow. We were sad to see her in this state. She'd been an adoring mother and grandmother in spite of her inflexible attitude to adoption.

Her condition worsened. The hospital staff said she might not last the day. Bryan, who had just left for business in Napier, had been phoned and was driving back immediately. I held my aunt's hand and told her what she had meant to us. I had loved to visit and was always made to feel special. My parents were at her bedside as Bryan arrived with his wife, Dianne. They moved into the ward lounge so Bryan and Dianne could say their final goodbyes privately.

Suddenly Dianne rushed into the lounge. She looked pale and shocked, and burst out to my mother, "Is this true? Tres has just said to Bryan, 'You're not my biological son, but you are my son and I love you very much.'"

"Oh no! Yes, it *is* true. Oh, why has she told him now!" My mother couldn't believe what she was hearing.

My aunt lived two more days and was too weak to discuss the adoption with Bryan, but each time he visited his mother she said, "Here comes my own dear son."

My mother told of the conversation she'd had with my aunt three days before she died. Tresna had first asked if she was dying, then had said in her fading voice, "There's one thing... would you do it for me? I made a promise to Bill that I wouldn't tell Bryan he was adopted because Bill wanted him as his own son. I wanted to tell Bryan, but... I'm going to meet Bill now. After I die, will you tell Bryan that he is adopted?" My mother told us how she was taken aback and immensely concerned at the request, but to comfort my aunt she had said she would tell him, wondering to herself when and how, and thinking that it was too late to tell him now. It would be too much of a shock for him. How could he deal with it at his age? He was forty-eight. And he would never be able to talk it through with his adoptive parents.

My mother later told Bryan all she knew about his parentage, and how the matron of Bethany had said that his mother was a lovely girl and she would be pleased to call her her friend. But no one knew the names of Bryan's parents. His mother had taken that knowledge with her to the grave.

Yes, Bryan was very shocked, and angry that he hadn't been told. But he was equally distressed that all the family had known about the adoption, everyone except him and his wife and children. He didn't want to discuss his feelings and said he would not try to trace his mother - if she was alive she would be an old lady and he wouldn't want to intrude on her life now. He remained a close member of the family but never talked with us again of his adoption. Three years later he died of a brain tumour.

His children wondered about their genetic roots and medical background and contacted Births, Deaths and Marriages, now located within the Department of Internal Affairs. They were advised that they couldn't be given Bryan's birth mother's name unless the adoptive parents and the birth parents were all deceased, or one hundred and twenty years had passed since Bryan's birth. Even if his birth mother was still alive and had placed no veto on releasing his original birth registration details, Bryan's children would still not be given her name.

I couldn't believe the one hundred and twenty-year rule and checked with my local office. They confirmed the information given to Bryan's children. 'Pursuant to S76 of the Births, Deaths and Marriages Registration Act 1995' they would have to wait until the year 2060 to contact their grandmother.

Ken took one last fishing trip. In January 1990. His speech was now just soft unintelligible sounds, but I usually understood what he wanted. The two of us camped for a month, in our camper-trailer, on the beaches of the east coast bays between Gisborne and Opotiki. Ken fished each day and we cooked up the takings from the sea on a little fire we made each night on the beach. Sometimes we just sat on the sands and watched the sunset. We both knew what we were facing and that this would probably be our last holiday together. We were pleased we'd spent the superannuation all those years ago and had that wonderful family time together in England.

One day we called in to a marae to find out where we might find a tawhero tree or some matipou leaves that we could boil up. Ken still felt that homeopathy and Maori medicines were helping his condition. An old Maori woman was seated outside, talking to a circle of Maori teenagers. We walked tentatively over to her, with our request. She left the group and took us into her office: "Aunty Ruby, we've got a couple of Pakehas looking for a tawhero tree. Any idea where they can find one?" But Aunty Ruby at the other end of the phone didn't know of any and the Maori woman on the Gisborne marae next rang the Department of Agriculture who advised that Rotorua was the closest area that they grew in. We would revisit our tohunga there.

"But try my brother Rangi in Te Araroa on the way," said our Maori helper. "He knows all about Maori medicine. It's all we used when we kids were growing up." She looked at Ken's staggered walking and she knew he couldn't talk, and the concern showed. We thanked her for her efforts. "That's what we're here for," she smiled at us, and walked back to her waiting group of young people.

Katrina and Aaron looked after the house while we were away. They had encouraged us to have this holiday together and we knew they'd be all right without us. Half an hour after we returned there was a knock at the front door. It was one of Aaron's friends. He looked surprised to see us.

"He's in his room," I said and the friend slithered down the hallway. The knocks kept coming and I wondered how so many legs could fit into the bedroom. Presently Aaron and friends emerged. "We're just going out for a bit."

"You're very popular tonight," I said to Aaron.

I think we might have arrived back a night early.

The following month Aaron applied for the Massey University Aviation Programme, sat psychology flying tests to determine whether he had the right temperament to be a pilot, and was accepted for the course. He continued with his temporary employment as a porter at the Quality Inn until his aviation studies began in May.

# Chapter Fourteen

CHRISTCHURCH
9 March 1990

Dear Katrina

Well, here it is at last, the letter I have waited twenty years to write - the old heart is beating a bit faster at the prospect!

During November last year I wrote to the Social Welfare Department and asked them to be ready to start looking for my daughter on 1 December and after these few months they presented me with a name - Katrina Maree. Born Lower Hutt Hospital, 1 December 1969. Actually you were registered as Rachel Susan McLean - did you know that? But Katrina's a lovely name - I now have a twenty-year-old daughter named Katrina!

And you have a birth mother named Glenis Rosemary McLean. I am thirty-eight years old, and I'm a kindergarten teacher, which I have been since 1974. I have no other children - I was unable to have any more after you.

Oh Katrina - what do I say? I have a thousand questions, but now is not the time. Except, how do you feel? Have you been expecting this? Are you pleased to get it? I'm sure you're experiencing the same range of emotions I felt yesterday when they gave me the information I have waited so long to hear. Thank God she's alive and safe was the first one. Over the years one fervent hope I have had is that your parents stayed married and happy, and that you wouldn't be living in a 'broken home'. I'm not sure, of course, but it appears your Mum and Dad are still together, and I'm glad about that.

Will you write to me, Katrina? I am so longing to hear from you, but I understand it must be a shock to you. Perhaps one of your first questions might be "What does she want from me?" Please don't feel threatened. What do I want? Contact. I'd love to see you. Answers to a thousand questions. Friendship really, I guess. I'd like to fill in some gaps for you too, and answer the questions you're bound to have.

I'm enclosing a recent photo - taken at kindergarten so excuse the backdrop. My thoughts are very much with you and I really look forward to hearing from you. Please do write. Or if you're

brave enough, ring collect.
Love, Glenis

"It's from my birth mother! Oh Mum, it's from Glenis. That really is her name. She's written to me." She sits on her bed and reads the letter to me.

I feel slightly shocked. We should have been expecting it, Katrina is twenty and neither she nor Aaron had considered putting a veto on their own birth registration. But we hadn't expected a direct communication from her birth mother. We thought that Social Welfare acted as an intermediary, advised that the birth parent wanted contact, gave us time to prepare ourselves. But hadn't we been preparing ourselves for the past twenty years? We had always hoped that when the time was right we would meet. But is Katrina ready for this? And what does Glenis feel about meeting us, the adoptive parents? Her letter is addressed only to Katrina. I feel the need to be a part of this coming together.

The tears trickle down my cheeks as Katrina reads the letter to us. Is that because of her composure, or Glenis's letter? Both, I think. Ken smiles his gentle smile and nods. Aaron has very little to say.

Lower Hutt
18 March 1990

Dear Glenis,

I wasn't surprised to get your letter, but I was surprised you'd found me before I found you! I hadn't planned to start searching for another year or two, and it never really occurred to me that you'd start looking before I did. Now that you have found me I'm really pleased - I just don't know where to start telling you what I've done in the past twenty years, or what to ask you. I suppose it's best to start from the beginning.

I have really neat parents - Robyn and Ken, and a brother Aaron (also adopted) two years younger than me and we all get on really well.

In December 1978 our family went to England for three years on a working holiday. Aaron and I went to school there, in West Surrey. Our school was very regimented but I learnt French from the age of eleven and we even put on a play entirely in French for our parents. Every school holiday we toured around somewhere new in Britain and we also spent six weeks towing a camper-trailer around Europe. On our way back to New Zealand in 1981 we campervanned around the United States for three months.

I started learning piano when I was six and continued with it until 1987. I still play now, though only casually. Whilst in England Aaron and I went on a music camp at Milton Keynes run by Avril Dankworth, sister of jazz trumpeter Johnny Dankworth. We stayed in tents in the grounds of the home of Johnny Dankworth and his wife Cleo Laine. I became interested in the clarinet at the camp, and continued with it back in New Zealand. I also tried the saxophone but had to give it up as I ran out of time to practise. Too many social activities! At the moment I'm trying to teach myself the guitar. Aaron plays the trumpet.

I went to Hutt Valley High School for four years, then decided to work for a year before going to Teacher's College. I never actually got there, because while working for a chartered accountant who gave me time off for seventh form Spanish at High School I heard about YFU (Youth for Understanding) International Student Exchange Programme. I decided to go to Argentina, because of the Spanish, and saved furiously for the programme fees. I spent 1988 in Esperanza, a town of thirty thousand people, six hundred kilometres north-west of Buenos Aires. I lived with a family and went to school there, and had a really cool time.

Back in New Zealand in 1989 I decided that I didn't have the patience to be a teacher so I took an interim job with Thomas Cook Business Travel as a receptionist typist. I'm still here, though now as a travel consultant. I really enjoy it.

I'm also still involved with YFU as a returnee and organise lots of social activities for current and ex-students. At the moment I'm busy organising a two-week trip around the North Island for forty students in the August holidays. Next month I'm going back to Argentina for a holiday. I can't wait.

Another thing I can't wait for is meeting you - there's so much I'd love to ask you. However, I won't be back from Argentina until the beginning of May. I'm really looking forward to the break as the year's work is catching up on me. Anyway, maybe we could see each other in the May holidays as you won't have kindergarten then.

Well that's about all I can think of to say at the moment. I've enclosed some photos so that you can see what I looked like at different stages.

I look forward to hearing from you.

Love, Katrina

He is deteriorating faster now. He has more difficulty swallowing, in dealing with the congestion in his throat and lungs, and often chokes. The community health team from Lower Hutt Hospital visit us regularly, the speech therapist, the physiotherapist, the dietician. They give him exercises for his throat and chest, exercises for his limbs, food supplements for his thinning body, show me how to massage his wasting muscles. He disregards the soft food suggestions, preferring to struggle with normal foods, with cheese on toast for lunch.

His mind is very sharp. He is frustrated at not being able to express himself verbally and bangs the table. Frustrated by tongue muscles that won't move to allow him to articulate his thoughts. His hearing and eyesight are sharp. Compensation for what he has lost, we are told, and we have to turn down the television volume to very low so that it doesn't disturb him in the bedroom when he's trying to sleep.

Lower Hutt
20 March 1990

Dear Glenis,

You have been in our thoughts many times over the past twenty years, and as Katrina has passed milestones and been successful in so many areas of her life I have often thought, if only Katrina's mother could know how happy and well-adjusted she is. We have had a happy family life together and Katrina has packed a lot into her twenty years.

Firstly, we would like to say that we have never stopped thanking you in our hearts for Katrina. She has brought us continual joy and happiness. She is a sensitive, intelligent and caring daughter and we couldn't have loved her more if she had been born to us. Aaron was born in April 1972 and he and Katrina are really good friends. Aaron is also a great kid.

We first told the children that they were adopted before they themselves could talk and it has never been an issue or a problem.

The story of their adoption was told as a loving bed-time story. Katrina remembers sprawling across our bed and saying, "Tell us again how you adopted us." We told them that their mothers loved them so much and wanted only the best for them with both a mother and a father to bring them up. I can understand your fervent hope that Ken and I stayed together.

I know that times have changed since Katrina and Aaron were born. Social pressures to give up babies for adoption, and lack of financial support for the unmarried mother, are no longer an issue, and we were indeed sad to read that you have been unable to have any children since Katrina. We have always told our children that we would support them if they wanted to meet their parents, and we have also wanted to meet you ourselves.

Ken and I grew up in New Zealand and I went to Thailand with my parents and brothers when I was sixteen. I stayed there for several years, working at the New Zealand Embassy, attending university, and teaching English and piano in a Thai school. From there I went to Europe where I met Ken who was doing his own bit of travel. We married in New Zealand in 1965.

Ken worked as production manager with a footwear company and was with them for fourteen years before we took off for Europe for our second working holiday there. This was an interesting and exciting event and probably explains why Katrina has chosen travel as a career. When we returned home to New Zealand we turned a craft hobby into a full-time business which we have operated from the house.

Sadly, Ken was diagnosed about eighteen months ago as having motor neurone disease. He has lost his speech and can walk only with difficulty. Like me, though, he is looking forward to meeting you.

Love, Robyn

P.S. Katrina was really pleased to get your photo and tried to work out which features of yours matched with hers.

Christchurch
25 March 1990

Dear Katrina,

Thank you so much for your lovely letter. I guessed what it was before I even opened it, so I started to cry and went to Dad for a hug - he lives with us. He was totally bewildered of course, because he knew I hadn't opened it. Then when I did open it I looked first at the big sheet of photos and then when I saw one or two particular photos of me looking out, I was away again! It was a real shock to see me in someone else's life! I always felt when I was pregnant with you, and when I had you with me for the first week, "It's just you and me, kid, no one else had anything to do with this," and it would certainly seem so after seeing those photos!

I have an aunt living down here - Edna - and she rushed out yesterday to have a look at the photos, and she couldn't get over the resemblance. Not now, so much, but in your teens.

Anyway, enough. I was so bowled over by the enthusiasm of your response, and the obvious effort you went to, to give me an overview of your life, I was quite overcome. What wonderful parents you have, and what a life you have led! If it wasn't for the resemblance I might have thought we had a case of mistaken identity - I hate to tell you, Katrina, but I don't have one tiny ounce of wanderlust in my entire body. I'm a real stay at home, me. I love to be at home in my house with my animals. But I appreciate the travel bug in other people - I love to hear them talk about their travels and go through their photos. And what a travelling life you have had - everyone who has read your letter has said, "She's certainly been around!"

There have been a troop of people through the place, come to see the photos. Even Harry the plasterer had to look at the photos and say how lovely you are!

I just can't believe I have such a daughter - so adventurous and accomplished, so vivacious and enthusiastic, all such a credit to you and your parents. My initial reaction was that you don't need me in your life, but then I wouldn't have it any other way either.

This letter is really supposed to be just a note (but I warn you, I'm notorious for my long letters!) to thank you so much for the photos and wish you a wonderful holiday in Argentina. Argentina - just fancy! Now I'm trying to remember all the things I've read about this place, although if I recall, most of them were pretty worrying!

While you are away I'll take the time to adjust to all the news, and write you a long letter telling a few details you might be interested in, and answer Robyn's lovely letter.

In the meantime I'll enclose some photos of my childhood for you to ponder. I'll fill you in on who's who in a later letter.

Have a wonderful holiday, Katrina - take very good care now, you hear? I'm so impressed with you I'm bursting!

Lots of love, Glenis

They arrange for hand rails on the stairs and in the bathroom, and a plastic chair for the shower. He accepts the railings but gets angry about the chair and waves it away. Kay brings him a little electronic keyboard on which he can type out messages. He fiddles with it and waves that away too. He writes me notes about what to buy at the shops, what he is thinking. He falls on the workshop floor and I ban him from entering it again. All that glass. I massage him daily to try to keep his muscles moving. He's still caring for his canaries. I worry about him going down the concrete steps to them.

Christchurch
7 April 1990

Dear Robyn,

Thank you so much for your lovely letter - I really can't tell you how much it meant to me. Katrina's letter was wonderful of course, bubbly and lovely and fresh and exciting and a joy to receive, but your letter was written woman to woman and touched me more than I can say. Your generosity of spirit is astounding and obviously all of that has come through in Katrina. She seems a really lovely girl, but how could she fail to be after the amazing life you have given her!

I cried buckets of tears the day I received your letters, but you know those are the only tears I have ever shed over Katrina. Except, I remember, the day I left the hospital - I was going down in the lift with one of the nuns who had come to collect me, and I recognised my baby's cry in the nursery - I cried a little then. But I am basically a sensible person - I have never been in any way neurotic about Katrina. I didn't get all emotional on her birthdays, or maudlin about the baby I had given up. In my first teaching job, in Edgecumbe, there was a boy called Michael Watson, whose birth date was 1 December 1969, and I was very interested in his development, with Katrina in mind. I drank a toast to her and to you on her sixteenth and twentieth birthdays, and I talked about her freely when the topic arose, which it often does in my job with all the talk of pregnancies and babies that kindergarten mothers engage in. I was what you might call very adjusted about it all, and for two good reasons.

The first and most important one was that I seemed to know that I could trust you and Ken completely. Not that I knew who you were or anything about you but I had given my beautiful baby to you and I just knew I could trust you to love her. After all, she was in a splint when you chose her, and that didn't worry you. That you have succeeded so well in giving her a loving family life full of adventure and excitement was more than I could have dreamed of, so my trust was well-placed.

The other reason was I made a bargain with you in my head - I agreed to stay completely out of your lives until she was twenty, but I was unwavering in my determination to make contact when she became an adult. When Katrina was about seventeen I went to Social Welfare to talk about tracking her down, really for my father's sake after my older brother's death. My other two brothers had both died in accidents and I was the only child left in my family. The welfare officer encouraged me to start my own search immediately because he said the longer you leave it the colder the trail gets. I thought about it, but I decided against it. Interference from me was not what you needed bringing up a teenage daughter.

I had no other children of my own, but I did bring up a stepdaughter from three years to sixteen years. Her name is Alix and she is in the sixth form at Avonside Girls' High, and to all outward appearances I did a good job. She is extremely bright, very attractive, lots of confidence and independence, very capable and accomplished and highly though of by peers and adults alike. But I know that our relationship was fraught with tension and clashes - we never overcame that invisible but insurmountable 'step' barrier. I saw, also through my job as a kindergarten teacher, the friction and disruption to children's lives caused by the 'other parent' having weekend access to their children and I vowed that I would never do that to you.

So you see, I really do appreciate fully that you have been able to love Katrina as your own and I admire you tremendously for taking her so completely into your family.

Another thing I want to say is when I look at Alix I see so many things about her that are directly taken from me -

mannerisms, attitudes, abilities (a letter from Alix reads like a letter from me - the similarities are quite amazing), her interest in words and language - lots of things. Of course there are many things that are different (hence many of the arguments) but I have seen first-hand how much of someone's personality is assimilated from the environment and family influences. Therefore I expect that much of Katrina's personality reflects you and Ken (certainly her interest in travel, and the wonderful ability with music that you have instilled in her) and I'm more than happy, that's the way it should be.

There are many times of course when I have wondered and worried. Because of family circumstances in my life I worried quite seriously that she might not even be alive, I worried that you might be separated, I worried that she might be into drugs, or like me, had a baby, at seventeen, but they were brief thoughts and my first always won out. I hoped she would be close to her grandparents, that she'd stay on at school past fifteen, that she would be open and articulate, that she would push forward and accept challenges rather than be timid and hold back, that she would be close to you and most of all that she'd be happy. And it appears that all those hopes have been fulfilled many times over. What more could a birth mother ask?

Finally, I'd just like to say you're a real hit around here. I have shown your letter to all my friends, who are every one of them mothers, and they've all come out of it with tears in their eyes and goose bumps all over. It was a very moving letter!

I was shocked to hear of Ken's misfortune. To have led such a very active life and then contract a disease like that - the adjustments must be extremely difficult for him and you. I'm sure you have the strengths and supports to make the adjustments, but my heart goes out to you both, having to cope with this, with so much life left to live.

I hope this letter conveys to you some of the gratitude I feel - it comes from the heart and is echoed strongly by my mother and father, who are just as excited by all the good news. (There's only really one other grandchild in their lives - Susie, who is nineteen).

Congratulations on your wonderful daughter. I look forward to meeting you both and hope it will be soon.

Love, Glenis

Katrina stuffs the paua shell key rings and trinket boxes into her suitcase and smiles at us.

"Only three hours to go and I'll be on my way back to Argentina." She lays a T-shirt decorated with puffy sheep on top of a small machine that clamps ID tags on to cows' ears.

"Trust Papi to want something like this. I hope I've got the right one. The guy from Federated Farmers said there are about two hundred different types of tags and most have different clamps. What does a city girl know about choosing farm equipment?"

I laugh. "You'll probably end up helping him clamp them on to his cows. Give Mami and Papi and the children our love and tell them we'd love to meet them some day. By the way, do you realise you've got three mothers now?"

She looks quizzically at me.

"Glenis, Mami and me."

"Wow, I have too. I wonder what my Argentinian family will think of Glenis contacting me. I remember they thought it really strange when I told them I was adopted."

"Did they?" I help her lift the case off the bed.

"Over there it's only poor or very underprivileged families that have to give their children away. Adoption doesn't normally happen. If the girl gets pregnant she gets married right away. And the family are always very supportive. Got the keys? We should be going."

Christchurch
19 April 1990

Dear Katrina,

How are you? Where are you? Did you have a good Easter? I thought of you. I had a lovely weekend but as usual I ate too much chocolate, and as usual it was over far too quickly. Last Easter I was sick and spent the week alone (well except for Dad) but this year was much better.

A couple of weeks ago I had the weekend to myself, so I decided to spend it writing to you. Actually, first of all I started making a tape for you, then I abandoned that and got up at ten o'clock at night and wrote you a long letter and then I wasn't brave enough to send that either! I think I'll take it with me and show you when we meet.

I finally had to give in and send all your photos off to Mum. I hate not having them, and I don't have too much faith in N.Z. Post, but I couldn't delay it any longer. By the time she has shown all her friends and skited about you all over Whakatane, heaven knows when I'll get them back.

I'll tell you briefly a few things - I was born in Invercargill on 27 December 1951. I went to fourteen schools but did most of my secondary schooling at Teschemakers, a Catholic boarding school just out of Oamaru. After you were born I did two years at Canterbury University, and then two years at kindergarten college also in Christchurch. My first kindergarten job was in Edgecumbe, and I lived in Whakatane for twelve years.

My parents were a mismatch from the beginning, and finally separated in 1977. After a year or so of moving around, Mum followed me to Whakatane, and has bought herself a lovely flat up there. I hope she stays there - she is a very forceful person - she and I get on best when she's in the Bay of Plenty and I'm in Canterbury!

In 1984 my husband and I moved from Whakatane to Christchurch, and I guess now I'm here to stay. Dad stayed in Invercargill until I went down and forcibly removed him three or four years ago, and now he lives with us. He has a little cabin out on the back lawn and has fitted in very well. They are both very, very excited about you, and can't wait to meet you.

You know, it's not even easy for me to say what my interests are. I guess principally I'd have to say my home and my animals. I have two dogs, Petal, my beautiful fat black spaniel, the apple of my eye, and Poppy, a mongrel who wandered into kindergarten a couple of weeks before Christmas. She's an Alsatian cross - possibly with a Huntaway. She was little-ish when I met her. She's biggish now. Drives Dad crazy. She is on heat right now, so she's off for her op tomorrow. No breakfast for Poppy - poor love, she's no idea what she's in for!

Then there's Turbo, my fat tabby cat - he's the old man of the family, about ten years old. He's feeling paranoid at the moment, because we have two visiting cats, Gus and Minx, and they have usurped all my Tubby's favourite places.

On top of that, there's Tessa across the driveway. She's an old black Lab, and lives here more than at her house. We all love her and anyone in Kaiapoi would swear I own three dogs - if we take one dog we have to take three. So one of my largest time-eating occupations is walking the three dogs.

That done, then I love to spend time at home. I can waste hours just pottering around. Music plays a large part - only records, I'm afraid, not instruments. I love movies, I love to eat out. I'm reasonably good at talking - I seem to spend hours doing that.

I live with Keith now, a childhood sweetheart, a situation I'll explain in more depth when I see you. Keith is a musician from way back. My house is full of guitars and PA systems and amplifiers and speakers and microphones. Keith also plays the sax, and the piano. A keyboard is the next thing we must buy, although he's nowhere near as good as you must be. He's very good on the guitar though - really knows what he's doing. So these days I spend a few nights in pubs and halls whenever the boys are playing a gig. That's still a novelty for me though - I've only been living with Keith a year.

I am not restricted to seeing you in the May holidays as I'm having the winter term off from teaching. Since I will be quite flexible, I will leave the plans up to you. I can come up to Wellington to see you, or you can come down here, or if you'd like to make it completely neutral territory we could get a motel in Picton (my shout) - I'm quite happy to fit in with whatever you'd like. I'm just really looking forward to meeting you!

What do you think? Would you like to arrange it? Just let me know where and when, and I'll be there.

I hope you had a lovely holiday. I thought of you so much. Write and let me know what you think.

Love, Glenis

Aaron phones from Palmerston North. He's loving the course. He got ninety-seven percent in Meteorology and ninety-one percent in Navigation. He must be working well.

I visit him a week later, unexpectedly, at the flat that he shares with three other would-be-aviators. He is alone in the kitchen. An open recipe book sits propped up behind the sink taps, a great quantity of thinly-sliced raw steak is scattered along the chipped green Formica bench, next to this a dish of white flour, a bowl of beaten eggs, a plate of dried bread crumbs. His hands are coated in the mixture. I can't believe that this is my son, he who wouldn't boil water if he didn't have to.

"How many for dinner?" I ask.

"Just the four of us, Patrick comes from a farm." He opens the cupboard. "Look at all the preserved fruit and jams his mother sent back for us. Do you want to stay for dinner?"

He doesn't think he'll be down for the reunion with Glenis. Too much emotion, he says. I ask him to come, please.

Lower Hutt
24 April 1990

Dear Glenis,

Many thanks for your lovely long letter. I must admit that I shed a few tears as I read it.

I felt quite privileged to be part of the adoption triangle as you expressed your feelings on how you had dealt with, and come to terms with Katrina's adoption.

I smiled as I was reminded how she had been in a splint when we first saw her. We were really excited about her from our first visit though and I went to the hospital each day to learn how to look after her in the brace, prior to her being 'released' to us. I was quite relaxed about caring for a new baby as we had previously had a foster baby for four months.

I really appreciate the fact that you didn't contact Katrina when she was in her teens. Being adopted has always been a natural part of Katrina and Aaron's existence and Katrina hadn't dwelt on it much. However, after she was interviewed for the Youth Focus article (which I'm enclosing) she said she was forced to think deeply about the issue. Teenage years are vulnerable ones and she wouldn't have been ready to handle contact. In some ways she's probably still not ready for it, but I'm probably just being a protective mother here!

Your letters and photos have done the rounds of the family and they are looking forward to meeting you. My brother Brent, and his American wife Julie, can relate to what is happening with us. Last August Julie got a call from an adoption agency in the States to say that her birth daughter was looking for her and wanted to meet her. It was a real shock to Julie who had given birth twenty-one years ago, three years before meeting Brent. She was unmarried and had told no one except her parents, the natural father's family, and later Brent. She had given a false name so that she couldn't be traced and put the birth completely out of her mind. After the phone call, they decided to tell their children and the rest of the family and close friends. Three weeks later her daughter Sarah came out from the States with her adoptive mum. The whole episode was quite draining on Julie and has left her rather unsettled. Sarah had been searching for Julie for a year and had to go through the courts to get access to files. The adoption search laws for the State of Washington appear to be much more restrictive than ours.

Katrina and Aaron were the only grandchildren for my parents for about ten years and they have always had lots of love and attention from them. Ken's family lived in Hamilton and Auckland so we didn't see so much of them but did enjoy holidays together. Ken's mother had died of a neurological disease before I met him. After Ken was diagnosed with MND he discovered that his mother had died of the same disease and that it is hereditary in about ten percent of cases, so you can imagine how thankful we are that our children are adopted.

We scrutinised the photos you sent Katrina and thought the ones of you at twelve could be Katrina - it was quite uncanny. By the way, she is left-handed too, as is Aaron, and Brent and Julie's two children. Katrina, as she is now, looks quite similar to the photo of your mother taken some time ago (studio photo). Your father has very similar features to Ken which may explain why everyone used to tell Katrina how much she looked like her father - not knowing she was adopted.

Argentina was a great experience for Katrina and she was so looking forward to seeing her host family and friends again. Before she went we discussed about meeting up with you and wondered about the weekend of 12-13 May. Katrina gets back on 2 May.

We haven't heard from her since she left New Zealand but this isn't surprising as the Argentine postal system is notoriously unpredictable.

We look forward to meeting you soon Glenis. It still seems a little unreal to me after all these years.

Love, Robyn

# Chapter Fifteen

FRIDAY, 11 May 1990

"IT'S ON TIME at 7.30pm." Katrina drew a deep breath and we walked away from the arrivals monitor at the Ansett airport terminal and over to Gate 24. The doors swung open. Businessmen emerged with black attaché cases, important faces and purposeful strides. Straggling small children and distracted parents, a platoon of Japanese visitors and their cameras. Katrina held my arm, waiting for her first glimpse of Glenis. What would she be like, I wondered? How would our personalities mix? Can a mother and child separated at birth slot back in to each other's lives twenty years later? But the letters had helped considerably, and the phone call from Katrina to arrange the date. We weren't meeting a stranger, we already had an understanding of each other, had time to get used to the situation.

An attractive lone figure with Katrina's brown curly hair walked through the door and over to us. We hugged and walked to the car, suddenly feeling relaxed. We talked as if what was happening was very normal, as one would when a friend who hasn't been seen for many years arrives for the weekend. Glenis told how she had cried for ten minutes on Keith's shoulder before boarding the plane in Christchurch. She wasn't normally emotional, she said, but the enormity of the occasion had overtaken her.

Glenis spent the evening with us. Questions. Answers. A sharing of thoughts and feelings.

"Yes, congenital hips is in the family." "What did you know about us?" "Do you think we've got the same eyes?" " I didn't like the lawyer, he was scathing. I had questions for him, but couldn't ask them. He wouldn't even look at me."

Ken was pleased to be part of the reunion. He couldn't talk but he could watch and listen and convey his emotions in his own way. Aaron had phoned to say that he would be arriving down tomorrow, but might stay with his friend Duncan.

"I was really concerned when I made enquiries about you last November," Glenis said to Katrina as we drank cups of tea around the table. "Social Welfare came back to me with the information that you were on a benefit and had now gone overseas."

We were incredulous. How could they get it so wrong?

"I worried that you were in the same situation as I had been. Single and with a baby."

"I did go to Sydney for four days," said Katrina. We laughed. "How did you find me?"

"They gave me your phone number of twenty years ago and said that it appeared that the family was still at the same address. They told me to have an intermediary woman anonymously phone the family and get the details of where you were. She got such a shock when you answered the phone."

"Yes I remember the call," Katrina said. "I thought it really strange. When I answered the phone the woman at the other end asked to speak to Katrina, and when I said 'Yes, that's me,' she said 'Thank you very much,' and hung up!"

So it was the Department of Social Welfare who advised that adoptive parents be by-passed, be excluded, when birth mothers seek initial contact with their children. It was only twenty years previously that Child Welfare, its predecessor, had told us, as new adoptive families, to exclude the birth parents from *our* lives.

Katrina drove Glenis down to her motel that evening, the accommodation pre-arranged in case the reunion was difficult. It was the first time they had been alone together. "We chatted all the way down and got on pretty well," smiled Katrina on her return. "I'm going to pick her up in the morning. We'll probably browse around the Queensgate Mall."

She returned with Glenis at midday on Saturday. They both seemed relaxed. "We did the shops," said Katrina as she stirred the saucepan of tomato soup for lunch. "When I was there I thought, 'People will think I'm with my mother,' and then I thought - 'She *is* my mother!'" She grinned at me. "You know it's not considered cool to be seen with your mother at Queensgate? Or your aunty, or your grandfather for that matter."

The family came for the evening. Cousins, aunt, uncle, grandparents and Aaron. Glenis coped admirably with the onslaught. We all liked her. Aaron felt comfortable with the occasion and decided to stay home for the rest of the weekend.

Sunday was Mother's Day. The significance of the day had escaped us until the day before. Katrina bought Glenis a 'To a Special Person on Mother's Day' card. We asked Glenis if there was anything special she would like to do. "I'd like to see the Rosanna Hostel again," she said, "and could we drive past the doctor's house where I lived for two months?"

Glenis told us of her arrival at the Rosanna Hostel for Unmarried Mothers, twenty years ago. Penniless and pregnant. It had been a twenty-six hour journey for her and her large suitcase. Train from Invercargill to Christchurch, ferry to Wellington and a taxi to Rosanna. Her first trip to the North Island, a seventeen-year-old, three months pregnant and alone, leaving Invercargill before her pregnancy was visible, her mother wanting the pregnancy kept secret.

The nuns at Rosanna weren't expecting her, her mother should have booked her in through Catholic Social Services, she could stay only three months at the hostel - the maximum time allowable in one period, she was told. The nuns took her initially for a month then found her a family to stay with for two months, a gynaecologist and his family. She was treated like a servant by the wife, did all the cooking and cleaning and was paid two dollars a week when they remembered. If visitors arrived she was banished from their sight. She should be aware of the shame of pregnancy in an unmarried state. She was glad to return to Rosanna for the final three months of her pregnancy.

Katrina looked tentatively at Glenis. "What about... my father?"

"Your father had no idea that he was soon to become one. I never saw him after I left Invercargill." She hesitated. "Because of the circumstances at the time I told him that I was coming up to Wellington to do a course. He doesn't know of your existence."

"Oh." Katrina bit her lip. "Can you tell me anything about him? I know he was a technician and likes music."

"Does he?" said Glenis. "I didn't know him very well. I think I concocted most of the information I gave Child Welfare." She looked serious. "I can't remember much about him. I can give you his name, though. I've told no one his name, not even my parents."

Katrina nodded. "I'd like to try and find him some time, now that I've met you."

We drove into Tyndall Street and looked up at the imposing old wooden house, surrounded by lawn and trees. The Rosanna Hostel signs had disappeared long ago. It looked like private accommodation. "See all those steps leading up to the front door? I stood there at the bottom with my large suitcase, feeling like something out of a Dickens' novel. I still remember the day. Mother Euphrasia came out of the front door and looked down at me and said, 'What are you doing there?' I said, 'My mother sent me. I'm pregnant.'"

We stared at the house trying to imagine what had been. Glenis looked at Katrina. "Katrina would you mind... if I took a picture of you outside the house?"

"I'll take one of both of you," I said. They stood together on the bottom step where Glenis and her suitcase had stood twenty years earlier, and smiled for the camera.

"See these hills behind the home? I carried suitcases up and down them for three days in the hope that you would be born by the first of December and I could get U.E. accredited and not have to sit it. I'd been doing it by correspondence. It worked."

The doctor's house wasn't far away. A white 'character' home from the early 1900s, set back from the road amongst flowering trees and shrubs. I stared at it as memories flooded back. "What was his name?" I asked Glenis. It was the gynaecologist whom I had visited all those years ago when I thought I was pregnant and wasn't. The one who told me that Tuesdays, Thursdays and Fridays were for pregnant women only, and that I should make a Monday or Wednesday appointment.

We parked outside and from our car watched a Rover being backed down the long driveway. It slid through the gateway in front of us. Glenis stiffened. "It's the witch," she said, as the woman drove away, unaware of her curious onlookers.

We drove on ourselves, past the Tutukiwi Orchid and Fern House and the sunken garden where local musicians entertain Sunday afternoon strollers when the weather permits.

"How long did you look after me in the hospital?" asked Katrina. "Was anyone with you when I was born?"

Yellow marigolds and purple pansies fluttered in royal display outside the War Memorial Library.

"I had you beside me for a week. I hadn't expected to look after you but the matron insisted. She said it would be better for me to do so.

And then I thought how you could go from one set of loving arms into another, rather than just having a variety of nurses looking after you for the first ten days. I wasn't allowed to breastfeed you, though, and no photos were allowed of our babies. I remember a friend taking a photo. She slept with it under her pillow and was totally upset at having to part with her baby - she couldn't handle it. But I realised in hospital what a full-time job looking after a baby was. It was a twenty-four-hour job. As a seventeen-year-old I didn't have the wherewithall to cope."

Past Homestead Golden Chicken and wafts of crumbed wings and thighs. Over the Ewen Bridge. A kayaker stroked his way down the river.

"The nurses at the hospital were good to me. And the gynaecologist. There was one young nurse who had just got engaged. She was lovely. She sat beside me during labour and held my hand."

On to the railway bridge and up the hill. Winding, winding through the native bush.

"Did you just stay a week in hospital?" asked Katrina.

"Yes. The nuns came and collected me. I stayed four more days at Rosanna, waiting to sign the adoption papers, then I went to Christchurch and worked as a waitress until varsity started."

And back into suburbia. Wooden houses of assorted hues and shapes punched into the hillside.

We took Glenis back to the airport at 7pm. Most of the jigsaw pieces had come together. Just the father was missing. Would he be easy to find?

# Chapter Sixteen

ANOTHER letter came.

Christchurch
18 May 1990

Dear Katrina, Robyn and Ken,

Thank you for your letter, Katrina, which I received today. Those dates are fine for you to come down, and we're really looking forward to it. I'm glad you didn't have to juggle work time to do it.

Thank you also, all of you, for a lovely weekend. I really enjoyed it very much - I liked the low-key approach, the easy pace of it all which gave all of us time to absorb everything. I returned very happy and wondering what on earth I had been so nervous about!

I had a good flight home - bumpy for the first and last minute, but for the rest of the time we were above the wind.

I've had a lovely relaxed week, but I'm still officially on holiday - next week the work ethic will raise its ugly head and my conscience will spring into action. Who knows, I might even get sick of such idleness!

Actually, I was going to take a photo of my cute husband lying on the couch, eyes shut, listening to music, with cute Poppy lying sprawling across his chest breathing into his Jewish nose, but instead it turned into the Great Camera Hunt. I realised eventually I must have left it in the back of your car. Don't worry about sending it down - just bring it with you when you come. There'll be plenty more man-and-dog photo opportunities!

On Wednesday I rang up about my Market Research job, now that I'm taking a term off from teaching, only to find that they're not doing training sessions for another six months. They actually told me that they'd bring me in for one-to-one training, but they obviously have enough people. So I spent Wednesday afternoon totally panic-stricken and chose that opportune moment to do the bills! However, Keith is quite determined he doesn't want me to work in a factory, and I have my name down for relieving teaching, so we'll see how we go. Makes life interesting anyway!

Everyone loved the Argentinian pasties you sent down, Katrina, especially Dad. He was most impressed. Dad's really excited about meeting you. I must arrange it that Susie comes out while you're down - relatives are fairly thin on the ground for her too, so she'll be glad to welcome another into the clan.

Well, the menagerie is getting demanding - two cats are using stand-over tactics on me, wanting their tea, and the dogs are frolicking - there go the ornaments on the coffee table. I'd better go and feed them, and get the father's tea while I'm at it.

Thank you again for a great weekend, and we're all looking forward to the 15th.

By the way, here's that information that Social Welfare sent me after I went to see them a few years ago. You can keep it if you like - I made a copy. It's a glowing report of your first eight months - you obviously made a good impression! It set my mind at rest when I received it.

Bye for now,

Love, Glenis.

We read the report.

*Thank you for your enquiry of 1 September 1986 seeking information on your daughter Rachel,"* it began. So, I thought, Glenis wrote to them about her Rachel, who became our Katrina, the day the Adult Information Act 1985 came into effect. The report continued:

*I am able to give you non-identifying information from these records, but Rachel's name and address must remain confidential to this Department. We have no up-to-date information available on Rachel beyond 1972 when this Department ceased contact with her adoptive family.*

*Most of the information is about her adoptive parents rather than Rachel herself, in view of her very young age. I hope this information will be helpful to you, however.*

*Rachel Susan McLean, born 1 December 1969 at Lower Hutt.*

*Birth details : Full term, normal delivery.*

*Birth weight: 8lb 3oz*

*Normal early progress. Very fair skin and brown hair.*

*On 15 December 1969 Rachel went into the care of her adoptive parents.*

*They were a New Zealand-born European couple who had been married for four years and had no children. The couple met while overseas and had a close loving relationship. They were financially secure and owned a three-bedroom new home. They loved children and had done some fostering for the Department before applying to adopt.*

The information gave details of our ages, education and employment, then listed progress notes from home visits:

*21.1.70 Parents delighted with baby who has a congenital hip dislocation and is in brace until end of month. Going for X-rays. Nice little baby - light brown hair with reddish tints.*

*23.1.70 Lovely contented baby. Brace off now and X-rays show all OK.*

*29.1.70 All well. Baby perfect.*

*30.1.70 An interim order of adoption was made in the Lower Hutt Court.*

*06.3.70 All well. Baby very contented. Quite attractive - fair hair, very fair lashes and eyebrows (scarcely visible). Nice plump baby - well proportioned. Parents absolutely devoted to her.*

*16.4.70 Very sweet baby. Very fair, clear skin, one inch taller, one pound heavier than average. Plunket reports good. All family including grandparents, etc delighted.*

*25.6.70 Quite a change in baby. Has lost all her fairness, has good skin colour and should tan in summer. Hair mid-brown but still quite bald. Healthy-looking child and above average weight. Contented and pretty little girl.*

*28.7.70 Baby progressing well - pretty and happy. Very good likeness to adoptive father. Will tell child she is adopted, want to familiarise her with the word 'adopted' and explain gradually.*

*13.8.70 A final adoption order was made in the Lower Hutt District Court.*

*8.12.71 The adoptive couple applied to adopt a second child. Rachel described as a delightful little girl with dark blonde hair, fair skin, blue eyes. Close relationship with parents.*

*April 72 This couple adopted a baby boy.*

*31.5.72 Rachel an attractive, outgoing little girl, very active.*

*We have no further notes on file relating to Rachel's progress. Our contact with this family ceased in March 1973 and the family did not adopt again.*

*The file has been noted of your willingness for contact and we should be able to advise you in the event of any approach to the Department from Rachel or her adoptive parents.*

*When Rachel reaches twenty years of age you will be able to request that a social worker approach her on your behalf under the provisions of the Adult Adoption Information Act 1985. She, at that age, will be able to apply for her original birth certificate which would show your name and her birth name. You have the right to veto this information if you do not want it disclosed.*

*I will be returning Rachel's file to Lower Hutt so suggest you refer any further correspondence to that office. If you would like to talk things over further, please contact me on any Monday or Wednesday.*

The letter was signed with the name of the social worker.

We were impressed by the detailed reply to Glenis's enquiry.

"It's funny reading about me as a baby," Katrina said. "I never did tan though."

"Yes, it's interesting seeing how your progress was recorded. It seems such a long time ago. But where was the social worker who was supposed to approach you on Glenis's behalf?"

He can't swallow enough food for his needs and is getting so thin. The dietician speaks of a gastrostomy tube through which he can be fed liquid meals directly into the stomach. He won't have to worry about choking and he might even put on weight. He can think of nothing worse, the end of his meat and vegetables and cheese on toast. The end of his independence.

I massage him daily to try to keep his muscles active. He's still walking but his speech has entirely gone. The tongue muscles have simply stopped moving. I become a full-time translator - I seem to understand everything he wants to tell me. His body language is so expressive, too expressive sometimes. He rejects Kay's offer of a small keyboard that translates typed messages into male or female American voices. He doesn't need it, he writes on a scrap of paper: he has me. He rejects the notion that he is dying. We all do.

Medi-Care, who he's been insured with for twenty-five years and seldom claimed from until recently, are refusing to pay for his doctors' visits as they say he now has a chronic condition. And we've just heard that his sister who has had multiple sclerosis for four years has died from choking. He still doesn't want the tube.

He asks me to sell his canaries.

Lower Hutt
27 May 1990

Dear Glenis,

It's a lovely clear winter's day and I'm sitting at the dining room table enjoying the view. Our lounge ranch-sliders were finally put in last week and the room looks so different. We just need a balustrade around the patio now.

It was so good to have the weekend with you. Amazing really how 'easy' it all was. I think I was just as excited by everything as Katrina was. I feel as if we have known you for years and there was certainly a feeling of relaxed togetherness. Even Aaron, when asked how he felt about the weekend, commented that it was good, and maybe it would be all right to meet his birth parents some day!

I have mentioned to several friends about Katrina meeting you, some of whom didn't know previously that she was adopted, and most of them have had tears in their eyes, and been quite moved. In turn they have all had their own tales of adoptee/birth mother meetings, some of which are good, others negative.

I have a busy week this week. I'm Area Co-ordinator for YFU in Lower Hutt and have been organising a week in Lower Hutt for a group of adult Mexicans visiting New Zealand as part of an adult exchange. They arrive tonight, seventeen of them. We've just discovered after working out a hectic itinerary of marae visit, Marlborough wine trails, Explorer Bus trips, farm visit, Southward Car Museum, craft shops and Vogel House for dinner (Prime Minister's residence but without the PM - the Government hires it out to fund-raising groups) that most of them are in their sixties and seventies. I hope they can hack the pace. My main concern is the Latin Americans' laid-back attitude to time - that they'll miss the ferry or all the connections for the Explorer Bus.

Katrina is looking forward to her trip to see you on the 15th. She felt really comfortable and happy about the way our weekend went, and any concerns of mine about how she might cope were needless. She is now interested in meeting her father, but realises this could be a tricky situation.

I've enclosed an article from the Hutt News regarding the adoption conference held over the weekend you were here. I bumped into one of the organisers last week and told her how successful our meeting had been. She said that she had thought she had her act together, but the adoption conference was very heavy and she discovered that she had a lot of unresolved conflict. She is an adopted person who had a negative meeting two years ago with her birth mother. I read that she wants to ban adoption. Katrina also read the article and disagreed vehemently with the idea of banning adoption. She said she has never wished she wasn't adopted. I think that those with negative experiences can spend so much time analysing and discussing their situation that they end up in a worse state than when they started.

I'd better finish here. I'm starting to scrawl my writing. Hope to meet up with you again soon, Glenis. It's a pity we have that expensive stretch of water between us.

Love, Robyn

# Chapter Seventeen

MONDAY, 9 July 1990

HE IS BECOMING WEAKER. He chokes so often now that I need to be with him while he eats. Soft foods only, now. He has trouble breathing one night and a *locum* doctor visits. She calls it heart failure and gives him an injection. There is nothing more she can do for him, she says. Perhaps we should get him checked out at the hospital later on, she says, and goes away again. We lie awake together most of the night, wondering if he will still be alive in the morning.

At the hospital he is put in a general ward 'for observation'. They don't really want him. They tell him that he has arrived too late, at 4pm, to be listed for an evening meal. Just something soft will do, I say. Mashed vegetables. An egg. Sorry, they say, it's too late. We'll send the dietician up to see him tomorrow. There's a takeaway across the road, you might be able to get him something there. I walk down the stairs and across to Golden Eagle Takeaways and read the menu. Chicken and cashew nuts. Stir-fried beef in oyster sauce.

My husband is very sick in hospital but they can't feed him, I say. Is it possible to cook me a poached egg? The shopkeeper sympathises and produces the egg, specially cooked, not normally on the menu.

The hospital serves him cornflakes and toast for breakfast the next morning and he can't manage the toast. He hasn't seen the dietician yet. I take him some lunch. He still hasn't seen the dietician. She arrives the following day at my insistence, the day they say he can go home again. Five doctors in white coats and stethoscopes are gathered around his bed. They look like a scene from *The Singing Detective* and I expect them to break into song as they did in the television movie. He has motor neurone disease they say, and the weak heart is a result of that. They nod and smile serious smiles and walk away. I take him home again that afternoon.

The community health dietician visits and is concerned that he weighs only 50 kilos which gives him a Body Mass Index of 16, and less than 15 is classified as emaciation. She asks whether he is eating extra butter and sugar as earlier suggested and taking the food supplements. He doesn't like butter and sugar, and the powdered supplements only increase his congestion, I say.

They suggest again that he has a gastrostomy tube inserted into his stomach. He could still swallow by mouth if he wanted to, but this would be supplementary feeding which he really needs. He could put on weight again and start feeling better, not so weak. And I should have a break, they say. There is a Physically Disabled Unit at the hospital and he can go there for two weeks, after the tube is inserted into his stomach at Wellington Hospital, and the unit will build him up for my return.

He doesn't want to go. He doesn't want me to go away. I plead with him that I need a holiday. I'll stay with his other sister in Hamilton - I won't be too far away. He agrees to the tube as long as he can also keep eating by mouth, and finally agrees to a stay in the hospital.

Aaron phones to find out how Ken is and how we are coping. His course is going really well and he's about to start on his practical training. Flying in a four-seater Piper Warrior.

Katrina returns from a successful weekend in Christchurch. Warm welcomes by her new grandfather and the rest of the family.

"Everything seems to be finalised for our YFU trip," said Katrina. "We've got forty exchange students going, and the bus takes forty-four people so with four supervisors we'll be just right for seats."

"It should be a great trip," I said. "Two weeks of sightseeing around the North Island, white water rafting down the Tongariro River, thermal pools in Rotorua, a night on a marae in Waitomo. I wish I could come."

"Yes, and we've got a good mixture of nationalities going - the Scandinavians, the South Americans, quite a few Japanese and the North Americans. Wendy and Andrew are coming with me as supervisors. Andrew will be good, he's a policeman, but we still need one more person. I can't think of anyone else who is free for two weeks in the August holidays."

"What about Glenis?" I said with a sudden spark of inspiration. "She has holidays from kindergarten then. I wonder if she would be interested in swapping pre-school kids for high school students for a couple of weeks. She'd be good value as a supervisor." I smiled at Katrina. "And it would be a good opportunity for you to get to know each other better. It's difficult with her being so far away down in Christchurch. I think she's got you up there on a bit of a pedestal. You only get to meet her in snatches. What do you think?"

"Hey, yes. Do you think she would do it?" She paused. "She doesn't like travelling, though, and it wouldn't be a very restful break for her."

"But she would have two weeks with you. She might consider it."

Katrina phoned Glenis. She wasn't home and Katrina left a message with her boarder about the intended trip. Glenis contacted Katrina the next evening, unsure about whether she would consider it. She couldn't think of anything much worse than taking forty pre-schoolers in a bus around the North Island for two weeks, even with the strong draw-card of Katrina's presence.

"But they're all teenagers!" Katrina laughed. "You must have got the wrong message. Sixteen- to eighteen-year-olds, all from other countries, here on exchange."

Glenis agreed, with a small amount of trepidation, that she would go as a supervisor. It would be quite a new experience for her, this homebody who once wrote that she didn't have one ounce of wanderlust in her whole body, whose idea of happiness was being at home with her animals.

"Forty teenagers on a bus for two weeks?" she confirmed with Katrina.

27 July 1990

I return from holiday, well cared for, and he is overjoyed to see me again. I am surprised to see him sitting in a wheelchair. He was walking, perhaps staggering is a better word, two weeks ago, but has lost the use of his legs since his hospital stay. He felt unsafe walking in the wide hospital corridors and the nurses didn't have time to walk with him, to massage him, to keep his leg muscles going. He 'says' he saw a physiotherapist only once. He still has strength in his arms and hands and can write. My friend Caroline has visited every day and taken him for walks. How good she is - she had never met him before, but offered to be there for him while I was away. My parents did the same.

He can't swallow now, either. He shunned the red jellies offered to him, wanting his normal pureed meats and vegetables, so the nurses drip-fed him all his meals through the tube. But his throat muscles needed to be kept working. Even a small amount of swallowing would have helped. What has happened to him?

A nurse shows me how to feed him. How to hook him up to the machine. Each feed mix takes one hour to drip-feed into him, she says, and he'll have to be fed every other hour, to get enough nutrients into him. Or he could have continuous feeding through the night and that would mean fewer day time feeds. She helps me put him and the feeding machine and a wheelchair into the station wagon.

I get to the top of our driveway and haven't the strength to lift him from the car to the wheelchair and up the steps to our house. I leave him in the car while I fetch a neighbour to help me. We get him inside and I run out to the mail box and trip up on a bit of low concrete wall that I've never tripped up on before, and am unable to walk on my twisted ankle. I hop back to the house and ask him if I can borrow his wheelchair to move around in. The situation is becoming farcical.

Katrina comes home from work, sees me in the wheelchair with a swollen ankle, says "My family!" and bursts into tears. The physiotherapist visits Ken and arranges for crutches to be delivered for me. ACC, the Accident Compensation Corporation, advises that I can have twenty hours' home help for two weeks because of my injury. Just when I really needed it, too - I'm impressed with my timing. Ken doesn't qualify for the home help, it wasn't an accident that cost him the use of his legs.

The feeding machine keeps bleeping. Warning sounds that the milky mixture is not feeding through properly. He can't be fed at night because of the continual noise from the alarm and I spend all day hooking and unhooking him to the machine. Katrina can't cope with his inability to walk and his tube in the stomach and says, "Please don't ask me to feed him." I cuddle her and we comfort each other.

The nozzle at the end of the tube sometimes comes off when he is in bed at night and his stomach contents leak out over the sheets. I complain to the community health team and to the company representative supplying the feeding machine, about how easily the nozzle comes off. I am told, confidentially, that Ken has been given an unsuitable tube for feeding into a stomach and the nozzle is just a make-shift one - both are defective for the job required, but Wellington Hospital wanted to use up their old stock of catheters. Ken's anger has also been used up and he has become resigned and patient. For my benefit, I think. Or perhaps it is just that he is too weak to fight any more.

His breathing is irregular, and a masseur, whom he had visited regularly, comes to see him at home. He seems to massage him in just the right places and his breathing improves. The masseur says to call him whenever he can be of help and he'll come straight up. He refuses to take payment. The community health physiotherapist who now visits twice a week says that there isn't much point in her coming if we have someone else giving him massage. I tell her we need all the help we can get.

Nancy, from St Aidans Church on the Hill, tells me they have organised a help roster. Someone different turns up every morning for three hours to do whatever needs doing, and someone different again arrives with a meal each evening. My time revolves around the feeding machine and seeing to his personal needs.

The beeping feeding machine finally gets changed. Hoorah. I discover that the discarded machine was not the model recommended for him by the supplier.

The district health nurses come every day to bath and dress him. One morning I find him dressed in my jeans, blouse and sweatshirt. Dressed in my clothes that were lying on the bed ready for me to get into. We laugh about it together. Except that Ken's facial muscles hardly move and his voice makes a strange sound and I know only by instinct that he is laughing. Different nurses visit in the evenings and help me prepare him for bed. I learn that Social Welfare will pay for a night nurse for eight hours a night, seven nights a year. Seven nights in a year that I can have some sleep without worrying about a feeding machine, and whether he is still breathing. I book a night nurse.

The house is full of people coming and going, people caring.

"I've just been up on my first flight. It was fantastic. We flew over to the Wairarapa and practised straight and level flying."

"That must have been exciting. I'm looking forward to a flight with you. When you've had a bit more practice. But Aaron, I think you may need to come down very soon and see Dad. He is deteriorating very fast. What is your schedule for this week?"

"Is he?" His voice faltered. "I've got exams for the next three days, so I'll come down on Friday. That's four days away. Will that be all right?"

"That'll be great. I'll tell him you're coming. He'll look forward to seeing you and hearing all about your flying."

"Happy Wedding Anniversary for tomorrow."

"Thanks, love."

Why didn't I give the phone to Ken? Why do I forget that he can listen on the phone, can listen directly to Aaron's news, without me relaying everything to him? But we are not used to the idea of someone talking their news into silence on a telephone and I never suspect that he will die before Aaron sees him again. He is hanging on to life so tightly. He is not dying. No, he is not dying. He writes that he doesn't want to leave us.

Tuesday, 14 August 1990

Today is our twenty-fifth wedding anniversary. I want to relax and just be with him but the feeding machine controls our day. Ken is pale and his breathing is laboured. He is becoming agitated. I tell him that an acupuncturist is about to arrive. I'd booked him a few days ago - we'll try anything. The acupuncturist lies Ken down on the lounge sofa. He inserts little needles into him and burns herbs. Moxibustion, he calls it. The room smells like a Tibetan temple. The needles are removed after an hour and Ken sits up. The colour has returned to him, and he is breathing easily. Feeling much better. We make an appointment for the acupuncturist to return on Saturday.

My parents visit us for some of the afternoon. My father helps me lift him from his wheelchair on to the commode and I don't see the tube looping around the arm of the wheelchair until it yanks out of his stomach. He now can't take in food at all, and how long before the hole in his stomach closes up? I phone the doctor who says to try and push it back in, and he'll come up this evening as soon as he can if we still have a problem. I phone my nurse-friend Barbara who tries to get it in, without success. Ken's face is white.

An occupational therapist arrives to enquire whether we need more railings now that he is in a wheelchair - did someone forget to tell her? - and decides the bedroom would be a good place for one. Nancy and Caroline arrive unexpectedly at the front door with flowers, an anniversary cake, a bottle of wine, hand cream for Ken. We sit at the table, Barbara and Caroline and Nancy and Katrina and Ken and I, and celebrate our silver wedding anniversary. I put a piece of cake on his tongue and he savours the taste, then I remove it. Katrina gives him a droplet of wine.

The doctor arrives and pushes the tube back in. He gives us a card for our wedding anniversary with a personal message inside. On the outside is a picture of a tall totara tree. "That's how I think of you," he says to Ken. "You are a strong brave man." We continue with the party. Nothing is normal, everything is made normal. We take photos, and laugh, and pass the cake.

Everyone goes home. He asks me to wheel him into the lounge, to the window, where he sits and gazes over the lights of the city. Imprints on his mind. Imprints on my mind. I kneel beside him and we hold hands, in silence.

Two days later an ambulance arrives at the house. Wellington Hospital have said they will replace their leaking gastrostomy tube. The gold chain around my neck gets caught in the arm of the wheelchair as I help a friend lift it into the ambulance. The chain snaps and breaks. Ken points to the road. A tiny, almost indiscernible part of the chain lies there. He is pleased as I climb out of the ambulance and retrieve it.

The surgeon wants to send an endoscope down his throat into his stomach to see exactly where to reinsert the tube. Make sure it doesn't cause a rupture as he inserts it, which could cause peritonitis, his muscles would all seize up and he'd probably die. They've already seized up, I think. I tell him he can't, Ken can't swallow, he will gag and it will distress him. The doctor puts the instrument away. I hover round the bed and ask him to show me the new tube before he inserts it. It's the same type as the old one. "He's not having that," I say. "I want the correct one, not just old stock. That's been the whole problem." The doctor goes away for twenty minutes and brings back a different one. Inserts it through the hole in Ken's flesh. Tells me I can take him home after he has slept a couple of hours to allow time for some of the anaesthetic to wear off.

Two hours later Ken wakes and I ask the receptionist to call an ambulance for his return trip home. But Ken is still drugged and I realise I won't be able to manage him at home that day, and the seven night-nurse allocations are used up. I ring the hospice from a phone at Wellington Hospital and they say yes, he can go there for the remainder of the day and sleep there overnight. He goes reluctantly, his first time there. I show the hospice staff how to work the feeding machine and tell Ken I'll go home for a rest and come back later.

I return four hours later and Ken is pointing to the feeding machine and waving his arm at me. I ask the staff when he was last fed and they say they are really sorry but someone is dying of cancer in the next room, isn't expected to last the night and they haven't had a spare moment to feed Ken and could I do it? They apologise again.

He must be so hungry. I hook him up to his machine and stay with him until it's time for him to sleep. The nurse brings him some sedative. He waves it away - he doesn't need it tonight. "The hospice doctor has prescribed it," the nurse says. "He's still quite dopey from the anaesthetic," I say. "I don't think he needs it." She phones our own doctor. He says to reduce the medication by half.

"This will help you sleep," she says again as she puts the liquid on his tongue. He takes it reluctantly. I kiss him goodnight and he points to the other bed in the room. I know he is asking me to stay with him for the night, but I tell him that I desperately need a good night's sleep, that I'll be back in the morning, that Aaron will be down from Palmerston North to see him tomorrow and we'll have the day together as a family. He nods grimly, and squeezes my hand. I don't want to leave him but I have to get some sleep.

I arrive home as the phone is ringing. It is the hospice. "Does he usually have shallow breathing after the sedative?" "No," I say.

The phone rings again. It is the hospice. "I think you had better come down." I can't start the car and I flood it and Katrina is out for the evening so I run to Barbara, my nurse- friend neighbour. She drives me to the hospice. We walk up the drive and see that the lights are out in his room. He has died.

Aaron arrives at the hospice from Palmerston North at 2.30am. Katrina and I are still with Ken, waiting for him. He'd sobbed on the phone when my parents rang him but his first question had been, "How's Mum?" and then, "Why did Dad have to die tonight? I wanted to talk to him when I came home tomorrow and tell him that I'd look after Mum and Katrina." We leave Ken at the hospice. Our house seems dark and empty.

"Do you think he died because I left him, or because of the sedative?"

I ask my doctor the next day.

"Probably too much sedative for him," he says. "His heart had become very weak."

We arrange for Ken to come back home in his casket, and we are able to say our goodbyes. I'd never thought of having the casket at home but suddenly I can't just leave him in a morgue. Here, I can still look at him and touch him and talk to him. And Aaron can see him again at home. Say goodbye. Tell him all the things he missed out on saying. I didn't really get to say my goodbyes, either. Not in words. Katrina had told Ken just a few days ago how much she loved him and what a great father he'd been.

He looks so well lying here in our bedroom, the old familiar Ken. Looks just as he did before he lost so much weight. I'm always visiting him here. "Doesn't he look well," I say often to the children.

"Mum, he has died. He's not there any more, it's just his body," Aaron finally says. Gently.

Katrina rings friends and family to tell of our loss and organises the household. She is coping so well and is so supportive. I don't know if she is accepting his death yet.

My brother Lindsay and his new wife Catherine want to send me a return ticket for a holiday in England. I say that I can't come - it is too soon, and too generous. "We need you here," they say. "You can babysit our new baby sometimes." I tell them I'll think about it, perhaps I'll come in a couple of months.

How can I thank family and friends enough for loving support?

I waved goodbye to Katrina and Glenis as they clambered aboard Mount Cook Coachlines with their forty foreign students. Excited students, babbling in a variety of languages. I hoped that it would all work out and that the diverse nationalities would integrate well. It was only ten days since Ken had died but I thought the trip would be a good break for Katrina, away from the sadness for a little while. And she was planning to meet Lorna, her new grandmother, who would come to Rotorua.

A few days later I received a letter from Whakatane.

Dear Robyn,

Just a note to tell you how much I enjoyed my day with Katrina and Glenis. I arrived in Rotorua at 10am as planned and when I got out of the car to meet them it was to find I stood eye to eye with Katrina. It was lovely seeing them both together. I think nature learns a little in creativity coming down the years for I am sure Katrina is a mite prettier than either Glenis or I was at that age.

It was nice to see Katrina relaxed, yet quietly in command of her job with the students - no fuss, just taking it all in her stride.

I am happy that she brought joy to Ken, whom I'm so sorry I did not meet. I am sure Katrina will bring you many happy hours yet and will help you through this sad period.

Having the three of us together for a day has made such a difference to my life. The relationship between Glenis and me is quite magical. Some deep abyss has been bridged and a mighty invisible wall toppled - nothing tangible. I don't want to shout or cry but my mouth feels as though it wants to smile, just a little bit, all the time. A strange feeling for me, and I think Glenis feels it too. And I know we both have you and Ken to thank for this and I am so sorry I could not do this personally to him. Perhaps this coming summer I shall have the pleasure of personally thanking you.

The videos of your English sojourn and trips through Europe I enjoyed immensely - I only wish I could have been with you through it all. I have fun just pretending I was there. And the tape of the children talking and playing their instruments when they were younger was lovely too.

I trust that you and your parents continue to derive much pleasure from your handiwork that is Katrina, and Aaron as a brother. I look forward to some day meeting them too.

Love from Lorna

I appreciated the letter. Yes, I would like to meet her too. She had lost three of her four children in tragic circumstances - it seemed hard to comprehend the magnitude of that loss - but now a granddaughter, who had been farewelled so long ago in sad circumstances before she was even born, had come back again. It must have been a very special happening for her, meeting Katrina.

Ten days later a coachload of new friendships returned to Wellington with smiles on their faces, and tears of farewell running down their cheeks. They'd all had a great time, the students had loved the trip and behaved themselves most of the time, the four supervisors got on well, Glenis survived the experience admirably, and Katrina and Glenis enjoyed getting to know each other.

Katrina had lost her father to whom she was very close and who could never be replaced, but a new relationship was beginning in her life, with someone who would also love and care about her very much.

# Chapter Eighteen

*"RED VOLKSWAGEN 1959. Excellent body, new paint, no rust, runs well. Collector's item. Only thirteen owners.* What do you think?" said Aaron, kneeling on the floor over the Cars for Sale pages of the *Evening Post.* "It's not a bad price, either."

"Thirteen owners?" I looked up from the front page of the paper. Hungry Iraqi troops had eaten nearly three-quarters of the edible species in Kuwait Zoo. Lower Hutt City Council ended its discharge of raw sewage into the harbour at midnight last night.

"I think I'll have a look at it now that I've sold the Viva and while I'm down here for the weekend." He grinned at me. "I could come and visit more often if I had a car again. And the motor bike isn't too good in the wet, getting from lectures at Massey out to the airport. It often won't start."

"That's because it's a mongrel bike. Bits and pieces of spare parts. An impulse buy. It's not cheap if it doesn't go."

"Volkswagen beetles are a classic car."

I sighed. "Just be sure you check it out well."

He took a friend with him to look at the vehicle. The friend also liked the bright, new red paint and jaunty look of the little car and Aaron became the fourteenth owner.

"Do you want to go for a quick spin?" He gazed proudly at his new acquisition sitting outside our house. I lowered myself into the passenger seat. It seemed a long way down, and the windows seemed very small, particularly the back one, but the car had a cosy intimate feel about it. Nothing much in the way of dials on the dashboard, just a speedometer and mileage gauge.

Aaron revved the engine and with a throaty roar we were off down the hill and on to the Western Hutt Road. Within minutes the car began to splutter and jerk, and the engine cut out as Aaron pulled over to the side of the road. I looked questioningly at him. "Damn, it must be out of petrol," he said. I looked for the petrol gauge on the dashboard. There wasn't one.

"It's all right, Mum. This model doesn't have a petrol gauge. There's a reserve system on these cars. Should be a lever under here somewhere."

He felt around under the seat and found what he was searching for. A quick turn of the reserve petrol lever, a turn of the ignition key, and nothing happened. Total silence, not even a faint stirring of the motor. "Won't be a minute," he said, as he took a screw driver from under the seat and scrambled under the car. Within a few seconds the engine spluttered back into life and Aaron reappeared. He brushed down his clothes and grinned.

"What was all that about?" He had bits of grass and gravel sticking to the back of his sweatshirt.

"It's just the solenoid. It's a bit temperamental, apparently. But it's OK. It's not difficult to get it going. I just need to press it with this," and he put the screwdriver back under the seat.

"But do you have to climb under the car each time to do it? How often will this happen?"

"I'm not sure but I can get a new solenoid some time."

We drove to the petrol station. He felt around in his back pocket. "Have you got any money? I left my wallet behind."

I felt in my jeans pocket. One solitary coin.

"This is embarrassing," Aaron said. "Is that all you've got?"

"It'll be more embarrassing if you have to climb under the car to start it again."

"Fifty cents worth, please." Aaron turned to the petrol attendant waiting beside the window and dropped the coin into his hand. We roared out of the petrol station.

I picked a rose out of the garden, one of Ken's roses, and gave it to Aaron as he was leaving to go back to Palmerston North. He drove back with it on the ledge of the Volkswagen dashboard.

I sold the terrarium business. I didn't have the heart or the energy for it without Ken. The next thing to be sorted out was the accounts. I'd written to the Department of Inland Revenue in February 1990, explaining that the business was not generating income due to my husband's terminal illness and that I had been unable to organise the accounts in time for this year's income tax returns. Could I have an extension of time? Three months later a letter from the Department of Inland Revenue had arrived in the letter box. "I have no record of having received Your Return of Income which is now overdue. A Return of Income must be filled in by the due date under the Income Tax Act

1976. If I do not receive an early reply, I may assess your tax without information from you. You will then be liable to pay this Default Assessment. Yours sincerely, D R Henry. Commissioner of Inland Revenue." Hand-signed. How did D R Henry, Commissioner of Inland Revenue, have time to hand-sign all his 'payment overdue' reminders?

I'd written back. Same message except that my husband was worsening and I'd do the accounts as soon as I could and didn't they get my last letter? No reply from Mr Henry.

In August 1990, another "I have no record of having received your Return of Income which is now overdue..." In November 1990 I received a letter from Mr Pollard, District Commissioner of Inland Revenue, the name typed but not hand-signed. The heading in red ink read, "Final Notice. Request for a 1990 Return of Income." In black, "I have no record of having received your return which is now overdue. Under the Income Tax Act 1976 you are required to furnish such a return. As you have failed to furnish this return within the time required you have committed an offence. You may be prosecuted without further notice. In the event of you being prosecuted and convicted you could be liable for a fine of up to $6000."

I wrote back immediately - had they still not received my letters of 17 February, 5 June and 21 September 1990? I told them that the business had not been operating since May 1990, that my husband had died in August, that there was no tax to pay, that I would sort out balance sheets for the accountant as soon as I could.

A week later a letter arrived for Mr K J Shaw. I opened it. This time it was from Ken's insurance company. "Dear Mr Shaw, We have no record of your quarterly life insurance payment due 24 October 1990. You may have inadvertently forgotten to pay it. We will allow you to make payment by 24 November 1990, after which time, if such payments have not been received, penalties may occur. We look forward to an early reply."

I wrote back to them explaining that Ken had died and that they had paid out his life insurance to his estate two months ago. "Please amend the records."

I received no reply. Why did you have to die, Ken? Life doesn't get any easier.

But in many ways life was getting easier - I was spending longer periods without so much sadness. On the occasions when I felt overwhelmed by grief and wondered whether life was worth continuing I would remember my children and the need to be there for them - they were always there for me. Katrina, who had intended to go flatting before Ken died, had postponed her plans for a while and was living at home with me. She came home from work each evening with little stories of the day's happenings. Aaron kept the promise to look after us that he had made to Ken, and he often phoned, or drove down from Palmerston in his shiny red Volkswagen for a weekend.

Sometimes we talked together of life without Ken. Aaron said he'd had trouble sleeping at nights after Ken died but was now coping better. He had found it helpful talking about his loss with an older aviation student at Massey whose father had died the previous year.

Katrina didn't show her grief, wasn't tearful, and I still wondered if she had accepted it. Can we ever accept death? Do we need to cry? Ken was the closest person any of us had loved and lost. I knew that if we bottle up our grief it becomes more difficult to deal with.

And what about the unresolved anger within *me*? I knew I wasn't dealing well with Ken's being given the sedative and dying ten minutes after I left him. I was angry with the hospice doctor for prescribing it when Ken was already sedated - had the doctor even seen him? I was angry at hospice staff for giving it to him, and with myself for not supporting Ken in his rejection of it. I knew I was being unreasonable about the hospice staff. Ken had just been landed on them - they had taken him in at one hour's notice because of my desperate situation, and they probably had more understanding of cancer patients than MND patients. And I knew he had to die soon but I was still distressed that Aaron had missed him by a day and we had been cheated of that family time together. I was aware that I often spoke about it, perhaps spoke about it too often, but I seemed stuck on it. I asked my brother Brent, a trained counsellor, if he would talk about it with us.

"If you don't deal with this anger you won't progress in your grief," Brent said. "It is perhaps time to move on."

"I don't seem to be able to."

"I suggest you write a letter to Ken, tell him of the things you are telling us. Talk about everything that is hurting you."

I nodded.

"And then if you wish to, you could light a match to the letter. As an act of healing, take the ashes to Ken's grave and scatter them there. Think of it symbolically, as a form of release for you."

"Yes, maybe that would help."

We talked more of Ken and dealing with our loss.

"I know I don't express myself through tears and talking the way you do, Mum, and as you think I should be doing, " Katrina said. "I loved him and I miss him but I have seen his mental anguish, his frustrations at having all ability, except the ability to think, taken from him, and I see death as a release for him. I didn't want him to suffer any more."

"Everyone grieves in different ways and just because it isn't expressed outwardly it doesn't mean that it is not being dealt with," Brent said.

The tears did come later for Katrina. At unexpected times such as when introductory music for Country Calendar, a favourite programme of Ken's, played on television after she hadn't heard it for many years. And sometimes she dreamt that he was alive again, and woke to incredible sadness when she found out it was only a dream.

I didn't write my letter. Somehow I didn't need to. The anger had dissipated once I knew that there was a way of dealing with it. And I knew that Katrina would be all right.

One evening I received a phone call from Aaron. "I've just spent most of the afternoon in the Palmerston North police cells. Unlawful arrest, I call it."

"What happened?" I couldn't imagine what he'd done.

"Well, my car registration was overdue a couple of months back and I was charged a fine of two hundred dollars. I was broke at the time. Still am, really. However I held back on some of the flying fees and paid the overdue car registration, and wrote to the traffic department here telling them that I'd had other things on my mind lately. I told them about Dad and was there any chance of letting me off the fine, just for this time. They said it was too late for them to cancel it - the charge had been forwarded to the Justice Department, and suggested I make an appointment with the judge at the court to put my case. Just a private hearing, I thought."

The police cells? Gentle Aaron. He wouldn't have hit the judge.

"Did you see the judge today?"

"Yes. I got a crazy one. The court workers had been on strike all morning and there were hundreds of people milling around. I was due for a 9am hearing but didn't get taken till 1.30pm. I had no idea I'd have to stand up there in the dock like a prisoner and plead my case."

I chuckled inwardly, but not too much as I still wasn't sure what his problem was. "Was anyone else in the court?"

"Yes. It was full of people and there were lawyers hanging around. But here I was, stuck up on this podium and the judge was sitting down across the way and said to me, 'Shaw, how do you propose to pay this fine?' I told him of my situation - poor student, extenuating circumstances - and he said, 'Shaw, you can do two hundred hours' periodic detention,' and I told him that I couldn't do that because the Massey course I'm on runs through weekends as well, and I have no free days. So he said I'd have to pay the fine. I told him I had no money. He said I could pay it off at twenty dollars a week. I knew my student allowance wouldn't cope there so I said I couldn't manage that much. I offered five dollars a week. Very politely, of course. The court started tittering a bit and one of the lawyers was grinning.

"The judge muttered about the five dollars and this is where he went haywire. He told the court policeman to put me in the cells. I was taken downstairs and locked into a tiny pink room of about four square metres. It was already occupied by a couple of heavies. Tattooed, scowling, smelling guys about twice my size."

"That's awful," I said. "They can't just lock up people."

"This judge can."

"How long were you there for?"

"About three hours. The only things in the cell were a blackboard with mis-spelt obscenities on it and some chalk. And these two guys. They were drawing graffiti on the walls and farting and pretty tough. I had to pretend to be one of them. A police van finally arrived for them and they were taken away. I was let out then."

My mother sent Aaron the two hundred dollars when she heard the story, together with a little note that she wouldn't pay the fine again and next time to pay the bill on time, but she didn't want him having to do periodic detention with those sorts of ruffians.

The new registration wasn't used for long. The Volkswagen was hit from behind by one of the students on the aviation course - I hoped the student was a better pilot. The accident spoilt the look of the vehicle and caused internal problems but the offender said he had no money to pay for repairs, and Aaron sold it cheaply to a mechanic. "I think I might get a bigger car next time," he said. In the meantime it was back to the mongrel motorbike.

It was time I made the effort and got the terrarium accounts together. Inland Revenue still hadn't acknowledged my letters and I didn't want to be 'prosecuted without further notice'. I checked payments against bank statements, and bank statements against cheque book butts, and did monthly reconciliations. I added up mileage from the vehicle mileage book and wrote down 'square footage of house' details. A friend suggested a good accountant. The previous one had handed our returns to an outworker who'd made so many mistakes that I'd ended up advising *her*.

I arrived at the accountant's office with the vehicle mileage book and a large black folder containing my A3 size sheets of loose ledger paper. Cash In on one side of the ledger paper, Cash Out on the other. One for each month of the year. He greeted me warmly, and took me into his room. There were books and papers everywhere - on shelves, covering his large desk, and in piles all over the floor. I walked carefully over to the chair opposite his desk, trying to avoid the mathematics on the carpet.

I explained that my accounts were twelve months overdue and the reason why. "When did Ken die?" he asked. "Last August," I said. And then I felt the tears coming. And they wouldn't stop coming. I was normally very controlled with strangers, in fact was quite controlled most of the time but I just sat there with all my papers in front of me and sobbed. The accountant just sat and looked at me - a combination of sympathy and empathy and helplessness. I'd never met him before, I'd been in his room only two minutes and what a fool I was making of myself.

I needed to check out some details with him, and with blurred vision I stumbled through the ledger pages. I couldn't find what I wanted, the months became mixed and there was no space on his desk to spread out my Cash In and Cash Out sheets. The accountant saw my flurries, my mixings and general disorder and offered the floor. Where on the floor, I wondered, as I gratefully knelt down out of sight amongst his workings. He shuffled some free space around and said, "What say I just go out of the room for a bit and give you time to sort everything out." I nodded gratefully and slotted February back in after January and August after July and wiped my eyes again and blew my nose. We started all over again ten minutes later and I thought he was the nicest man.

It would have been Ken's fiftieth birthday on 18 February 1991. I felt especially sad. A window-enveloped letter arrived in the mail addressed to him. If it's the Inland Revenue, thank goodness the accountant is working on my tax details. But it was the insurance company again. "Dear Mr Shaw, Your premiums are now well overdue. Could you please pay immediately. Penalties will incur. If you wish to discuss the matter, or have a problem with payments please contact this office." I wrote back yet again. Ken couldn't discuss the details. He was dead. I felt like repeating and repeating the word for them. Had died last August. Didn't they recall paying out on his life insurance? Today would have been his fiftieth birthday. What happened to the letter I wrote last November? How could they make such errors?

That night I lit a candle for Ken and wrote to him. I poured out my grief. It sometimes felt as if I'd been grieving forever but I suppose it had started three years ago when the neurologist gave him that death sentence. I told Ken of my aloneness. My emptiness. How I missed his love and wisdom now gone, but what great support the children, and family and friends were. I blew out the candle and went to bed feeling much calmer.

The following day I received a phone call from the manager of the insurance company. A very apologetic phone call and could he come around to see me? He arrived with a large bunch of flowers and more apologies and said that they were altering their computer system so that the situation wouldn't happen again.

Two weeks later I applied for a job at the Correspondence School Library and was appointed. My first permanent job as an employee since before the children were born. A forty-seven-year-old widow with limited school library experience, and they wanted me. I was amazed, and excited, and concerned as to whether I'd manage the computers.

I loved the job. Choosing books for high school students who were unable to attend school for a variety of reasons - illness, remoteness, school phobias, school expulsions. Writing a letter with each posting and reading the student's comments on books sent. Liaising with teaching staff for curriculum and recreational reading. Sharing in the choosing of books for purchase. I began to feel alive again and that life was worth living.

# Chapter Nineteen

THE QUEEN'S BIRTHDAY weekend arrived with its public holiday on the Monday. Aaron was busy flying. Katrina was away with Tom, a builder friend whom she'd known for several years. She had been visiting him the night Ken died, and the friendship had since grown. "He reminds me of Dad a lot," she'd said.

Everyone, it seemed, was out of town. It was ten months since Ken had died and I'd been coping reasonably well for a few months now, but suddenly the sadness hit again. Friends rang for a chat and heard my stifled sobs and said, "Come up to us right now." I hopped in the car and we talked and laughed together and I forgot about my emptiness.

But the heaviness and dullness returned as I walked back into the empty house. And then the phone rang. It was 10.30pm. Who is calling at this time of night? Intruding on my space. Intruding on thoughts of the evening just spent with my friends.

It shrilled on. Could I just let it ring? I succumbed to its insistence with a weary, "Hello."

"Hello. It's Roger Cooper here. Sorry about the late call. I've been trying to get you all night."

"Oh, hello. I've been out." Nice man. Terrible timing.

"I'm having trouble getting the family together before August for the movie of our canal trip. Alan's going to be in Nottingham until then."

"And Katrina will be away in July. It doesn't matter. We can leave it until August. It's only two months away."

"How about *we* catch up on the last decade? Do you feel like going out to dinner somewhere?"

It sounded like a date. Why did he have to ring tonight? I didn't want to think about anything else tonight. And I wasn't ready to go out with an unattached male, wasn't ready for a new relationship.

But I was rushing myself. This wasn't a new relationship. This was an old friend whom I didn't know very well, just asking a simple question. Why was I stammering and stuttering and swallowing my words? Frantically trying to work at an answer.

Roger Cooper. I had first met him and his family in 1978 through a mutual friend - a Malaysian Colombo Plan student whom Roger's parents and mine had befriended some twenty-five years earlier - and we had discovered both families were soon departing for Britain, Roger's to Cambridge, and just 'somewhere in England' for us. In Britain our two families had shared a narrowboat, the *Ploop*, on the canals of the Cheshire Ring.

Then just three months ago I'd bumped into Roger again, at a plant and pickles stand at the Martinborough Fair. It was our first meeting in more than ten years - a chance encounter amongst the thousands of visitors, the ceramic pots, the mustards and jams, the 'hand-crafted' clothing and wooden clocks. We'd talked, exchanged news. He'd been disturbed at my news of Ken. I told him that Katrina had seen his son Alan on television the previous year, discussing the Australian origin of the kiwi. I didn't tell him that Katrina had wowed about this good-looking molecular biologist son of his and had suggested I ask the Coopers up for dinner.

We'd talked about our boat trip together all those years ago. I asked if he thought his family would be interested in getting together to see our old movie of the canal trip. He thought it a good idea. He would be in touch. I chuckled all the way home. Katrina will be so impressed with her scheming mother.

"But I like Tom now," she'd said when I told her of plans for the Coopers to visit.

Roger had phoned me a couple of times since our meeting, trying to find dates when we'd all be in town at the same time. I learnt that he was on his own. We'd talked about grief on our second phone call. He told me of his grief at the break-up of his marriage six years previously but how he felt that working through it had made him a stronger person. I told him that I'd rather remain weak and go without the grief.

"You may not want to go out." His voice broke into my agony. My deliberations. I liked the man. That was my agony. But not yet. It was too soon.

I suddenly remembered a work 'do' I had coming up. Formal occasion. Lots of people.

"There's a Sri Lankan evening for the Dalai Lama." It splurted out.

Silence at the other end... then, "A Sri Lankan evening?... for the Dalai Lama?"

"Yes, he's coming next year."

"Next year?"

"Yes."

"A Sri Lankan evening? What happened to Tibet?"

"Oh it's a fund-raising dinner. My friend at the library is a Buddhist. The Sri Lankans are cooking. The money is going towards his visit."

"Are you going, or are you just selling tickets?"

"No, I'm going. It's in three weeks. You're welcome to come if you'd like to."

He sounded confused, but said he'd come.

I got off the phone and threw up.

A week later I was still churning. I couldn't eat and was losing weight. I visited my doctor. I thought he might have a homeopathic cure for my confused state of mind, this emotional tight-rope I was walking.

He listened to my story. "Should I even *think* about going out with someone else so soon after Ken's death?"

"How do your children feel about it?"

"They don't mind. They're rather amused by my twitterings."

"Well," he smiled. "I'm a romantic. I'd go for it."

I must have looked surprised. He leaned back in his chair and clasped his hands behind his head. "But don't wait two more weeks. Phone him up and suggest something a little earlier. Save you churning for another fortnight."

"You think so?"

"Yes. Good luck. Let me know how it goes."

He stood up and shook my hand. I bounced out of the surgery.

But what if he says, "No," when I ask him?

"What do you think about me ringing Roger earlier?" I asked Katrina. She had become the mother. I was the teenage daughter with all the insecurities. "The doctor said I need to ring him and go out earlier. Not wait another two weeks."

She looked up from her book and saw me pacing the room. "Then you'd better do what the doctor says."

I looked up Roger's number in the local phone book. Dialled, and let it ring. And hung up again before he could answer. I'll do it tomorrow, I thought. More time to practise what I'm going to say.

I hung on to the phone the next night. Had the words all ready. Shot them at him when he answered the phone. "Wondered if you'd like to go out sooner. The Sri Lankan evening isn't for another two weeks." There. Done it.

"No, it's OK," he said. "I don't mind the wait."

I must have sounded deranged. Now I've really blown it. Damn the doctor.

Roger arrived fifteen minutes early for the Sri Lankan evening for the Dalai Lama. I wasn't ready but felt at ease from the moment he walked through the door. All my doubts seemed to drop away. I would enjoy myself.

Katrina entertained him in the lounge while I slipped on a long skirt and some lipstick. "He's easy to talk to," she whispered to me in the bedroom just before we left.

We got lost trying to find Wadestown. Goodness knows why, we'd both lived in the Wellington area most of our lives. But Roger kept taking wrong turnings and I kept misdirecting. We must have been too busy talking, and enjoying the newness of a night out.

The Sri Lankans provided wonderful curries and we were among the last to leave. I asked Roger in for a coffee as he pulled up outside my house. He declined, said he'd better get home, and drove off. What happens now, I wondered?

I wanted him to know how much I'd enjoyed the evening. Could I write and tell him that? I certainly wasn't going to ring him. I wrote out a full page of thoughts and meanderings. No, too much there. He doesn't need all that.

Aaron phoned to see what I was up to. I told him of my night out.

"Do you like him?"

"Yes, he's very nice."

"What did you talk about?"

"Oh, Crown Research Institutes and his job as a paleontologist and Zen Buddhism and his marriage break-up and Dad dying and DNA."

"Sounds interesting. Are you going out again?"

"I don't know. I'd quite like to. What do you think?"

"Sounds all right by me."

I got the foolscap page down to two short paragraphs. I'd spent four nights on it and time was running out. I knew that he was leaving in two days for a two-week conference in Australia.

"What do you think this sounds like?" I read it out to Katrina.

"It's good."

"He wouldn't object to this?"

"No, Mum. It's fine." She sighed.

I walked to the post box across the road and my fingers hovered in front of the slot. I opened them slowly and let the letter drop, then immediately wished I hadn't.

The next morning I asked Katrina to shoot up to Belmont. "I don't think I should have written to him. Can you just take it out of his letter box for me, before he gets to read it?"

"Mum. Just relax. I'm not going up there. The letter is OK."

Katrina was now spending all her free time with Tom. It seemed strange, just the two of us in the house, and the way our lives were moving. A mother and daughter and these new entanglements.

Roger rang the day after he got my letter. I wasn't home and Katrina took the call. She told me he was just leaving for Australia. A week later I got a Gary Larson card from Sydney - an elephant with a squashed human on its backside. Was that funny? He said he'd appreciated my letter and maybe I'd risk going out with him again sometime and meanwhile it would be good to get our two families together in August. The card didn't tell me too much, but he must have felt reasonably relaxed to send me a picture of an elephant that hadn't watched where it sat. I still felt as if I was walking an emotional tight rope. I hoped I'd jump off before too long.

Downstage Theatre were performing *The Taming of the Shrew*. I really wanted to see it and bought two tickets for the last night of the performance, scheduled for two days after Roger was due back in New Zealand. I'd never bought tickets for an unattached male before. If Roger didn't want to go I'd find a female companion. I phoned him the day after he arrived home. "Thanks for your postcard," I rushed. "I've got a couple of tickets for the *Taming of the Screw* if you're free and would like to go." The title didn't seem right as it fell out. He laughed while I blushed, and said he'd look at his calendar.

We enjoyed being out together again, and decided to buy tickets for a performance of Piaf in two weeks' time. In the meantime, the families were to converge at Roger's house on the top of the Belmont hills for the great movie show, our seven-day narrowboat trip together on the canals of England in 1980. Aaron came down from Palmerston North and drove up the winding Park Road with Katrina and me. How would the evening go? Roger's family didn't yet know we'd been out together. My children were probably sick of hearing about it.

It was good to see his family again - Alan, now twenty-six and Julie, a secretarial student, aged twenty-four. His former wife came down from Waikanae for the occasion. Roger cooked up a curry and we laughed as we watched the 8mm sound movie with commentary just like a real travel film. Children raced to unwind the canal locks, we steered the boat through tunnels and across aqueducts and some of us collided with road bridges.

Roger gave his family no indication of a developing relationship between us and didn't talk of our two nights out. I wondered what I really meant to him.

I had my answer at Piaf. We talked over dinner for two hours before the performance, the longest talk we'd had. The apple and rhubarb crumble we ordered never got started on - there didn't seem to be time to eat. We talked about our lives and about personal relationships. He'd not met anyone he wanted to be involved with emotionally in the six years since his marriage ended. Julie, his daughter, had been living with him for most of that time. She'd recently gone flatting but often returned to stay with him. Hers must have been the female voice I'd heard laughing in the background during one of our early phone calls. I'd wondered who it was. Alan was quite independent, had been so for several years.

We held hands through the Downstage performance and I felt as if I were sixteen again. When we pulled up at my house Roger said, "We seem to get on pretty well. Do you think we might have a future together?"

"Yes," I glowed.

We were surprised at ourselves. Only three times out together and talking like this.

"I don't think I'm known as being impulsive," he said. And how could I know I wanted to be with him for always? I still didn't know him very well - we hadn't even kissed! But what I saw I really liked and I had no doubts about our future together. Two months ago I was never going to remarry and now I had unexpectedly fallen head over heels in love.

We soon realised we'd not had a daytime date. "Maybe you'd better wait till then before you tell your family about us," I joked. So we arranged to meet for lunch one noon. I waited for him in his office at the Institute of Geological and Nuclear Sciences in Lower Hutt. Book titles such as *Carbonate Depositional Environments, Ontogeny and Phylogeny, International Code of Zoological Nomenclature* lined the floor to ceiling shelves and I wondered about life with a scientist. I'd dropped science as a subject in the fifth form and knew nothing of extinct fossils, of Ordovician graptolites and Cambrian trilobites - his research fields - until last month, when I'd searched the Correspondence School library for information, and had memorised the relevant pages. And what would he think of all my little brown bottles of homeopathic remedies and my trend towards organic foods and tofu? Not to mention meditation and creative visualisation. And can an agnostic scientist live happily with someone who believes in the importance of a spiritual dimension to their life? I flicked through a copy of the Sceptics Society magazine sitting on his desk. They didn't seem too happy with UFOs or bending spoons, and homeopathy and acupuncture got them really mad.

At 12.30pm he still hadn't appeared. I wandered into the hallway and gazed at the Geological Time Table wall chart on the wall. Paleozoic, Mesozoic, Cenozoic. Cambrian = 515 to 575 million years ago, Ordovician = 425 to 515 million years ago. I read on up the scale, filling the gaps in my science education, repeating the foreign names and the millions of years hopefully to memory so that I could subsequently impress him. At 12.45pm a colleague appeared. I explained I was waiting for Roger. "I've been here since midday. Do you know if he's in the building?"

"I haven't seen him, but he has been known to be a little forgetful." He paused, unsure whether to tell me. "He did call a staff meeting once and forget to turn up." I must have looked dismayed. "Oh, but I'm sure he wouldn't forget *you*."

I went to work at 1pm. At 2.30pm a very apologetic Roger

telephoned. He'd forgotten. I couldn't believe it. I'd thought of nothing else for three days, and all this scientific knowledge I was storing away, and he'd forgotten. "Could we make another time?" he asked. "I promise I won't forget again. I'll set the alarm on my watch."

He had to set an alarm to remember me! Yes, life with a scientist might be challenging. I wondered about life with an absent-minded one.

I discovered later, when parading my new-found knowledge of geological time scales, that the wall charts were out of date.

I asked my children how they would feel about me marrying Roger. They said they were pleased to see me so happy. Roger told his family of our relationship and our desire to be married, all in one go. He told them he hadn't wanted to talk about it any earlier in case it didn't work out. They were totally surprised, had no idea, but were happy for us both. We told my parents. "I'd been praying for you to find happiness again," my mother said, "but I didn't expect my prayers to be answered so soon." My friends and family must have wondered if I really knew what I was doing. We'd been out only three times and still not in the day time, but if they had any misgivings they said nothing, only wished us continuing happiness.

Aaron and Katrina sent us a card and wrote, "Best wishes for the future. You deserve each other." Julie made us a card with pink and purple paper hearts on and "Congratulations. Wishing you all the best." Alan said he was delighted to see his father having a new life.

We wondered when to marry. It was now August and Aaron would probably graduate in December but we didn't know the date. January, everyone was away. It would have to be November or February. "I didn't think my mother would be leaving home before me," Katrina said, "but make it November. I couldn't stand you mooning around the house any longer."

One fine November morning we negotiated a steepish bush track and stood on a tiny unrailed bridge under a nikau palm in secluded native bush reserve off Park Road in Belmont. All four of our parents were there, sitting on camp chairs in the little lacy- green amphitheatre, with its peeks of blue sky through overhead palm fronds. Female friends and relations dug their heels into the ferny bank so they didn't slide. My mother watched my feet, waiting for a fateful backward step into the creek below. Julie and a friend played violin and flute duos. The birds twittered as the minister, in long cream robes, talked about new beginnings and we exchanged our wedding vows. Our children joined us beside the bridge for final blessings.

We held an afternoon wedding reception in a marquee on the lawn of Roger's hilltop home. We'd earlier transported an old red telephone booth from a friend's garden to a car parking area at the bottom of Roger's drive, glued a red heart-shaped notice 'R & R TAXIS Phone Booth' on the door and hooked up an intercom service between the phone booth and Roger's house. Aaron stuck an authentic 'taxi' sign on his ancient white Ford Falcon 500 station wagon, donned a chauffeur's cap, and ferried guests from the phone booth, up the long winding narrow drive to the house and marquee. The fluffy blue poodle off Katrina's bed sat proudly on the Falcon's front bonnet, blue cardboard hearts on the car windows and Blue Poodle Taxi Company lettering on the front windscreen. Part of the neighbour's fence got knocked down while Aaron was trying to negotiate a difficult bend. "Wouldn't you think the taxi company could have sent a more suitable vehicle," murmured a guest. Our daughters provided a musical item, Roger's son Alan gave a humorous 'parental' speech, Katrina's Tom dispensed the drinks.

At 7pm, as more guests were arriving for an evening barbecue, Roger pulled a calf muscle and couldn't move. We drove off to hospital where the nurses told the groom he'd need to be in plaster up to his thighs, then relented and sent him home on crutches - just as the last guests were leaving. And so we began married life.

Katrina and Tom bought a flat in Belmont - not married, how times have changed, I thought - and Roger and I sold our two houses on the western hills for one on the eastern hills of Days Bay, close to where Roger had spent his youth. Our new home nestled high into the hills overlooking Wellington harbour, with access by winding path through native ferns and beech trees or in our own cable car with seating for two. We talked endlessly for the first year, filling in the gaps. Getting to know each other. Learning about our earlier lives. Talking about relationships and feelings. Me hearing about evolution and him learning how to pronounce homeopathy. We discovered that we'd bought identical stoneware pots from the same stall at the Martinborough

Fair, the only purchase for each of us on that day, and had attended the same cocktail party at the New Zealand Embassy in Singapore in March 1963.

There were still no doubts about our commitment, only a sense of wonder and amazement that we had found each other. We were probably total bores to everyone else and our children had to put up with the embarrassment of their mooning parents.

"You were so busy getting to know Roger that first year that we were almost forgotten. And we couldn't have a conversation with you without Roger's name popping up at least three or four times," Katrina said.

"It's not good, being so besotted," Aaron said.

How could I do that to my children who were always there for me when *I* needed *them*?

And it wasn't until after our marriage that we realised the extent of Roger's and Julie's emotional dependency on each other which evolved after Julie's mother left them, and Roger's over-protectiveness of his daughter. Life wasn't meant to be too easy and it took us several years to work it through.

We heard the Dalai Lama speak at the Michael Fowler Centre. After all, he had some responsibility for this whole affair.

# Chapter Twenty

AARON turned twenty. He hadn't put a veto on his birth registration and we wondered if Social Welfare would write or phone to say that his birth mother wanted to meet him. He felt happier now about contact than he had in his teenage years. He'd seen how the relationship between Glenis and Katrina was developing, how they had become good friends, how Glenis was low-key and non-demanding. But he was very involved with his aviation studies and social life, and said he didn't yet feel the need to search for his mother.

I wondered about his parents. About his mother. Where was she? What was she doing? Was she married and did her husband know of Aaron's existence? Did Aaron have half-brothers and sisters? Would she want him to contact her? Had she placed a veto on his birth registration?

Aaron completed his course at Massey and graduated with a Diploma in Aviation, a Commercial Pilot's Licence and one hundred and fifty flying hours. Not enough to get a job as a pilot - it was perseverance that was the extra factor required there.

It was good having him back in Wellington. He worked in a variety of temporary clerical jobs, any spare cash going into extending his flying hours. Then he got a job with Ansett NZ as part of the ramp staff, working out loading levels, running backstage operations, loading luggage into the hold of the aircraft and dreaming of the day when he'd be responsible for the other end of the plane. He was appointed Ramp Staff Union Representative. Our only intellectual, they'd said, when they knew he had attended university. He moved into a rickety flat in Ghuznee Street with four friends and 'borrowed' my video and small television. "Have you got a spare washing machine?" he asked. "I should make further contributions to the flat."

Later, wanting to be closer to the airport, he moved to shared accommodation at The Crescent in Roseneath. They had million-dollar views of Oriental Bay and Wellington harbour, and a maid to clean the house, two hours a week.

At twenty-two years of age Aaron still hadn't been contacted by Social

Welfare. If he wanted to find his birth parents he would probably have to be the one to do the search. Six months previously he'd picked up an application form to obtain a copy of his original birth certificate but hadn't completed the form as yet. Life was still rather busy... maybe he'd do something about it later.

One evening Katrina and I were watching television together, and a high-jumper appeared on the screen. A high-jumper with the same name as written on the data-entry card, the card that had been furtively handed to me all those years ago by my friend in Births, Deaths and Marriages. We turned the volume up and stared at her. Yes, she had the same shaped face and slim build and colouring as Aaron, looked very similar to him, and was about the right age. She must be his mother! She was interviewed for five minutes about her prowess on the sports fields and in recent competitions. Aaron, who is good at sport but would rather ride than walk, obviously hadn't inherited all her genes, but Katrina and I agreed that as he looked so much like her she must be his mother. Wow! He would know where to begin if he ever wanted to search.

Aaron was still working for Ansett and honed his aeronautical skills by hiring small planes and flying friends around the country for cheap weekends away. He replaced his Ford Falcon with a 1967 Holden HR, a huge tank of a car with leopard-skin seat covers and wings out the back. The closest he'd get to owning an aeroplane, I supposed.

"By the way, I've been offered a job in Botswana when I've got five hundred hours." He grinned at me. "Only two hundred to go."

Katrina was now also employed by Ansett NZ and enjoyed the contact with Aaron. While he loaded the planes she flew in them, tending to politicians and businessmen and harassed mothers, checking that their seats were upright for landing and their tray tables stowed away. She brought us snippets of life in the air - the politician in business class who propped her legs high against the plane walls for the entire trip, the overseas visitor who hoiked into his serviette and gave it to her to dispose of. One day she was asked to escort a dying man down to Nelson. It was to be his last trip to see his family. She supported him and delivered him safely to his family but was in tears afterwards - the man's condition had reminded her so much of Ken's last days. Ansett sent her a letter of appreciation for the way she had looked after their passenger.

"Funny things happen, too," she said. "I've just been given some 'lipstick for lovers'. It's brown, chocolate-flavoured stuff. This woman phoned the airport yesterday, sounding really weak and feeble. She'd got off the plane feeling so ill that she'd forgotten to collect her bags, and as she lived at the Hutt I said I'd try and track them down and drop them off on my way home. When I arrived at her house a guy came out with this lipstick still in its box." She laughed. "She must have wanted to give me something and it was the only thing she could find."

Katrina and Tom decided to marry and Katrina asked Aaron if he would escort her down the church aisle. He bought a dark-green pure-wool suit at Vance Vivian's sale for the occasion. "I got it for two hundred dollars," he said to me. "Down from seven hundred. Good, eh. It's a nice suit. Only problem is it's about four sizes too big."

"It's not cheap if it doesn't fit," I said. We seemed to have had conversations like this before.

"I've found a really good tailor. He's going to fix it for me."

A few months later, on a sunny afternoon in May, Katrina alighted from the hired deep-blue Rolls Royce with its white satin ribbons and attendant chauffeur. She looked the proverbial beautiful bride in cream silk gown with lace overlays, attended by three bridesmaids clothed in forest green silks to match the bridegroom's jacket. I looked at my two children as they walked down the aisle together, Katrina's arm through Aaron's, and thought how lucky I was.

Glenis and her family had flown up from Christchurch to share in the celebrations. Glenis's mother, Lorna, her father, George, and his girl-friend, Joy. Glenis, so proud of her daughter, sat at the table with us. Roger, coping well with his ever-extending family, gave the parental speech and talked of all that Katrina and Aaron had been through with the loss of their father and the change in their mother's life. He told stories of Katrina's growing up years, from information I had given him. We toasted Tom's and Katrina's very apparent happiness.

Katrina was able to visit Glenis in Christchurch more easily now that she was flying. They had kept in contact by mail and phone, but it wasn't the same as being able to visit. A special bond was developing between them, but there were no divided loyalties for Katrina. She was loyal to each of us and loved us in different ways. She asked Glenis endless questions about her background and family and laughed about the differences between Glenis and me.

"It's really funny," she said to me one day. "You and Glenis are opposites. She loves pets and hates to travel and you love to travel and don't like pets. But it's quite nice to have people with opposing interests. And I used to hate biggish dogs but since I've been going down there I quite like them." She laughed. "Glenis got another dog to replace the one that she had put down last year, and I chose the new one. It was like 'Adopt a Dog'. It's a young collie-cross and very bouncy. Glenis doesn't really like it because it's so naughty. Hopefully it will come right. She blames this dog on me but deep down I think she likes it."

I smiled. Fancy Katrina choosing dogs for other people!

I also felt a special bond with Glenis. We shared a love of Katrina and were each interested in her well-being as only a 'parent' can be. But I didn't feel threatened by Glenis's entry into our lives. She was non-intrusive and happy to let the relationship develop at its own pace. Katrina still needed me in the same ways that she had before, and she also needed me to be supportive of her relationship with Glenis. But how could I not be happy that there was someone else in her life who would love her without qualification, without demands, and who would always be there to support her if she needed it? But in a different role from me. I was still her mother. Nothing had changed that. In fact our relationship had deepened. Yes, I was happy.

Katrina often visited us on her days off. "How do you introduce Glenis to friends and work colleagues?" I asked after she had returned from a weekend in Christchurch.

"It's complicated," she said. "Sometimes I just say this is my friend Glenis, but if I know them reasonably well I might say this is my birth mother. It depends if I feel like going into details because they'll want to know the whole story - how I met her- that sort of thing. And sometimes when referring to her I say, 'my mother who lives in Christchurch' and they say, 'but your mother lives in Days Bay'."

"There's no word in the English language for this kind of relationship is there."

"No, except for birth mother and that's too long. And it doesn't have very good connotations." She thought for a bit then smiled. "But for Glenis, I am her daughter. There are no two ways about it. Plus, I'm the only daughter she has. The only child she has. She doesn't think of me as not being her daughter, although she knows full well that I don't think of her as a mother. She understands completely. She's really proud of me." She smiled and lowered her voice. "It's quite nice."

At the Citizen's Advice Bureau in Lower Hutt I noticed a pamphlet compiled by the Department of Social Welfare in 1987, and entitled *Adopting a Child - Some Questions and Answers.* The last page was headed, *The Adult Information Act 1985*:

"This allows adopted people over 20 years of age to receive a copy of their original birth certificate, which will normally show the details of one or both of their birth parents provided that they have not placed a veto on the release of this information.

"It also allows the birth parent(s) of an adopted person over 20 years of age to approach the Department of Social Welfare and ask for a social worker to try and locate their adopted child and see if he/she wishes to have contact with them."

Yes, where was the social worker for Katrina? Glenis must have slipped through the system.

May 1994

Katrina now wishes to find her father. "Just curiosity," she says. "I don't look totally like Glenis. I just want to know what he looks like." I go with her to the Registry of Births, Deaths and Marriages in Lower Hutt and we check the New Zealand electoral rolls. It's not a common name. He's not on the rolls. Glenis doesn't know any of his family but remembers the name of his friend who ran a trucking company. But the company's not in the yellow pages and the friend's not on the electoral rolls, either. Katrina writes to her birth father's employers at the time of her birth. They advise that he left their employment to go to Perth, Australia, in 1972. Three years after she was born. We phone international directory enquiries for a Perth listing. No one of that name there. We try Sydney, Melbourne and Brisbane. Not there. I check the Australian electoral records when we visit Roger's parents in Queensland. Not there. He could be anywhere. He may not be alive.

Back at Births, Deaths and Marriages we check the deaths registered in New Zealand since 1972. He hasn't died in New Zealand. He hasn't married here, either. Katrina applies for his original birth certificate and finds out the names of his parents. They are not on any electoral rolls in New Zealand. And there's no record of them dying here. We ask for suggestions from an official at Births, Deaths and Marriages, but they are unable to discover any further identifying information. We have reached a dead end in the search for Katrina's father.

He'll never search for her. He doesn't know of her existence.

# Chapter Twenty-One

THURSDAY, 30 June 1994

"Widespread reports of storm damage continue with roofing iron lifted, trees uprooted throughout Wellington and surrounding suburbs, and yachts breaking free of their moorings. The Met office warns that heavy rain is likely to continue for another twenty-four hours." I turned off the radio and gazed out the window. The blackness was punctuated by forked flashes which lit up the beech trees, the dark harbour waters and Somes Island. Beyond the harbour, stretching across the night, the lights of the motorway blurred and twinkled in the torrential rain.

"It's a wild night," I said to Roger, snuggled beside me on the couch. "Aaron's on late shift at the airport. I hope he gets home from work all right." An angry squall of rain lashed at the windows, and the cabbage trees swayed back and forth like windscreen wipers. The phone rang. A young guy for Aaron. He didn't give his name. I told him Aaron was working, gave him the phone number for his flat in Roseneath. The wind screamed at the beech trees, snapping off large branches as if they were delicate twigs. "I hope he didn't take the motor bike," I said.

Friday, 1 July 1994

I awake to a hushed stillness. The broken branches on the paths are the only reminder of the evening storm. I wander through the trees, looking for suitable material for my next floral art lesson. I need something for a 'modern European design' where the leaves are layered, and flowers or plant material stream down the front of the arrangement. I'm to create a passive and an active area. It sounds like English grammar lessons. The phone rings as I walk back into the lounge.

"Hi. It's Aaron."

"Hello love. I was just going to call you. How did you get on with the weather last night?"

"It was pretty wild, wasn't it. Work was shocking. Planes and passengers delayed all over the place. We loaded and off-loaded the same luggage several times. The planes couldn't get off the tarmac." He pauses. "You'll never guess who has just rung me."

"Air Botswana?"

"No." He doesn't laugh. "Mary."

"Mary?" I don't think I know anyone called Mary.

"I was asleep when the phone rang at ten thirty this morning and just ignored it. Went back to sleep. I was pretty tired from last night. It rang again about ten minutes later and in the end I picked it up."

Why is he giving me a detailed description of the phone ringing? And who is Mary?

"I'm afraid I wasn't my usual sparkling self. You know what I'm like when I'm only half awake."

"Slurred and grumpy, huh?"

He laughs. "After she said her name was Mary she said she wanted to ask me a few personal questions. I wasn't in the mood for market research and got a little bolshy with her."

"You don't have to answer these researchers. You can just say you're not interested."

"Well, I decided to do my own market research. Ask the questions instead. Every week or so we get these researchers phoning the flat." He pauses. "I told her that Mary was a nice name and asked her if she was married and where she worked. Then I asked what her husband's name was. And his surname. It was something unpronounceable. I wondered how she could remember it." His voice is quiet. Subdued.

I am mystified. Why isn't Aaron laughing? I can't understand why he is talking like this. Telling me something that he would normally have found amusing, and being so solemn about it.

"I discovered her husband was an accountant. I was going to ask which salary group Mary fell into and whether she was aged 15- 36, 37-58, or 59-103 but she sounded so nervous and asked if I could just tell her if I was born in Upper Hutt on the 16 April in 1972, so I said I was and let her off. I thought I'd overdone it a bit anyway."

"You probably had. But who is Mary?" I am still totally mystified by his phone call.

"You'll never guess. It was totally embarrassing." He pauses again. "She's my birth mother."

"Your birth mother!" I feel hot and cold. His birth mother. My mind locks on the words. Poor Mary, it would have taken so much courage to pick up the phone and make the call and she must have wondered what on earth she'd struck at the other end. But why didn't Social Welfare contact Aaron first? A phone call from his birth mother was not what we were expecting. "Oh, Aaron, how do you feel?"

"I felt really stink at first. The way I'd been having her on. But she sounded very nice. We talked for a bit. I've got two half-brothers aged twelve and seventeen. She lives only fifteen minutes from my flat. She asked if she could meet me. We're going to work out something for this weekend."

"Oh Aaron. It's quite exciting, isn't it! Mary must have been relieved that there was no veto on your name. And she lives so close. And you've got two half-brothers. I'd love to meet her. D'you think she'd mind if I come too?"

"I'm phoning her tomorrow. I'll ring you back."

Mary. She has contacted Aaron. She wants to know about him. I feel a bit stunned but Aaron seems to be coping well with it. He sounds really pleased, apart from the false start. If she had given him her maiden name as well he would have known immediately who she was, known she was his birth mother. But how does Mary know the telephone number of his flat? I vaguely wonder about the phone call from the young male last night. He didn't give his name. But if he was related to Mary why would he have rung, and not Mary?

I phone Roger with the news. Aaron is going to phone the rest of the family. Then I fiddle with the flowers that are lying on the bench, waiting to be arranged. The block of oasis has soaked in water for long enough and I cut and shape it, and push it into the top of my imitation Grecian urn vase. Where is a small flower to poke in it? "Smallest flowers, lightest colours at the top," the tutor had said.

But I can't stop thinking about Mary. It seems unreal that she is about to become an actual person. No longer a fantasy figure, to be talked about with wonderings and imaginings, and a strange mixture of detachment and closeness. The scrap of paper listing her physical features and interests is still in an envelope in the writing desk. I take the envelope out of the drawer and remove the paper from inside it. A half-sheet of foolscap paper torn in two some time before the parental details were recorded on it. The first piece of paper I found after the phone call from Child Welfare all those years ago. The paper is yellowing at the edges.

I read my notes, hastily scribbled down in red pen. Scribbled down before I forgot the facts, jumbled up the features. Mother aged 21, unmarried, brown hair, blue eyes - no, not blue eyes. Blue eyes is crossed out and green-grey eyes written above it. Height 5'6", slim build, four years secondary school, sports (ballet, tennis), works in office, South Islander, very nice girl. Listed below are the details of Aaron's father. Aged 24, dark blonde hair, blue-grey eyes, height 5'8", four years secondary school, UE, likes sport, supported mother with finance, New Zealand Police Force, now in USA. We weren't sure if that was for a holiday or forever. Mrs Nolan the adoption officer hadn't known. So many questions can now be answered.

I turn the paper over and read what's left of a typed message from the Maungaraki Ratepayers' Association. Tree Planting on Street Berms: Residents are advised that on application to the Director of Parks and Recreation, residents' names will be noted and, at the appropriate time, trees will be planted on the berm outside their properties. A note about joining cubs or scouts, or becoming a cub or scout leader. A reminder about subscriptions being due. Fifty cents per household. They would be collected at the AGM.

I had wanted to thank Mary so long ago for her son - how could you ever 'thank' anyone enough for their child - and let her know that he was loved and happy. I had wanted to thank her for the baby clothes she left with him at the hospital. The smocked nightgown, the napkins, the shawl, the jacket and helmet she'd crocheted. They were so tiny they didn't fit him even at ten days of age. I had kept them, though, in sheets of tissue paper which were now also yellowing at the edges. But thanking wasn't permitted then. I had felt cheated of the right to communicate with my new baby's mother. Now I can thank her myself.

I move an apricot carnation down a little in the arrangement. It is amazing what a few floral art classes can do for a bunch of flowers. But what about the phone call? What is Mary thinking about the conversation with this newly-found son of hers? She must have some misgivings. He's normally very pleasant on the phone although he does like to kid his friends along sometimes. He's good on Chinese accents - just as well Mary didn't get one of those. It was only last week that he'd rung a friend who worked at Westpac Bank, claiming he was the Chinese landlord. He'd complained about the noise coming from the bank, up through the air-conditioning ducts to his seventeenth-floor penthouse suite, and his friend had apologised and said he would speak to someone about it. And what about the phone call he made to another friend at Foreign Affairs, claiming he was from the Indonesian Embassy? He had discussed the Timor situation with her, and she'd sounded startled at some of his political suggestions and wanted to pass him on to her supervisor. But this is different. This is his birth mother.

But I'm so pleased she has contacted him. Glenis found Katrina and now Aaron will know that he isn't forgotten either. I hope Mary will want to see me, too. As with Glenis, I need to feel a part of the reunion.

# Chapter Twenty-Two

SUNDAY, 3 July 1994

Oriental Bay curves around the bottom of the Roseneath hills. Victorian villas line up against the hillside. Across the road an intimate sandy beach and palm trees. Angle parks entice Sunday drivers to stop and look at the view and watch the fountain playing off shore, the yachts leaning against the winds.

I drove past the palm trees and the parked cars and the old band rotunda and turned right into Grafton Road, following the twisting narrow roads upwards as far as The Crescent. Everywhere houses jostled for views of harbour, yachts, inner-city buildings and the Picton ferry. Everywhere concrete steps leading up or down from street-side letterboxes. Concrete steps tripping into native bush. Invisible houses. Visible houses in pinks and creams with corrugated iron roofs. Stucco houses painted white with leadlight windows, red brick houses with brown tiled roofs.

Aaron's shared flat was an old two-storeyed wooden house, painted sky blue. It overlooked Oriental Parade and its sandy frontage and beyond that the harbour and port activities. He was waiting for me. We would meet Mary at the Opera Restaurant just beyond the Parade. Her husband and sons would be with her. Katrina was coming too. We decided that Roger and Tom should remain at home. Five people may be too much of an onslaught for Mary.

Aaron was feeling nervous - it was only two days since Mary's initial phone call. He was still adjusting to the idea of meeting his birth mother. And what would his half-brothers be like? Would he look like them? What would they think of the idea of an older brother?

We waited at the top of the restaurant stairs. Aaron's new family arrived. Mary knew Aaron as soon as she saw him. "He looks so much like his father," she said. I had been carrying the wrong image of Mary. She wasn't the high-jumper on TV. I wondered for a few seconds if we had the wrong mother.

Introductions were a formality. We hugged and were led to a table for seven, conscious of the intensity of the occasion. We felt an immediate rapport. But where should we start in this search for information? This quest for identity. The beginnings of a new relationship, we hoped, for Aaron and Mary. There were twenty-two years to catch up on. How could so many years of living be translated into a lunch-time of conversation? We looked at the menu. There wasn't time to decide about food yet. We wanted to talk. To look at one another. To absorb. Aaron looked so much like the seventeen-year-old called Robert.

Aaron asked Mary how she'd found him. She wasn't sure what triggered off the search, she said, but she knew she wanted to find him. Her husband was supportive. They had talked firstly with a counsellor to see which was the best way to go. The counsellor said they couldn't just knock on doors, they needed to go through the proper channels. Through Social Welfare who were experienced in handling these matters.

Mary smiled at Aaron, "I started looking for you just over four months ago. In February. I got a letter from Social Welfare on the 16 April, your birthday, telling me that there was no veto and that your name was Aaron. Until that time I hadn't known if you were still alive. I'd never known whether you were well and happy." Mary's eyes were moist. I felt the tears in my own eyes. "After that they were hopeless. They said you were living in Auckland."

"Auckland?" said Aaron. "I've never lived there."

"They told Glenis - that's my birth mother - I was living overseas." Katrina shrugged her shoulders.

"They said they'd sent a letter to someone of your name asking them to come to their Auckland office for a confidential interview."

"Really?" We were amazed. Aaron and Katrina looked at each other. They could imagine the situation. Letters arriving with Social Welfare Adoption Service headings. Confidential interview. Some guy out there suddenly thinking he's adopted and nobody told him.

"Nothing happened and I wondered if the letters had been received - there was a letter from me too. Social Welfare had asked me to write a letter for inclusion with theirs to this Aaron in Auckland. Actually, I asked them to give me some idea of his occupation. 'Am I writing to a philosophy student or a truck driver?' They said that shouldn't make any difference. 'He's your son. Just write to him.' And I said, 'He's not my son. He's someone else's son.'

"Anyway, I heard nothing back and Social Welfare did nothing more about it. Finally we did our own research and discovered your surname and checked the Auckland electoral rolls and telephone directory service. We rang the Aaron in Auckland with the same surname as you but his birth date and middle name were different. He hadn't even received the letters from Social Welfare."

Not even the same birth date? Why do they get it so wrong?

"I phoned them the next day and told them and asked why they didn't check the name via Directory Service weeks before. They said, 'We are very sorry about this but we're very busy.'

"I decided Social Welfare were too hopeless to deal with." Mary looked at Aaron. "They never did locate you." Her voice was husky. "We found out your address by other means, within two hours, and using public facilities."

We listened quietly to Mary's story. The waitress arrived with pad and pencil to take the order. We apologised. "We haven't had time to look at the menu yet," we said. She smiled and said she'd come back.

I asked if it was Robert who'd phoned on Thursday night. It was. Social Welfare had sent Mary a list of advice for birth parent reunions. They advised against birth parents speaking to the adoptive parents when tracing their children. Advised them to phone anonymously. Adoptive parents feel threatened and don't always pass messages on, they said. It's a good idea to use a younger person to obtain the phone number from them. The adoptive parents will think it's a friend of their adopted son or daughter. I felt a surge of anger towards Social Welfare. Their secrecy practices still continued only they were now working against the adoptive parents.

I nodded and said that I wouldn't have felt threatened. We talked about Robert's call.

But why don't Social Welfare see the adoption process as a triangle with all parts of equal importance? Adoptive parents have feelings that need to be considered, too. I would have loved Mary to have phoned me and said who she was and asked for Aaron's location. I would have told her. I would have been excited to hear from her. I wouldn't have hung up on her.

And how can Social Welfare so blatantly generalise about adoptive parents? I too could generalise and say that if adoptive parents have cause to feel threatened when birth parents find their children, it is because they are by-passed in the initial contact. I took a sip of juice and listened to Katrina telling how she ate the spare vegetarian meal on a flight last week, then found it wasn't spare.

The waitress returned. We apologised again and examined the menu. Chicken crepes smothered in yoghurt and blueberries, homemade paté with hot toast and chutney, mushroom crepes, beef lasagne and vegetarian cannelloni, exotic salads. The waitress smiled again and said she'd come back. We commended her on her patience. I wondered if she had overheard the conversation, was aware of the occasion. We made our selections. Mary and I chose the smothered-in-blueberries chicken crepe.

Aaron sat back and talked with his new half-brothers. They looked a trio. Fitted in well together. I felt proud of Aaron, the way he was handling all this. I could see he was pleased with his new family. Mary was sometimes quiet, sometimes expressive. Often sad. Often looking at Aaron. She sometimes sat on her hands. "So that I didn't constantly jump up and hug him," she later said.

Her husband and sons seemed fairly lively. Good fun. The sort of family it was easy to relate to. We laughed and talked together about Aaron's years of growing up, funny incidents, Friday's phone conversation. "I'd rehearsed all night what I was going to say but nothing really sounded right during the rehearsal," Mary said. She smiled. "But I hadn't expected to be the one answering the questions. I thought he might hang up on me when I finally managed to tell him who I was - there was such a long silence."

We all laughed. "It was embarrassing," said Aaron apologetically.

The paté and crepes and lasagne arrived. They looked as good as they sounded.

"How long have you known about Aaron?" I asked Mary's sons. I couldn't stop looking at Robert. He looked so much like Aaron.

"Only three weeks," Robert said. "It's been quite a surprise."

"It's very interesting." Michael the younger brother grinned.

"The mushrooms are awesome." Aaron piled another helping onto his fork.

"It's taken this long for me to be able to thank you for Aaron," I said to Mary seated next to me. My voice quivered. "And I had wanted to thank you for the lovely little clothes you left for him but Child Welfare wouldn't let me."

Mary nodded. We both had tears in our eyes.

"They said you'd gone back to the South Island."

"Did they?" Mary's voice was reproachful. "I lived in Wellington after Aaron was born."

"I've still got them."

Mary was touched that I had kept the clothes. The family said they would like to see them. I had brought them with me just in case, along with several photograph albums of Life with Aaron, which were still in the car. I took the garments out of the tissue paper, the tiny jacket and hat beautifully crocheted in cream. We passed them around. Aaron at six feet in height seemed far removed from them. We each harboured our own thoughts. The waitress came to enquire if everything was all right.

"Aaron was only five days old when we first saw him," I said to Mary. "He still had the dents in his temple from the forceps, but even at five days he was a beautiful baby."

"I didn't know he was a forceps delivery," Mary said, "but that explains a few things."

"I can remember going to the hospital to pick up Aaron. I remember holding him." Katrina looked fondly at Aaron. "I sat with him on a little chair - a child's chair. I remember the room. It was a creamy yellow room and it had a dustbin, one of those foot dustbins."

"You would have only been two years and a bit then," I said.

"But I can remember it." She tilted her head to the side. "I can just picture it so clearly. There were only two chairs and a dustbin in the whole room. It was a round metal dustbin and the dustbin lid flipped up." We laughed.

"They make a good lasagne," Robert said.

Mary moved her fork around the chicken crepe and turned to me. "Were you told by Social Welfare about the family history of arthritis and asthma?"

"No." I shook my head. "Just your physical features and interests."

"I did tell them."

I looked across at Aaron. It possibly explained the asthmatic wheeze he sometimes had as a child and the hayfever he still experienced in the summer months. He must be wondering about the arthritis.

The waitress returned. "Would you like to order dessert? How about coffee? Yes?... So that's three coffees and two teas. Yes, we have herbal teas. Peppermint, camomile, lemon zing...?"

"Would Aaron like to find his father?" Mary turned to me.

"I'm sure he would, but you ask him."

Mary told Aaron the last contact she'd had with his father was a letter from him just after Aaron was born, but she would try and locate him through the family farm up north near Rotorua.

Michael looked around the restaurant. It was a classy place for lunch with its white linen table cloths and silver cutlery. Popular too, judging by the number of diners. A grand piano sat in the centre of the room. "Can I play it, Dad?"

"I guess you could give it a go. But you'd better check with the waitress first."

We watched Michael seat himself at the piano.

"How long has he been learning?" I asked.

"Only two months," said Mary. She shifted around in her seat. Her husband was grinning.

"They look a conspiring pair," I said to Mary.

"They're hopeless. They go to juggling classes together and fall over each other when they get home in an attempt to be the first to show off the new tricks."

A crashing version of "Oh When the Saints..." hit the keyboard. We were impressed. It took the other diners by surprise. Michael played only one verse. Don't give them too much the first time and they'll want more at a repeat performance.

"He's good for only two months," said Katrina.

"I hear you can juggle too," I said as he returned to the table. Aaron gently nudged him and indicated with his eyes the jacket potatoes on his plate. Michael looked at the potatoes.

"Don't even think about it," his mother said.

I smiled. Aaron already looked part of his suddenly extended family. I knew I'd never lose him. I loved him and he'd always be my son. But I knew too that he and Mary would need to see each other again. I hoped that for Mary it would be a very different twenty-two years.

We walked together back to my car. Mary took the photograph albums to look through at home and Aaron suggested he go to her house that week. They arranged to meet for dinner on Wednesday evening.

It all seemed to be working out.

# Chapter Twenty-Three

"I'VE PUT my name down for the Ansett Rugby Sevens team to Australia next month," said Aaron leaning on the bench and watching me peel potatoes for dinner.

"Rugby?" I stopped peeling. "But you haven't played rugby for years. Not since you broke your nose playing against Wainuiomata. You promised me you wouldn't play again if I paid the ACC excess."

"Yes but this is a free flight to Sydney. I've never been there. It's an international airline tournament for countries in the Pacific. It will be massive. And the accommodation is pretty cheap."

"They mightn't select you," I said hopefully, layering the potatoes and onions into a casserole dish and sprinkling the lot with grated cheese. "Do they know how unfit you are? You complain about walking up the path from the road to our house."

He laughed. "I won't damage anything. I'll start running next week. I've got a couple of weeks to get fit. Can I lift that into the oven for you?"

"I just hope your father gets to see you in one piece. Do you think you'll get to see him before you go?"

"Yes, I phoned him last night. I told you that Mary spoke with him a couple of nights after our lunch at the Opera and he'd been very pleased and interested to hear about me and wanted to come down and meet me as soon as possible. He's flying down next week. He sounded pretty rapt about it all on the phone. It's a bit of a bonus, my father wanting to meet me too."

"How did the dinner go with Mary?"

"It went really well. They're a nice family. It's good, isn't it."

"Yes. Let's know how it goes with your father."

I met Mary for lunch the week of the reunion. She was still on a high from the weekend reunion: from meeting him again in the week and knowing that he wanted to keep in touch. I gave her more photograph albums, childhood tapes of Aaron talking - "I want to be a fireman when I grow up" - Aaron singing his Aaron version of popular nursery rhymes, and the Oliver musical where he had made his public singing debut as Fagin. “I’m poring over the albums you’ve given me,” she said. “He looks so much like Robert growing up.” Her voice was wistful.

A lone fantail fluttered about the balcony, then flew off into the beech trees. Trails of ants marched from the balcony into the house, carrying specks of food, one of many colonies that had made our house their home. I wondered if they were ‘sweet’ or ‘savoury’ ants. They’d rejected the sugar and borax mixture I fed them each night to try to reduce the numbers dropping from the light fittings, so I’d concocted appetising pureed vegetable dishes of spinach, carrot and potato spiced with borax, and left them at strategic points outside the house. When they’d lost interest in these pureed offerings Roger designed a complicated system of water-moats and squirters to prevent them leaving the house for their favourite garden nourishments, and connected the squirters to a temperature\timer regulating system. “We’ll *starve* them into non-existence,” we’d said. It had become a game - survival of the smartest. The ants seemed to be winning.

I heard Katrina and Aaron walking up the path, their laughter and a squeal from Katrina drifted through the trees. Aaron had met his birth father the previous day and said he’d relate the happening to us. It had been just a father and son reunion. I was looking forward to meeting his father but didn’t feel the same need to be there as when the children met their birth mothers. And two males would probably be more communicative without me sitting there. I wonder if Mary would have preferred to meet Aaron just on his own. She seemed happy at the time with a family-type reunion.

Katrina and Aaron puffed up the last five steps. Katrina brushed at her damp trousers. “We were just laughing about your ants. You need to give us a timetable for the water squirters. I didn’t bring a change of clothing.”

“Every hour on the hour when the temperature reaches fifteen degrees or more. The ants don’t come out on cold days.”

“Like Aaron.” She sprawled into the nearest chair on the balcony. The fantail was still flitting in the beech trees. A pair of tuis rocked around the tallest branches. We gazed beyond the trees to the harbour below. Shafts of silver and turquoise sunlight striped the sea, shimmering diamentes floated amongst the green and turquoise waters. Waves sprawled over rocks on the promontory at the end of the bay, a gentle surge and splash of foam. Katrina turned to her brother beside her. "Now, tell us what happened with your father yesterday. What's he like? Did you get to the airport on time?"

Aaron leant back in his chair and clasped his hands behind his head. "We got on really well. He's quite funny." He spoke in his quiet gentle voice, then grinned. "I was my usual five minutes late and he was already waiting in the terminal. As I got there I saw him asking someone if they were Aaron and they said no, but then he saw me and he kind of knew it was me."

"What did you do then?" I wanted all the details too.

"We shook hands, bit of an embrace. I told him there was a nice pub on the waterfront where we could talk. He was pleased about that. We went to Shed Five. We talked for five hours before he flew back home."

"Five *hours*! You don't talk to me for five hours," Katrina said.

"That's because I see you all the time."

"What did you talk about?" I asked. "The past twenty-two years?"

"Not really. It was more about what sort of people we are. Just getting to know each other, not a history of our lives. What we liked. Family stuff as well. We have a similar sense of humour and outlook on life. He said he had often wondered about me and what sort of life I'd had. He wanted to know if I had a good childhood."

"Did you tell him you ran away from home when you were five? What was that TV programme that Mum wouldn't let you watch?"

"Tarzan."

"Yes. Remember how you got all stroppy with Mum, and Dad said, 'Be nice to your mother - you've only got one mother,' and you said, 'No, I can always go and get another one from the hardware,' from Derek's hardware shop across the road. Then you took your red rabbit and pyjamas and put them into your little cardboard suitcase and went downstairs to the rumpus room." Katrina laughed. "You took your red rabbit everywhere."

"Yes, I do remember actually. It was too cold to go any further. It was just to make a point. It was a pride thing really. I didn't really want to leave. But I didn't want to go back up the stairs either."

I smiled. One of his few acts of early childhood 'rebellion' that I remembered. "Do you look alike?" I too, was curious to know more of Aaron's parentage.

"There are some similarities. He's a bit shorter and heavier than me. I think I'm a mixture of Mary and John. And guess what. He's got two sons aged thirteen and sixteen and a daughter of eighteen. The sixteen-year-old son wants to be a pilot. His children don't know about me yet 'cause the sons are at boarding school and the daughter's at Waikato University. He's going to have to wait till they're home for a weekend."

"Watch out for the squirters," Katrina tapped at Aaron's knee. "They're due in two minutes."

"Did he say if he was in the police force in the States?" I asked. "How long did he stay there?"

"He was only in the States on a working holiday. His wife is American; she knows about me. He met her when he was over there but they have lived back here for about eighteen years. John's family estate runs a tourist complex on the farm; golf and fishing for the Japanese and they own about seven pubs in New Zealand. They've even got a rather decrepit airstrip on their farm."

The answers to the questions of so long ago.

"And you won't believe it. He's a surrogate father to Damien, from High School. John asked me which secondary school I went to. That's when he asked me if I knew Damien. I told him he's a friend of mine, that we were in the same class at school. John was a bit shocked. He said that Damien's father had been his best friend but he died when Damien was only two. I remember Damien going to a farm up north every school holidays. He was going up to stay with my father and none of us knew it."

We made plans for Mary and her family to come to our house for dinner one Saturday night and meet our extended family, as Glenis had done. Aaron's grandparents, cousins, aunt and uncle and Katrina and Tom. We were looking forward to the occasion.

A few days before the dinner we learnt that Aaron's father, John, and his wife would be down in Wellington on business during that same weekend. I hoped we could meet him on the Sunday. We talked about the proposed weekend activities with Mary and John and they said that they would be willing to meet the family on the same evening. I was concerned that it might be too stressful for them - reuniting for the first time in twenty-two years in the home of Aaron's adoptive parent, and in front of a room full of strangers? Their relationship had been severed under strained circumstances before Aaron was born and they had not seen each other since. But Mary said if John was agreeable to coming on the same evening, then she thought she would be able to handle it.

They must have been nervous about meeting up again. I admired them for even considering it. To come with their respective spouses to such an evening requires a great deal of courage and understanding and it can't have been easy. But Aaron appreciated it. We all did.

Mary and her husband and sons arrived first, and then everybody else seemed to arrive at the same time. To save lengthy and complicated introductions we stood in family groups while we sorted out who belonged to who.

The evening went smoothly. So much talking. The new families related well to the old families. Everybody seemed to interconnect. My brother's American wife, Julie, had some feeling for the situation as the mother of a baby given up for adoption. John's wife, also an American, looked and sounded like Julie. They got on well together - two Americans domiciled in a foreign land with their Kiwi husbands. And all the young people. Half-brothers, adopted brother and sister, family cousins. They chatted together and played with Roger's antique puzzles. What relationship were they all to each other? What relationship were Aaron's new half-brothers to Katrina? There was no concise word for that relationship. Roger certainly got more than he bargained for when he married me but was happy to be part of it. Yes, it was a special evening for our family.

While John was in Wellington, he introduced Aaron to his youngest brother, Patrick, a forensic scientist who happened to work with colleagues and friends of Roger's. He was only three years older than Aaron, and later lived in the same street as him. A few weeks after their introduction they found themselves at the same party. "We look quite a bit alike," Aaron said, "And it was quite amusing, all these friends of Patrick's kept coming over and staring at me from about three feet away, then walking away again. His friends all call him Uncle Pat now."

A few weeks later Mary and her husband held a large gathering at their home for Aaron to meet his new uncles, aunts, cousins, and friends of the family. It was difficult for Roger and me to remember which uncle went with which aunt, and which cousin went with which parent, but Aaron coped well as he chatted and joked with the roomful of new relations. He was getting used to the curious and friendly glances at his physical features.

The ramp staff at Ansett took a particular interest in the adoption reunion scenarios. They knew Aaron well and they knew that the attractive flight attendant with the brown curly hair was his sister. But it was only recently they knew they were both adopted.

"They were stunned when I told them. They couldn't believe that Katrina and I weren't natural brother and sister. Just from the way we look and act together. And they wanted to know all about meeting my birth mother and father. By the way, I'm in the Ansett team for Australia. I'm a bit busy this week, but I'll try and get a run or two in before we go."

"Are you going to have a practice game?" I was secretly hoping he might pull a muscle before the international event and end up as a supporter.

"No, there isn't time for that. We'll get it altogether on the day."

He didn't quite get it together on the day and returned from Sydney with tortured muscles. His first game of the tournament had been against the Air Pacific team, comprised mainly of hefty Fijians. He was proud of the fact that he got the first try of the match. After that it was a downhill slide. His muscles had seized up soon after he sprawled across the try line with the ball and he was forced to retire for the rest of the tournament. It hadn't stopped him enjoying the social life.

"Robbie and I got lost in the convention centre when we were looking for the evening reception for the rugby teams. We found ourselves at a high school class reunion. A bunch of thirty-year-olds reminiscing over tables laden with great food. The rugby lot only offered drinks and snacks so we stayed for the class reunion."

"How could you do that?" I asked him.

"We put on fake Aussie accents and complained about being left off the registration list. I was a bit concerned about whether I'd be able to pass for a thirty-year-old. The rather aged teacher on the desk apologised and wrote out name tags for us. After that it was just a matter of listening around for a bit. Picking up on teachers' names and anecdotes. We asked people what they'd been up to since we last saw them and dropped a few of the anecdotes into the conversation.

One of the guys remembered me! The food was awesome."

Are these genetic or environmental traits that my son is exposing? Can I blame them on heredity?

"We went with some of our classmates to a couple of pubs down at Kings Cross to finish off the evening. Robbie and I shouted them a round and confessed. Luckily they saw the joke. They thought it was quite funny. My life seems to be a round of reunions."

Reunions. Yes, they keep on coming for Aaron. He has just returned from visiting his father's farm and meeting a new half-sister and half-brothers and grandparents and aunts and more uncles.

"They all made me really welcome. This small eye tooth I have is a genetic trait of John's family. And he's the only one of the five brothers who hasn't lost his hair by the time he's thirty-five." He felt his blondish locks. "I hope I take after him, not his brothers.

"My eighteen-year-old half-sister looks the most like me. She was helping out at the lodge on the farm and a Japanese tourist staying there asked if she was the oldest child in the family." He laughed. "She said she didn't know, she used to be. The Japanese guy was a bit confused."

I was so pleased for Aaron that he had two biological parents to whom he could relate so well and who wanted to welcome him into their families. And that their spouses and children were also happy about contact. "That's four half-brothers, one half-sister, one biological mother, one biological father and each of their spouses - what do you call them? - two new grandmothers and one new grandfather that you've met, all in the space of a few weeks. Not to mention all the aunts and uncles and cousins, and your newish stepfather, stepbrother and stepsister. How do you feel about it?" I was concerned that everything might be happening too fast for him.

He grinned. "It's going to be a bit expensive for Christmas. But it's neat. Pretty exciting really. They're all nice people."

"I think I'll have another go at trying to find my father," Katrina said quietly. "I'd love to know if I have some half-brothers and sisters out there. Social Welfare in Wellington said they would help me but they've still done nothing."

I heard the wonderings about a small corner of her life. Her need now to find the missing piece. To see if she has half-brothers or sisters.

Aaron had been inundated with missing pieces. More than he ever bargained for and faster than he could pick them up, although he wasn't complaining. Yes, Katrina would be satisfied with just that one missing piece.

# Chapter Twenty-Four

SEVERAL MONTHS after the reunion Aaron was still pleased with his new families. "Knowing them is more than piecing together the jigsaw pieces. It's just good knowing them. I'm going to keep in contact with them. They're family. It's not just a friend. It's more than a friend."

He visited Mary and her family when work and social activities permitted. He played an occasional round of golf with Robert, the elder of his half-brothers, and enjoyed their company at sporting fixtures and family happenings. John in the rural north was less accessible but they enjoyed meeting whenever possible.

Mary and I often talked together on the phone and sometimes met for lunch. But I heard a sadness replacing the euphoria and elation. And then, as the months went by, deep feelings of loss and regret. Of wanting her baby back. How she had been told all those years ago to forget Aaron's birth and make a new life for herself, and for almost twenty-two years had not allowed herself to think of the baby she relinquished. She had lived in a world of denial, but now the grief which had been suppressed for so long was resurfacing with an intensity that she was not prepared for. The forgetting and burying could no longer remain forgotten and buried.

Mary wrote to Aaron of her Scottish-Irish Catholic background, her growing-up years in the South Island, her love of singing and dancing, her experiences at the time of his birth, her wanting to hold on to him - but, with no on-going financial support, her inability to do so.

"A Child Welfare officer visited me in the hospital and asked about my life history. She talked to me about how many wonderful parents were wanting children. I can't remember it being mentioned that I might be able to keep my baby. I wasn't an assertive person and was quickly learning that my feelings didn't seem important. I was just lucky everyone was helping me out of this 'mess'."

She told how she'd asked the officer if they would come back to her if her son's adoptive parents split up and the woman had said, "I don't think we do that sort of thing," and how the matron, a caring and supportive woman, had said, after the officer left Mary's room, "I can't stand those people."

"Signing the adoption papers was the saddest day of my life. The solicitor said hello very quietly and never looked at me. I had to sign the papers first, and then swear on a Bible. I don't know how I managed to repeat the words. Whoever thought up such an inhumane system? Why did I have to swear on a Bible that I would never look for my child? That I would relinquish all rights? Did they think I feared God so much that I thought He would strike me dead if I wanted to know the whereabouts of my son? I cried so much that day I made myself sick."

Finally, Mary wrote of her recent search for Aaron and the joy at reuniting, overshadowed by deep sadness and regrets.

Aaron was moved by her story and pleased to have a record of his earliest beginnings. He was able to understand something more of her trauma at giving him up for adoption.

We had known nothing of Mary's situation and her overwhelming desire to hold on to her son at the time we adopted him. We understood only that she wished to have a home for her baby. I asked Mary what prompted her to begin the search for Aaron. She wasn't sure. She just knew that she wanted to do something - she had a son whom she knew nothing about.

She had started to think more about him over the past year and wondered if he thought about her. He would never know how much she cared about him, might never realise he was still such a part of her unless she told him. She hadn't thought about what she might want from the relationship if she found him, but now that they had met she was worried that she might lose him all over again. She wished often that she had left it alone.

I think Mary and I each felt the need to talk over what was happening. Mary had just found her son, but he had been my son for twenty-two years. Could he belong to both of us? Could he be a son to each of us? My relationship with Aaron was good and I didn't feel threatened by Mary's entry into our lives, but I did want Aaron to be comfortable with all that was happening to him. I knew that, as yet, Aaron didn't feel the same emotional bond for Mary as she did for him. He needed time and space for the relationship to develop. The close relationship between Glenis and Katrina didn't develop overnight.

It wasn't until after Katrina began flying regularly with her job to Christchurch, several years after their initial meeting, that she stopped thinking of Glenis as only a birth mother and began to feel really close to her.

I told Mary that Aaron was really pleased she had found him. That he thought they were a neat family. That he enjoyed visiting her. That he was happy for her to call him her son. I sensed that wasn't enough for Mary. We talked about the reunion and she wondered whether she should have seen Aaron on his own for that first meeting, whether it might have helped bond him to her.

I hadn't talked very much with Glenis after she met Katrina because she lived too far away, had seemed more physically removed down in Christchurch. But there also seemed to be less of a need to do so. Glenis had accepted that adoption was best for her situation, had always talked about and acknowledged Katrina's birth in spite of advice to the contrary. She hadn't allowed herself to forget but had promised herself that she would look for Katrina when she was twenty, and had come back with the hope and expectations of forming a good relationship with her daughter. Mary had suppressed her feelings and the desire to talk about Aaron, hadn't properly grieved after losing him.

Can someone grieve for a loss if that loss is never acknowledged? And is it more difficult to grieve for a baby if a mother has seen it for only one hour as Mary in her pain chose to do? Do we have to 'know' a person before we can fully grieve for them? Was it any easier for Glenis who knew and fed her baby for one week?

"It's been very difficult for Mary since she came back into it," I said to Aaron. "She never wanted to give you up and is only now facing all this unresolved grief. And she is having difficulty working out her relationship with you, where she fits in. You're her son, she gave birth to you, but she's not your mother, she says. She doesn't know *who* she is."

"Yes, I don't know what I can do about it. It's really hard for her. I did say to her, 'If you've got three sons why can't I have two mothers?'"

I sat outside in the sunshine, thinking over what had been happening for us since Mary's entry into our lives. Thinking of Mary's and Glenis's situation as relinquishing mothers. Of other birth mothers who had lost their children. What must it be like to have had that little baby moving around inside you, and then nothing? To swear on the Bible that you would relinquish all rights to your child and never look for them. To be asked if you wanted to say goodbye to your baby. How can you say goodbye to your baby? To never know whether your child is alive, whether they are well and happy. Not to have had your child acknowledged. Not to have received flowers or cards in the hospital room when your baby is born out of marriage, but to have a room flooded with flowers when your baby's father is your husband.

I had read articles written by birth mothers many years after they relinquished their children, and was aware of an anger that accompanied the deep sadness. An anger that was part of their loss and unresolved grief. Anger against society for being judgmental, against Social Welfare for giving few choices, against their own families for their inadequate support, against birth fathers for having helped create the problem but not carrying the consequences, against adoptive parents for their infertility. I read that adoption was invented so that infertile couples could have children, that it was part of some bizarre social experiment. "Just because we were unmarried didn't make us unfit mothers," many birth mothers said.

I thought of how we, as adoptive parents, were at opposite ends of the rope all those years ago, with Child Welfare in the middle, making it work for Ken and me at one end; pulling Mary apart at the other. I felt a discomfort, almost a guilt, because we were the ones who benefited from the social climate of the period when we adopted our children. But weren't we told that there were so many babies out there who needed 'good homes'? So many babies of unmarried mothers. Sometimes too many babies. We thought we were needed. We were told we were needed, that the unmarried mother needed us as much as we needed her. Of course we mainly adopted our children for selfish reasons. The parental instinct has a lot to answer for.

Society's attitudes also affected married couples who had no children. In my parents' generation, and in much of mine, it was expected that girls grew up, got married, had children and stayed at home to look after them while the father went to work. It was expected that married couples produce babies. To be childless raised eyebrows. To be childless was selfish. To choose to remain childless and pursue a career was considered even more selfish. The pressure from friends and family for couples to have children within a few years of marriage was great.

We parents who were 'childless not by choice' had difficulty talking about our problems. Today, infertile couples can attend workshops with such titles as Infertility and Its Impact on Adoption, Treatment Options, Grief Reactions and Infertility, Managing Endometriosis, Positive Steps in Living with Infertility, Childfree Living and Moving On.

Ken and I had remained curious about our children's parents and hoped that if the children wanted to find them they would be able to do so, but I knew that not all adoptive parents felt this way. Hadn't we been told all those years ago, when the interim and final adoption orders were made, that we were the new parents and these babies were ours, and only ours, forever? We had been encouraged to believe that it was in everyone's interests to shut out the past. There had been no expectation that the law would change, that it would now be legal for adopted adults and birth parents to seek each other, that birth mothers and fathers would return as from the grave.

I thought back to the time when the Adult Adoption Information Act of 1985 came into effect, and how adoptive parents were suddenly being told that it was not in everyone's interests to shut out the past, and that they must put aside any fears of what a reunion may bring. They must now believe that birth parents can enrich the lives of the their children without replacing the families they grew up in.

And what about Social Welfare's suggestion that adoptive parents be by-passed in this reunion process? Without the support of the adoptive parents, how well was the relationship going to progress? I was aware that if I didn't support Aaron in his relationship with Mary, that if I felt threatened by her re-entry into his life, then his relationship with her, and with me, would be affected. He would be hesitant about having so much contact with her. Our relationship couldn't remain a totally honest one.

Friends asked if I felt threatened by Mary's arrival - she lived closer to Aaron than I did, saw him often. I said my relationship with Aaron hadn't changed. I was still his mother, and we were able to share this new, sometimes overwhelming, experience and addition to our lives. And I felt a special bond with Mary, as I did with Glenis, the reason for our children's existence. But sometimes it was difficult. I sensed she would have preferred I wasn't there as his mother. I wondered how it was all going to evolve.

The media seemed so often to include the word 'adoption' in its reporting. Or was it just that the word stood out more since Mary's arrival? But I hadn't found much reading material on the feelings of adoptive parents after their child was reunited with its natural parent. How had other adoptive parents reacted to this new extension to their family? It wasn't just a newly-arrived birth mother on the scene, it was also new brothers, sisters, aunts, uncles and grandparents. Birth mothers' 'reunion and afterwards' accounts spoke little or nothing of their relationship with the adoptive parents.

I found myself caught up in a situation that I wasn't prepared for: the intensity of the emotions that Aaron's mother was expressing, and her huge maternal drive towards Aaron, her need to have him close. Where did that put Aaron? Where did that put me?

"How would you feel about me writing about this?" I asked Mary one day. "There doesn't seem to be much written for adoptive mothers. And I wasn't really prepared for what you are experiencing. We seem to have been living and breathing adoption ever since you found Aaron."

Mary said she would be happy to be part of the story, would have liked to read more about what she was going through - the elation of meeting her child tempered by feelings of terrible loss and sadness, old wounds resurfacing, wondering where she now fits in. She said she had no idea of the emotions she'd be experiencing and sometimes wished she'd never come back into it.

And so this book was also born.

*Once the past is relived, the old wounds are opened and the grief the birth mother has suppressed lies undiminished, waiting for her. It is so difficult to resolve the grief she experienced on losing her child as a baby - a special kind of pain which no-one who has not been there could ever understand. [5]*

# Chapter Twenty-Five

A LARGE PATCH of Arum lilies interrupted the weedy wasteland near the oil tanks on the way to Days Bay. Just what I needed for my next WEA floral art class. "I'll pick some for you too on my way to the lesson," I said to Katrina. "You can hardly see them from the road. A couple won't be missed."

Katrina was good at this flower arranging and we enjoyed going to the classes together. But the lilies weren't so easily procurable in the black night and no moon. Katrina looked at my shoes and laughed as we met at the front door of the Community Resource Centre.

"Mum, where on earth have you been?"

"I should have taken a torch. I fell into a bog just before I hit the lilies. They took some getting... I had to lean over and stretch for them. I didn't dare walk in any closer - I might have been swallowed up."

She laughed again. "They're full of holes. A bit bitten around the edges too."

Yes, the lilies did look motley under the light. My shoes squelched as I walked down the passageway. The mud was drying on my calves.

"Are you going into class like that?"

"I'll keep my feet under the table."

Katrina walked behind me as we entered into the room. "I hope they've forgotten you're my mother."

She took two of the lilies. I had three. I jabbed flax behind them and arranged pine cones around the earthenware dish of my Christmas display. Katrina cleverly masked the worst of her holes with greenery. We admired the magnificence of our fellow classmates' yuletide arrangements.

Now, a week later, the lilies were browning at the edges and the flax was drooping. Katrina would notice them, tell me it was time I replaced them. She'd be here soon, she needed some greenery for our next class. I heard her walk through the front door.

"You've timed it well, Aaron's coming up too. He's playing golf at Hutt Park and said he'd call in after the game. I might ask him about helping us paint the roof."

"He won't have the energy for that." She looked at the lilies.

I laughed. "No. I guess he'll be worried about pulling another muscle."

Aaron found us on the path, gathering up evergreens and more flax. We walked back up to the house and looked out to the harbour waters. The sea was spurting white tops.

"Shame it's so windy out there. I thought we could hire a windsurfer and have a bit of a spin."

"I can't swim," I said.

"Mum thought you might like to paint the roof."

He looked out the window again. "Look at that catamaran sliding around. Quite dangerous on the roof in those conditions."

"Lindsay and Catherine and the children are arriving from London next week for Christmas," I said. "They've finally had their tickets confirmed. It'll be a large family occasion this year."

"I was just talking to Mary this morning. I told her I'd slip over on Christmas Day for a couple of hours. You'll all be half asleep in the afternoon after the turkey and plum pudding."

"That's a nice idea," I said. "It'll be her first Christmas with you. It's been quite a happening, hasn't it. All these reunions... the differing reactions of your new families to the situation. The emotions." I put a jug of orange juice and a can of cold beer on the coffee table. And water crackers with tomato and basil and cracked pepper - home baking had become a rarity in my house. I never did perfect the date scones. "It's funny, all the years we've had together and I don't think I've ever asked either of you what you really think about adoption. How it affected you growing up. We've just breezed through really, without a lot of discussion, and now, since Mary contacted you, Aaron..."

"We haven't really needed to talk much," said Katrina. "I probably said most of how I've felt in that Youth Focus article when I was seventeen."

"How would you both feel about me writing about your adoptions? Could I record your thoughts and feelings?"

"That looks like the end of the roof painting," Aaron said to Katrina. I smiled and switched on the tape recorder.

"I didn't know what it was like not to be an adopted child," Katrina poured herself a glass of juice. "I just thought it was completely normal. It *was* normal. Some kids who aren't adopted sometimes wish they could swap their parents, but it never occurred to me to wish I wasn't adopted. And Aaron and I looked so much like each other, and like you and Dad - we didn't stand out as different. We felt so much like brother and sister. Still do, but then we *are* brother and sister."

"Yeah, adoption was a non-issue," Aaron said. "It just didn't mean anything to me either. I wasn't emotional about it in any way. I didn't feel any different from any of my friends. I knew of quite a few kids who were adopted - it wasn't rare."

"I sometimes wondered what my mother was like but I didn't think of her as part of my adoption. She wasn't a mother figure, she was just a 'person' figure. I didn't wish I was with her or think, oh no, I haven't got her. She gave me up because she *couldn't* look after me... financially, emotionally and every other way... not because she didn't want to look after me. She was only seventeen."

"Did you think about your birth parents much as you were growing up, Aaron?" I asked.

"Not a lot, but I did think about them... probably equally - mother and father. Just curiosity, really, trying to picture them from what I knew about them. Meeting them is a curiosity satisfied - it's been just that something extra. It's a positive thing." He peeled back the top of the Lion Brown can. "It's an important part of your life - where you come from, why you look the way you do. Your ancestry. Because ancestry, I believe, is in your blood. Your family is always going to be your family but beyond that it's in your blood."

"And mannerisms," I said. "I think some of them must be genetic."

"I'm sure they are. I think this experience has proved to me that a lot of things like that are inherited."

"You're probably a mixture of John and Mary. But then you and Dad were very similar in nature - you were both quite laid-back."

"I'm a combination of four people rather than just two."

"You and I are quite similar in many ways, Mum - our reactions and the way we think. And when I'm with Glenis I sometimes get mistaken for her from a distance. The way we move. Our hair. There's a photo of Glenis on her fridge, taken when she was twelve, and I always think it's me."

"Yes, I know the photo," I said. "I thought it was you when I saw it, too. You didn't look as much alike in later years."

"Did your friends ever ask you what it was like to be adopted?" I looked at both the kids.

"No, they didn't," Aaron said, "because they knew me really well and knew you, and there was nothing different for them. They just accepted it as being normal. I never tried to hide it although more people seemed to know that Stewart Dempster was my great-uncle, and when I got bowled out early at cricket I sometimes got a comment, from people who didn't know I was adopted, about not inheriting his talent. My friends would kind of cringe, wondering what my reaction to this heredity remark would be. But it never worried me, it's just something people would say. If you're going to worry about things like that you'd probably spend your whole life in a state of worry."

"Most of my friends didn't know I was adopted," Katrina took a sip of juice. "I didn't talk about it much because I thought it was more a personal matter." She turned to Aaron and smiled. "We were a bit different there... But now, since Glenis found me, everyone knows and they think it's neat the way my life has worked out."

The ferry to central Wellington shuffled out from the wharf below us, cutting a V-shaped path through the harbour waters. The catamarans were juggling with the waves.

"Adoption can be an issue for some people who don't know much about it," Aaron stretched out his long legs. "It's just ignorance. When I stayed with a friend and her family up north after Dad died I was talking about Dad and the way he died, and how his illness may have been hereditary. Her father said, 'It must have been one of the only times you were glad you were adopted.' I told him, 'No. I've never thought of it as a bad thing.'"

"Some people think you can't love your adopted child as much as a biological child," I said.

"And they mix up adopted and fostered, which are different. They think you haven't had a normal childhood - you've been moved around."

"Or you've been adopted out because something happened to your mother when you were about two," added Katrina.

"Well, yeah. They don't realise it's from birth and it's all you know. That's the most common misconception that I've come across. For me there's no difference being adopted except that I've now got four parents instead of two. And that's a positive thing." Aaron reached for a cracker. The tomato slice slipped off as he leant back with it, and he wiped at his shirt front. "I didn't know anything about your difficulties conceiving until you talked about it a couple of months ago."

"And you never asked. Never thought about it?"

"Not really. It's funny because now I think it's quite a big thing. I guess it's just more understanding from an adult's perspective. As you become more mature you think about these things more. It must have been a really big thing for you."

"It was quite a traumatic time. Five years married and still no children. It just took over our lives because we were getting older and older. Twenty-seven and still no children - a bit different from today when couples are often both involved with careers and choose to delay having children until their thirties.

"It's understandable that some birth mothers saw adoptive parents as waiting in the wings to take their babies away. But we didn't see it as that - we were told that unmarried mothers needed homes for their babies - and many couples adopted who already had children of their own. Adoption was considered a solution for those unmarried mothers who couldn't look after their babies, a solution for Child Welfare who had to find homes for them, and a solution for those of us who couldn't have our own children.

'Normal' families were those with two parents, a mother and a father, and it was seen as best for the baby if it grew up in a 'normal' environment. When you children were small I hardly knew of any families where the marriage had broken up, and apart from the mother of our foster baby, Kirsty, I knew no single women who had chosen single parenthood."

"When was the DPB, the Domestic Purposes Benefit, introduced?" Katrina asked

"Not until 1973. The benefit was given to women living without a partner and caring for dependent children or relatives. It meant there was now financial assistance for unmarried mothers which would enable them to keep their children, as many wished to. The number of babies available for adoption dropped quite a bit within a couple of years."

"So, it came in just a year after I was born?" Aaron said.

"Yes. About the time contraception became more easily available. And legal abortions - they were hard to get until the mid-seventies. Illegal ones weren't safe.

"The seventies saw quite a few changes. It had been quite difficult to get the pill if you were unmarried, and women couldn't always rely on male co-operation with the condom." I sorted through a pile of books on the coffee table and opened up Anne Else's *A Question of Adoption.* "Listen to this. 'The pill came on the market in 1960 but many doctors refused to prescribe it, or the diaphragm, to any unmarried women. Those who did, got reprimanded by the ethical committee of the Medical Association of New Zealand who said in 1966 that 'the supply of contraceptives to unmarried persons, thereby facilitating the extra-marital relationships, is not in keeping with the highest principles of the medical profession'."

"Who are they to direct people's lives?" Katrina crunched on her cracker.

"Even Family Planning had an official policy until 1972 of not assisting single women with contraceptive advice unless they were about to be married."

"Really?" Aaron stretched out his long legs. "It's all a bit shocking, eh. Mind you, I suppose I can thank my lucky stars!"

"You wouldn't have had me for a sister, either."

"Now technology has moved on," Aaron said, "And there's more help, isn't there, for those with pregnancy problems. For those who really can't have children there are still babies available for adoption."

"One hundred and eighty-three stranger adoptions in New Zealand in the past year... that is, to adoptive parents who were unrelated and previously unknown to the mother. I've just been looking at the statistics. There were just over 2100 stranger adoptions the year you were born. A year after the DPB came in it dropped to 1800, and by 1979 it was down to 845."

"Is that right? But it would probably be proportional - those applying to adopt, proportional to those available?"

"I'm not really sure, but it would probably be an open adoption with the birth parents involved in the child's life in some way that was mutually agreeable - anything from sending occasional letters and photographs to contact on a regular basis. How would you feel about that?"

"No," he said. "So much conflict could open up there. And what if the mother's circumstances changed and she wanted her child back?"

"Legally she wouldn't have any claim. It would only be a moral agreement. Understandably there's much less trauma and sadness for the birth mothers, not having this total and final separation from their babies. I don't know how I would have coped with an open adoption. It's not something that I thought about, or was ever suggested, while you children were growing up. I think its success would depend very much on the adoptive and birth parents' compatibility."

"I think it worked out well the way we did it," said Katrina. She finished off the orange juice.

# Chapter Twenty-Six

WELLINGTON International Airport. Our bags were checked in, our boarding passes put safely in Roger's jacket pocket. Only goodbyes had to be said. I was going to be away from my children and family for over a year and wasn't looking forward to the parting although the prospect of a year in Europe was exciting. The German and Swedish Governments had awarded Roger science research grants and we would be living in Berlin and Lund.

"We'll come and see you in Europe," Aaron and Katrina promised as we hugged our goodbyes. "Good luck with the search for your father," I said to Katrina. "Tell us how it goes." I knew Social Welfare in Wellington had been unable to find out anything for her and at Glenis's suggestion she had phoned the Christchurch office a few months ago. They had taken details of Les's birth date and his last New Zealand address.

The plane roared into the air. We sat back in our seats and watched the hills of Wellington disappearing beneath us. I had a lump in my throat at leaving my two children but knew they would look after each other.

Berlin. "We've arrived," I wrote to the family. "A vibrant city of cafes, buskers, buildings ancient and modern - decaying classical, baroque, shining mirrored glamorous buildings - bombed remains of churches, a city trying to come to terms with re-unification." I told of living with Bernie, Roger's German colleague, and of the two fellow guests - young Nigerian and Chinese geologists out of their homelands for the first time. Johnson, the Nigerian, staying awake for the eight-hour plane trip to Berlin because he didn't want to miss anything, Hai-feng whose English was almost unintelligible. "Bachelor Bernie's three pots and one wok are being constantly juggled to cope with the demands placed upon them. Hai-feng cooks Chinese, I cook Western, and Johnson cooks straight from the chilli sauce bottle. Roger sneaked a taste of Johnson's chicken casserole one night and was left without taste buds for the rest of the evening."

Katrina wrote back of social activities and progress in her search. "Social Welfare in Christchurch have told me that Les has a sister up north, unfortunately without a phone, and two brothers without a New Zealand address. They are aware of another two sisters but haven't been able to trace them. They have suggested I write a letter for Les which they will send on to the sister without a phone, and they'll also try to get a local officer to visit her although they couldn't guarantee anything because the Hamilton office is so busy. In the meantime I'll write a letter of introduction that could be passed on to Les and which the Christchurch office will keep on file for me.

"By the way, Glenis and Mary met each other after you left for Berlin. Glenis told me they'd talked non-stop. She said if someone had asked her how she knew Mary she'd have had to say, 'We've never met before, but her son and my daughter are brother and sister'."

Our four months in Berlin passed quickly and we motored northwards and crossed by ferry into Sweden. The countryside was green and gentle, the skies were grey. Steep-roofed brick houses and half-timbered cottages huddled together into little villages. Lund, a university town founded more than a thousand years ago by Canute - King of Denmark, Norway and England - was to be our home for the next eight months. It was a town of narrow, cobblestoned streets and more than 37,000 students on bicycles.

Tom and Katrina joined us for a holiday, as promised, via the circuitous route of Argentina where they visited her host family.

"What's the latest on Les?" we asked, protected in our little apartment from the cold north winds.

"I'm still looking. Social Welfare in Christchurch never did hear back from the phoneless sister so they've given me her name and birth date. I found her address through the electoral rolls but I don't think I'll be brave enough to knock on her front door if I'm ever in Hamilton. They also gave me the name of an adoption support group in Christchurch who've been very helpful. They suggested I get Les's parents' marriage certificate and try tracking down the witnesses, seeing his parents have also disappeared without trace."

"I wouldn't have thought of that," I said.

"No. I got the marriage certificate. It was all quite exciting - all four parents of the bride and groom were listed on it. My four great-grandparents! But my great-grandparents were the witnesses! I thought, oh no, they won't still be around, but I searched the electoral rolls anyway, starting from 1949 when Les's parents got married. I found the groom's parents first, and then the bride's parents. As I went through the rolls I saw their occupations changing from 'married' to 'widow' for the women, and 'tramway motorman' to 'advertising serviceman', and 'engine-driver' to 'retired' for the men. Three of my great-grandparents disappeared between 1969 and 1981. I presume they've died. But Les's mother's mother is still on the 1993 roll, same address for forty-five years. When I saw that I thought, WOW!"

"What are you going to do?" I was living too far away to be able to help her.

"I decided I couldn't write to this old lady myself so Helen, a friend of mine who's your age, is going to write to her pretending she's an old friend of her daughter, Amelia - that's Les's mother and saying she wants to contact her again and could she pass a letter on."

We said goodbye to Tom and Katrina after a week of castles, white churches with square towers and Viking stone arrangements, and wondered what else might be discovered about Les.

Roger's daughter, Julie, was the next of the children to arrive. We made peppercake houses and put the traditional seven-candled Christmas lamp in the window. We watched beautiful blonde Santa Lucia contestants get crowned with lighted candles, and watched the wax dripping down their beautiful blonde hair, and their singing attendants carrying more candles to bring light in the darkness of winter. Everywhere in front gardens, trees were decorated with thousands of little white electric lights.

The snows had been falling throughout December and when Aaron and his girl-friend Susie arrived on Christmas Eve it was to a silent white fairyland of twinkling lights and glistening snow. "It's like living in a Christmas card," we said. We dragged the branch of an old tree inside after finding it half-buried in snow on the housing estate and propped it up in the lounge. We cut gold paper into angels' robes and white shiny material into wings and made hair of curled gold ribbons, and stapled everything together into angels and hung them on the bare branch with little Swedish decorations. We put our presents underneath the decorated branch.

"I hope you don't mind pickled herrings and rice pudding for Christmas dinner tomorrow," Roger said. "We thought we should have a real Swedish Christmas."

Mary rang Aaron on Christmas Day from New Zealand. She sounded bright and cheerful and said she was feeling much better about everything. "Susie and I have been seeing a lot of her and the family while you've been away," Aaron said. "I'm understanding more and more what she's been through."

Susie, who had entered Aaron's life just a few months after Mary found him, was having to cope with more than just a new relationship with Aaron. Adoptions and reunions and what happens afterwards had suddenly all became part of who Aaron was. It can't always have been easy for Susie but we could see how supportive she was of Aaron, and her zany sense of humour must have helped.

In January we received a letter from Katrina. "My friend Helen has just heard back from Les's mother. She lives in Sydney. She was quite confused, as was her mother - the old lady we wrote the original letter to. Les's mother is called Val. She has never used the name Amelia. She said to Helen, 'I'm not sure who you are. I'm sorry, but I don't remember you. How do you know me?'

"Helen has written back apologising for the deception and explaining that she was writing on behalf of a young friend who is trying to track down her father, and that Val is the young friend's grandmother. She gave Val a glowing report about me and said I didn't want to intrude on their lives but would just like some information about Les. Every time Helen phones me now my first words are, 'Have you heard anything?' But we're still waiting."

Roger's son Alan and girl-friend Sarah were the last of our children to visit, for reportedly the coldest winter in Sweden since thermometers were invented. The edges of the seas were whipped and frozen into troughs and peaks like icing on angel cake, and we crunched on the frozen waves and pulled our jackets closer to us. Then the kids left and the snows started to melt and the shops became full of yellow decorations and fancy eggs, and tablecloths and serviettes with chickens and daffodils on. And just when the Swedes were getting excited because they thought that spring was really coming, down came more of those little white crystals and covered everything up, all over again.

Another letter from Katrina burst through the slot in the door of our apartment. More of her search. "Val wrote back to Helen a few weeks ago saying that she had talked to Les, and yes, he knew Glenis, and no, he didn't know he was my father! Val said she would like to hear from me, too, so I sent her a letter and one to pass on to Les. Last week I got a letter from Val, welcoming me into the family as the twenty-first grandchild, then this week I received one from my father! He's written to me! He included photos of himself and his wife and their children. The son looks very much like me and the daughters do a bit, too. He lives near Brisbane. I've enclosed a copy of the letter for you to read. It seems hard to believe I've finally found him. I'll write back to him soon, but I don't want to rush him."

Caboolture
Dear Katrina,

After hearing about you from my mother I was thrilled to get your letter. I have carried it around all week, reading it constantly.

Wow. I thought it was going to be a breeze writing this, but ... I'm glad I found out about you. I wish I'd known earlier. Never mind, you're there now. I'll have to make this short because I'm getting the shakes (nervous).

I've been in Australia since 1974 and travelled all over the country until I met Wendy and we married in 1979. We have three children, Anthony fifteen, Kelly nearly thirteen, and Jacqueline eleven. And a pussy, one year old.

I drive a concrete truck for a job. I can't play the piano, but I read everything around.

Thank you for the photos - they stay with me.

Must post this now. Stay happy and please reply soon.

Love, Les

P.S. You've probably heard from Mum. She's rapt, and like me can't wait to meet you. Say hi to Tom.

"He lives in Caboolture," I said to Roger, while trying to read the letter through blurred eyes. "That's only fifteen minutes from your parents! It seems strange we couldn't find him through the phone directory or the Australian electoral rolls."

Katrina and Tom called in one evening soon after our arrival back in New Zealand. They sat on the couch, Katrina looking at Tom.

Expectantly. Tom took a deep breath and said, "Well, I guess there's no easy way for me to say this. I've recently found out I'm adopted, too."

We were stunned.

"How long have you known?" Roger finally asked.

"About six months. We thought it better to tell you when you got back rather than try and write about it. Katrina and I were on holiday in Gisborne and a cousin introduced me to someone as Tess and Cecil's adopted son. We couldn't believe what we were hearing but we said nothing and tried to carry on as if everything was normal. We certainly had lots of discussion about it on the way home in the car."

"How do you feel about it?" Fancy Katrina and Tom both adopted!

"Well, I was obviously shocked at first. And upset that I hadn't been told. Katrina was more angry."

"Yes, I was. Still am."

"But it was a bit of a relief. I was somehow expecting it. I'd often wondered whether I was adopted as I was growing up. My parents are much older. I'm an only child. One of my best friends had been adopted by his grandparents when he was a baby and they were about the same age as my parents. And I'd overheard a neighbour saying to Mum, 'Isn't it unusual that you and Cecil have blue eyes when Tom has brown eyes?' I kind of wondered then."

We'd idly wondered about it ourselves sometimes. Tom's father at eighty-one was older than Katrina's grandfather. His mother was almost seventy.

"I went to see Mum and Dad the night we got back from Gisborne. It took a long time for me to bring up the subject. I asked them if it was true, and they said yes. It was a very emotional evening. I learnt so much about my parents that night. How Mum had nursed Dad after the war and how they couldn't have children because of his war injuries. They'd been on the adoption waiting list for twenty years. Gisborne is a small town. It must have been political - someone didn't like someone. And it was complicated by Dad's injuries and subsequent work instability. Mum and Dad worried that I might feel differently towards them after I found out that I was adopted, and not being told about it. But, if anything, finding out has brought us closer."

"Why hadn't they told you that you were adopted?" I asked.

"Their attitude was that there would be a time and place. They said they didn't see it as a major issue. I suppose they just had trouble telling me. All my family knew but I don't think they were told not to mention it. They probably just thought I knew."

"Did it take you long to come to terms with this?" He was twenty-six. Very late to find out you are adopted, and from someone other than your parents.

"I think I adjusted to it very quickly. In saying that, I did think about it a lot. But I'm just the same person I've always been." He paused. "I would have been angry if I couldn't have talked about it with my parents. If I'd found out after they had died. But I was able to tell them how much I loved them and that it made no difference to our relationship."

"Do you think it has helped with Katrina being adopted?" Roger wondered.

"Possibly, but I don't think it has made much difference."

"I can't understand why he'd never been told," said Katrina.

"Have you any thoughts on looking for your birth mother?" I asked.

"I'm just waiting for the word from Tom to start looking for her," Katrina said. "I'm an expert now."

Tom smiled. "I haven't done anything yet. I don't want Mum and Dad to feel threatened, to think that now I know I'm adopted I'm going to replace them with someone. And there is the issue of telling people about my adoption before I could consider finding out more about my birth mother. The rest of the family don't know yet. We wanted to wait until you came home so we could tell you first."

"I think you've dealt with it in an incredibly mature way," Roger said.

"I think that's a credit to my parents."

We had supper and Tom and Katrina stood up to leave. We hugged Tom goodbye.

"Thanks for sharing all this with us."

He gave a wry grin. "Your family really collects them, don't they."

A few months later Tom decided to apply for his original birth certificate. He made an appointment with Social Welfare who explained the process and told him to write a letter with a brief history of himself and maybe a photo or two. "They said they would provide counselling if I wished and they also prepared me for the possibility that my birth mother had put a veto on my birth registration details."

"Did they suggest you have an intermediary person make contact for you?" I asked.

"No, they didn't, although Social Welfare did say that if I felt uncomfortable with direct contact initially, that they would do it for me. They also said they would help me if I have difficulty finding my birth parents."

Katrina found Tom's mother, Beverly, for him, and Tom wrote to her in Napier. Two days later a letter arrived in their letter box. A letter saying how pleased she was to hear from him, giving a brief history of her life, and an invitation to come and see her or phone at any time. She had never married and had no other children.

Tom and Katrina visited her three months later. "Beverly and I were both nervous but it was a very casual, friendly meeting. Not emotional. She is half-Jewish so that may explain my colouring. I'd like to spend some more time with her, get to know her a bit more but I don't feel the need for deep emotional stuff. She has never told anyone except her parents about my birth. She doesn't even think her brother knows. And she's told no one about my contacting her."

"Did you find out anything about your father?" Roger asked.

"Yes, he was a university student and is now married with three children. Beverly doesn't know where he is and I'm not sure if I'll ever find him. He has a very common first name, and his surname is Smith."

The old Rosanna Hostel in Tyndall Street had been a private stately home for many years and was up for sale again. Interested purchasers could contact the real estate agency responsible for its sale. Viewing was 'by appointment only'. Glenis was coming up for a few days and Katrina suggested they go through it together. Glenis could show her where she'd lived while waiting for her child to be born.

"I rang the real estate agent for an appointment and pretended I'd like to view the house on behalf of a rich relation in Britain who was looking to purchase property in New Zealand. The agent wanted to know how much he was prepared to invest so I took a wild guess and said $500,000." I chuckled at Katrina's audacity. "He said the property was expected to reach at least $650,000 and he'd send me a copy of the details to forward to Britain. I don't think he wanted to be bothered with semi-rich uncles in foreign lands. I told him that my uncle insisted that I inspect the property."

"You'd better wear your most expensive clothes," I said to her. "You'll need to look the part."

So Katrina and Glenis had walked up the steps together, seven years after first standing at the bottom of them for a photograph together. The owner showed them the Shand Kydd wallpaper and pointed out the rimu panelling, and the agent had followed along behind.

"Glenis couldn't talk to me about the old layout, the owner was right beside us, but then she went back to the bathroom and called out, 'Come and look at this, Katrina.' I suppose they thought we couldn't nick much out of the bathroom if we were left on our own - I think they were a bit suspicious of us. And so, in the bathroom with just the two of us, Glenis told me where everything used to be and how the hallway wasn't in the same place and how some of the rooms were changed around. The vegetable preparing room and the laundry in the basement were still the same. I don't think the estate agent was surprised that he never saw us again."

Glenis called in one afternoon to see me before she flew back to Christchurch. We talked about Katrina's search for her father and Glenis said she had worried that Les might not want to know Katrina, that he might not want to have anything to do with a daughter he'd known nothing about. We were all amazed and so pleased for Katrina that Les and his family had so readily accepted her.

"It's now eight years since you found Katrina," I said. "You've got quite a special relationship with each other."

"Yes, we have. I was so pleased when the five-dollar phone calls came in. We spend quite a bit of time together on the phone!"

"Looking back, what do you think about it all?"

"I don't know why society is so against adoption because it is such a good option. At kindergarten we see young girls, young mothers struggling to bring up their children. I think it's really sad that there is so much emphasis on unmarried mothers bringing up their children regardless of the circumstances, when there are people out there with so much more to offer the child."

"Not everyone would agree with those sentiments."

"Some women tend to personalise it and say, 'I could never give up *my* baby.' They're not rational about it. They don't step back and look at the benefits to the child. They look at only how they would feel about it.

"It's my philosophy that what goes around comes around. You brought up my daughter, I brought up my step-daughter, Alix, and now I'm doing a lot in bringing up Sharn, this little boy that I've become an honorary grandmother to. Ownership of children doesn't mean a lot to me. I have a global mentality - people are responsible for all children. Katrina is probably the achievement of my life but I don't own her, just as you'd say you don't own her.

"I went to a school reunion a few years ago and we were all talking about what we'd been doing with our lives. I was so excited that I'd just found Katrina and I told the group about her. The nuns looked quite uncomfortable and no one said very much, but afterwards four women came up to me and said they'd been unmarried mothers, too."

"It's still very difficult for many birth mothers to talk about," I said. "Tom's birth mother still hasn't told anyone about him."

"When people take steps to cover up things in one generation they make it so difficult for the next generation. And what is hugely important in one generation ceases to be important for the next.

"History is history. We can't change it. I know that all literature around is from birth mothers who have never come to terms with the adoption of their child. But adoption was the best option for my circumstances. I trusted you with my baby, and in my naivety I trusted the system. In hindsight, trusting the system was quite a risk, but it did work for us."

Katrina and Les continued to get to know each other by correspondence. For someone who didn't write letters he was doing very well. He and his wife had decided to tell their children about Katrina, and their two daughters wrote sisterly letters to her. His mother, Val, came to Christchurch for a month and Katrina enjoyed meeting the first of the new family.

Katrina and Tom decided to have a holiday in Noosa and arranged to stay the first two nights in Australia with Roger's parents and his sister, Pat. They lived just a short drive from Les's house in Caboolture, and about two hours from Noosa. Katrina wrote to Les of her plans. He said to give him a ring when she arrived in Australia. He didn't say anything about meeting her. She wondered if he was ready to.

"I called him the night we arrived at Pat's and he wasn't home," said

Katrina on her return to New Zealand. "He phoned me back at seven o'clock the next morning. Roger's mother told him we were still asleep. He rang back at seven thirty and we were still asleep. He rang again at ten thirty and said could he come over straight away?

"I was so nervous, waiting. When I heard that knock on the door I said to Pat, 'Can you answer it?' and she said, 'I think you should really answer it.' I opened the door and this guy said 'gidday' and walked in as if he owned the place. He turned out to be a friend of Pat's husband, and I had to go through all the agony again with the next knock. This time it was Les. He was standing there with his two daughters and he told me later they were there for moral support, too. Like me, he was really nervous but Pat was wonderful, especially as I'd never met her before, either, and we hadn't expected that the reunion would take place at her house. She made us feel relaxed, cooked lunch, looked after the girls and they all ended up staying the whole day."

"I'm so pleased it went so well for you." I could hear her excitement still, through the phone.

"The girls followed me everywhere. They thought it was pretty cool having this older sister. Les rang me a few days later in Noosa because he said he just wanted to talk with me again. He came up with one of his daughters for a BBQ on the Sunday and we had a good talk about ourselves and our lives. He's close to his wife and children but she's not quite ready to meet me yet. I learnt why we'd been unable to find him in Australia. When he applied for his first job there the boss told him he'd need to change his name if he wanted to work for him as he already had two Les's on the staff. So he became Ray, his second name, and stayed Ray. He's really nice."

"You're very lucky, aren't you. He could have been anything!"

"Yes, that's what Glenis said. She's really pleased for me. We spent our last night in Australia with Les and the girls, cruising the Brisbane River. We hugged goodbye when it was time to leave and he told me not to go out of his life again. He gave me a poem he'd found for me." I listened to her reading it. It was about paths converging and softly touching, about hearts moving close, and about 'the future preserving the warmth of this special time'.

# Chapter Twenty-Seven

I GAVE UP writing this book for a year after we returned from Sweden. Instead of being helpful, as was our original intention, it was causing old hurts to resurface, and Mary no longer wanted to be a part of it. There was too much sadness all over again for her.

Now, four years after reuniting with Aaron, Mary says she is a different person from when she first found him. "I don't think I'll ever be able to adjust to the fact that I lost one of my children, but some things can never be resolved. I have now accepted it and moved on."

We have talked together about the silence that birth mothers faced when they gave up their children for adoption. The loss that wasn't talked about. Society's attitudes. Mary said, "When my son Michael saw me grieving for the baby I lost he said that until he learnt about Aaron he had thought that mothers gave up their children for adoption because they didn't want them. I'm sure many people still think this. And they think that we as birth mothers thought it was the right thing to do. It is such an awful thing to have been through. I often think, how could I have gone through with the adoption? I still find it very difficult to understand how society expected me to do so.

"I found the grieving process so difficult when I came back into it - when I was reunited with Aaron - because, again, I wasn't allowed to grieve. I was often asked why I was so sad - I had Aaron back in my life, his family had welcomed me, and I was so incredibly lucky that my husband and children were so supportive. And I was often told that I wouldn't have the lifestyle I have now if Aaron hadn't been adopted.

"No one could understand that it wasn't my baby I got back - it was a total stranger called Aaron.

"It was so very difficult to be part of it all at times. I felt such a huge loss, and many times I regretted coming on to the scene again. It hurt so much being there. Denial was much easier, blotting it all out. And I had no way of telling whether it would get any better."

Mary and I talked about reunions that work, and those that don't, and she suggested that it was probably more a personality thing. That reunied birth mothers and adopted children may or may not get along with each other, in much the same way that children in natural families may not get along with their parents.

"I have a close, comfortable relationship with Aaron now," she said. "But it's the little things that trip me up, in having an oldest son that didn't grow up in the family." Like telling someone of her oldest son, Robert, then remembering Aaron and calling him her very oldest son, hoping madly afterwards that no one thinks she's crazy. Like Michael coming home from school and saying how the priest had asked him if Robert was his only brother. There'd been a ten-second silence before he'd said "yes" and the priest had said, "You don't seem too sure, Michael." Michael not mentioning Aaron in case his mother was uncomfortable about his telling the priest that she was a birth mother.

Mary's family also feel close to Aaron. Robert says he thinks of Aaron as his brother. Michael and Aaron have fun fights with all the brotherly affection there is between them. Mary's husband says he feels a special bond with Aaron. And I know Aaron feels the same love and affection for them. He says isn't it great that he can relate so well to Mary's family, and that he and Susie feel a part of it. They've all been on holidays together, and Susie and Aaron have stayed in their home on several occasions.

I have admired Aaron's maturity in the re-unification process. It hasn't always been easy for him, or Mary, or me, these past four years. But Aaron says he wouldn't have had it any other way, her returning to him.

Mary and I share the same son, and now, with the intensity of Mary's grief diminishing, we can sit back and relax together, and be thankful that he is a part of both of our lives. He has a different relationship with each of us and I know we will each be special to him in our own way. Mary as the mother who gave birth to him, and me as the mother who is his parent.

Mary said:

*"He is my first-born son, such an important part of me. I am looking forward to another generation. A new beginning with Aaron's children. It will be wonderful to hold another little baby in my arms, feel its soft face, kiss it at least one hundred times and tell it I am going to be one of its very best friends."*

# Chapter Twenty-Eight

THE FERRY was returning to the bay. A sprinkle of passengers alighted from the gangway. Aaron arrived up at the house a few minutes later.

"What's the latest on the Subaru?" Roger asked.

"It's still driveable. Amazing really, after being driven along the railway tracks. Just because it's a four-wheel-drive they think they can drive it anywhere. The police have taken fingerprints but I don't know if they'll find the guys responsible. Bit of a shock to get a call from them yesterday morning. I was still in bed and didn't even know it was missing. I went out by train to Porirua and picked it up. It was sitting beside the railway tracks. I'll get it checked over tomorrow."

"When does Susie get back from Vanuatu?" I asked.

"The end of the month. She's still got another three weeks' work up there."

"Have you thought any more about joining us in the Cobb Valley next week?" said Roger.

"Yeah, Alan and I have been talking about hiring a plane and coming down. We'd leave the plane at Takaka. Alan said he'll take us caving in the Honeycomb Caves at Karamea if I can fly us in there as well."

I gulped. Roger was doing field work in the area and it would be fun to have the kids with us but I wasn't sure if it was expected that I join the caving expedition. I knew that Roger's son was an experienced caver, more than capable inside a cave I was sure, but I'd never been caving, not the crawling-on-the-belly abseilling-steep-wall stuff. The Waitomo Caves with its board walks and glow-worm Cathedral Cavern that tourists could glide into by boat was more my style. And small planes felt like froth in the air but maybe they wouldn't need me to fill up the plane.

The tiny four-seater Grumman Tiger struggled down a gravel runway that was called the Takaka airstrip. Aaron gripped the yoke, forcing the small wheels to keep on the gravel. Strong cross-winds played with the plane, threatening to spill it onto the grass beside the airstrip. The engine sounded strained as if it was objecting to all efforts to lift it off the ground. The runway became alarmingly short in front of us. Alan in the co-pilot's seat looked straight ahead. A friend and I in the back seat drew deep breaths and willed the plane to rise. Nobody said anything. Slowly the nose of the plane tilted upwards and the rest of the plane rose with it. Not far. Not far enough. We'd only just cleared the fences and scrub at the end of the runway and it seemed we had levelled out. We were still only thirty feet above the ground. Shouldn't we be climbing? I'd never see Roger and the family again. I should never have come, but a mother has to show some confidence in her son's flying ability.

Suddenly as if injected with fresh spirit the plane spurted upwards. Upwards into turbulence in which we shuddered and rocked around and had to clutch our stomachs and the sides of the plane. Upwards, we were still climbing. I adjusted my headset. We all wore one so that Aaron could communicate with us above the noise of the engines, so that we could hear the words that pilots hear from traffic controllers. Except that Aaron was silent and except that Takaka doesn't have any traffic controllers. Dotted against the aeroclub rooms was a minute Roger, who'd stayed behind to continue with his mapping and look for his beloved trilobites.

Upwards, the plane was still lifting. Upwards, we were suddenly out of the turbulence. Aaron's grip on the yoke relaxed. He turned around to us. "All right?" He was calm as if all this was totally normal.

"Just," I muttered.

Alan grinned. "That was bloody exciting. What was the problem?"

"Cross-winds blowing us off the runway, there's no direct nose-wheel steering on this plane. We'll follow the coast down to Karamea so that we avoid the clouds and hopefully the turbulence."

We sat back and tried to enjoy the views of white whipped waves and rocky coast-line from six hundred feet above. Aaron sat with an aeronautical map of the region on his lap. He'd never flown into Karamea and was looking for land marks. And then the coast line disappeared into cloud at the time we needed to turn inland to the airstrip. No air traffic controllers out here either. "We'll go under the clouds," he reported to his three passengers as he swooped down a hundred feet into clear visibility perched underneath the menacing clouds.

But there were clouds banked against the land. We flew low over the sea, all eyes searching for an inland passage of clear sky. The plane droned on, droned on southwards. Cloud all around us and sea below us, we seemed so tiny and insignificant and unwanted.

"We'll have to turn back if we can't get through soon. There won't be enough petrol to go much further," reported the pilot.

All this trauma for nothing?

Five minutes later we spied the gap and the Grumman Tiger turned into it. The runway was soon in sight. "You're a good pilot but it's the worst flight I've ever been on," I said as I trembled out of the plane. My body felt heavy on my legs. Alan and the friend were wearing weak grins.

"Me too," said Aaron removing his headphones and switching off the plane.

I removed my prescription sunglasses and discovered I'd left my normal glasses back at Takaka. I'd have to wear sunglasses for the evening and in the caves tomorrow. Could be tricky in the caves but I'd never see anything without some optical assistance, even if it was tinted brown.

We stayed in a bush hut for the night. The walls were smeared with mosquito blood and black body parts. The candles burned dimly in a very dim room. Mosquitoes whined in our ears all night. The Honeycomb Caves had better be worth it.

We hired an Education Department school bus, Avis Rental hadn't yet discovered Karamea, and drove the yellow clapped-out vehicle into the rain forests housing the caves. Thick forests of lush ferns, epiphytes, dense canopies of dark green foliage, rocks and tree trunks smothered in lichen, thick carpets of moss. Wisps of light on pale shimmering leaves. The total effect was fantastic. Primeval.

At the caves Alan handed out helmets fitted with acetylene lamps. "It's the first time I've taken anyone caving with their sunglasses on," he said. For hours I squinted and stumbled my way through the formations, the finer details eluding me in my blackish world, the lamp helping only slightly. I squirmed on my stomach under ledges and squeezed through narrow passageways. I peered at moa bones in lesser caves. Alan gripped my hand in difficult stretches, the old blind step-mother. I brushed past wicked-looking three-inch-long cave wetas with equally long twirling feelers. No problem seeing them - they were only inches from my nose. I avoided abseilling the steeper walls and went the long way around. There were limits.

We flew back to Takaka without aerial incident. Back to a brighter sunnier world, for me.

# Chapter Twenty-Nine

SHE LIES THERE. Two hours old. Freshly delivered and wrapped in cotton sheeting. The midwife passes her to me. I've never held such a young baby before. "She's beautiful," I whisper to her exhausted mother and beaming father. She looks just like Katrina at fifteen days. I examine her tiny toes and fingers and wonder how the nails can be so neatly trimmed at just the right length for delivery. She opens her eyes and looks at me. I feel part of her already.

"Pretty bright for two hours," I say.

We are in the same hospital as Katrina was born in. The lifts and brown polished linoleum floors look the same. Except that I'm now in the delivery wing. I've never been in here before. Katrina is lying back on the bed. It has been a long thirty hours of labour. "I'm exhausted from the waiting," I say. "I'm not too fresh myself," says my daughter.

The waiting. Awake all through the night waiting for that phone call to say she has arrived. That mother and baby are both well. Unable to concentrate on anything the next morning. Looking at the clock. Worrying.

Then the phone had rung. Four hours ago. This must be it. She'd been in labour twenty-seven hours - since six thirty the previous morning. I'd rushed at it with a breathless hello, body tense, waiting to hear if it was a boy or girl, if mother and baby were well. A robotic voice had droned at me, "This is a reminder from the Lower Hutt City Libraries. According to our records you have not yet returned one or more items which were due back at the library eight days ago. Please return these items promptly so that others may use them. Fines are increasing at the rate of twenty cents per book per day."

The next phone call hadn't come. I couldn't wait any longer. We'd just got in the car and driven to the hospital.

And now she's here. Safely. I know Katrina will be thinking of her own birth. Of her other mother who had her for only a week; who lay in the same delivery suite but without a husband and parents and grandparents and friends and flowers and cards and support. Just a nurse to hold her hand.

"We've phoned Aaron." Tom says. "He's quite excited about his new niece, and he and Susie will be back from Christchurch on Monday. They've just bought themselves a car down there. He says they're cheaper in Christchurch. There's a bit of a problem though with the electrics. The wipers go when you turn the lights on and when you flick the indicator the windscreen gets washed but he said it was only $700."

"Uncle Aaron." I say the words out loud and smile at his new role. He'll be a good uncle. I pass the baby to Roger. He admires her too, then passes her back to her mother. "We'll let you sleep," we say, and leave the three of them together.

Back home there's a message on the answerphone. "Message received today at 1.15pm." While we were travelling to the hospital. It's from Tom. "Good afternoon. Is that Nan and Poppa Cooper? Our daughter was born shortly after midday and weighs 8lb 7oz."

There has been a lot of discussion about what baby Meghan will call her grandparents and great-grandparents. My parents are already called Nana and Grandad. They need to keep those names to avoid confusion. Glenis would like to be Grandma and her husband Keith would like Grandpa, and Tom's mother wants Granny and his father is going to be Pappy. Roger likes Poppa. "You two could be Moppa and Poppa," Katrina had joked. Then there's Glenis's mother, who has made the most beautiful christening gown, and Tom's birth mother and her mother, and Les who is already being called Grandad by his friends, and Les's mother and grandmother. And there might be Tom's biological father and his wife and parents. And what about Mami and Papi in Argentina? We hope that Meghan has inherited her mother's sharp memory.

Glenis is coming up from Christchurch to stay with us for a few days and become acquainted with her grandchild. She hasn't slept all night either. It's a double celebration for Glenis. Meghan was born on her birthday.

# Appendix I

# History of Adoption Legislation in New Zealand

THE ADOPTION of Children Act 1881, introduced as a Private Member's Bill, was the first adoption legislation in New Zealand. Its principal purpose was to give some security to the adoptive parent and child, as, prior to this, adoption had been a rather informal process. Nothing in the Act limited access to birth records.

1915: The Births and Deaths Registration Amendment Act 1915 provided for adopted persons' births to be re-registered, with the new adoptive details replacing the original ones - apparently to protect the adopted person from the stigma of illegitimacy. Issuing of the original birth certificate was restricted to certified purposes, though anyone could still inspect it.

1924: The Births and Deaths Registration Act 1924 made it a little more difficult to obtain a copy of the original certificate but did not restrict inspection.

1951: The Births and Deaths Registration Amendment Act 1951 applied the restriction in the 1915 and 1924 Acts to the inspection of the records as well as the supply of copies. Access was at the discretion of the registrar or Registrar General. As with the 1924 Act, records of parliamentary debate are not helpful on the reasons for this change.

1955: The Adoption Act 1955 allowed a birth parent to give consent to an adoption without knowing the identity of the adoptive parents. The Act also limited access to 'adoption records' though it is unclear why. The interdepartmental committee's report, on which the Act was based, included the recommendation 'that a Judge's or a Magistrate's order be required for the production or inspection of adoption records and then only on special grounds... the committee thinks that the records should be regarded as absolutely confidential and not disclosed to anyone except in particular circumstances.'

Advertising for babies became illegal after the 1955 Act and the period of consent was reduced from three months to ten days.

1961: The Births and Deaths Registration Amendment Act 1961 provided for adopted persons' birth certificates to be the same as for non-adopted people.

1969: The Births and Deaths Registration Amendment 1969 closed off access to original birth certificates to an even greater extent. In effect, it prevented the Registrar General from releasing information where to do so would contravene the principals of the 1955 Adoption Act.

1985: The Adult Adoption Information Act was passed. Birth parents and adopted persons had the right to officially seek contact with each other once the adopted person reached twenty years of age, providing no veto had been placed on the identifying information.

Reprinted from *Reunion - Adoption and the Search for Birth Origins - the New Zealand Story*, by Ann Howarth with permission of the author, and publishers Penguin Books (NZ) Ltd, Auckland 1988.

The 1985 Act came into force in September 1986. An estimated 50,000 New Zealand-born adults who were adopted by strangers, and their birth parents, were given the legal right to make contact with each other In the six months prior to the Act's enforcement, 653 adopted persons (nineteen years and over) and 2243 birth parents (with daughters or sons nineteen years and over) placed vetoes. In the year following the enforcement of the Act, 5834 adult adopted persons received their original birth certificate and 1128 birth parents requested the department trace their son or daughter. A further 2000 to 3000 birth mothers asked the Social Welfare Department to record that they would be happy for contact should their child wish to find them.

# Appendix II

# Historical Aspects of Illegitimacy and Adoption

NEW ZEALAND was the first country in the British Empire to make any kind of legal adoption possible - England did not pass a similar law until 1926. But at the time the 1881 Adoption Act was passed in New Zealand, the social attitude to adoption was one of hostility, due to concern that it might encourage immoral behaviour by allowing birth parents, especially the poor, to disown responsibility for their children. This hostile attitude, and the fear of inherited 'bad blood' and 'moral imbecility' were among the reasons why people were slow to take advantage of adoption. For at least fifty years, well over half the babies born outside marriage were cared for in other ways.

Several institutions ran homes for unmarried mothers, such refuges being a favourite form of charity for middle-class women. Pregnant single women were taken in before the birth, worked for their keep and stayed in the home in the months afterwards. After the mother left she would often have to place her child in care - finding a few shillings a week to pay a minder, or she might even pay a lump sum for the child to be taken off her hands permanently.

The social stigma attached to unmarried motherhood grew in the late nineteenth century as communities became more settled and increasingly concerned with respectability. The 1890s became a decade in which the country was seized by one of its recurring moral panics over the behaviour of young people and their parents. 'Concerns about the behaviour of young women in the 1890s was largely related to concerns about the "social evil" - prostitution - and illegitimacy. Between 1886 and 1896 illegitimate births increased from 3.12 percent to 4.8 percent of all live births. This increase occurred because of the increasing proportion of young women in the population and did not signify a real increase in illegitimacy but was enough to cause considerable alarm.'[7]

'The founding of the Society for the Protection of Women and Children in 1893 reflected the trend in the western world to see children as precious assets to the whole of society rather than as the property of their parents, or, more accurately, of their fathers. Children came to be viewed not only as small adults but as individuals who needed to be protected, nurtured, loved and educated'[8] amidst the best environments.

'Historian Margaret Tennant dates the first signs of an official shift in focus from original sin to "child life" back to the 1890s when population anxieties among white settlers gave rise to the view that even "illegitimates" of the right colour and quality were worth saving.'[9]

But right up to the 1940s few people saw adoption as the automatic solution to an out-of-wedlock pregnancy. Many believed that keeping an illegitimate child was a fitting punishment for a mother's sins and a warning to other women who might be tempted to stray. The view of unmarried mothers as 'fallen women' meant they could not be given financial assistance because it might encourage them to repeat their offence, or keep their babies. Unmarried mothers were not entitled to the family allowances introduced in 1926 and there was no specific provision for them in the Social Security Act 1938 - 'An illegitimate child is not a child within the meaning of the Act,' reported the *Auckland Star* on 17 November 1943. If mothers were utterly unable to keep their children, the usual alternative was institutional or, more often, foster care. The Society for the Protection of Women and Children was still commenting in 1943 that adoptions were rare as girls usually wished to keep their babies.

'Following the upheavals of war and Dr John Bowlby's work on "maternal deprivation", institutions, long suspect, fell completely out of favour as places to put young children, and even day nurseries were thought to do lasting damage. Foster care or 'boarding out' was too insecure and the state was usually left to carry the cost. By the end of the 1940s the 'best environment' for a child was seen as a permanent home with bread-winning father and stay-at-home mother; and the best way an illegitimate child could acquire this kind of home was through adoption.'[10]

But the Society for the Protection of Women and Children did not approve of the increasing practice of adoption of illegitimate children. 'The increase in illegitimacy led to new organisations such as the Motherhood of Man Movement, formed in 1952, and Childhaven, which helped unmarried mothers and facilitated adoptions. The Society was critical of these agencies. It believed that children should remain with their natural mothers and that everything should be done to make this possible. The Society also advocated equal treatment of illegitimate children under the Social Security system and argued that it should be made an offence to offer help to pregnant women on the condition that their babies be offered for adoption. Their views in this respect anticipated the shift in the 1970s towards single women keeping their babies and their support through the Domestic Purposes Benefit.'[11]

Reports of long waiting lists of adoptive applicants had begun to appear as early as 1949. Only about a third of all babies born at the Salvation Army's Bethany Hospitals, where many unmarried women had their babies, were available for adoption, and the waiting time for a baby was a year or more. In the 1950s adoptive applicants knew they might have to wait years for a baby. But by the 1960s there were signs that the shortage was rapidly becoming a surplus, and the average waiting time was down to six months. It was difficult for single mothers to find jobs that they could combine with parenting, cheap housing was scarce, child-care facilities were almost non-existent and there was strong pressure for single mothers to show concern for their children by offering them for adoption to a two-parent family.

The Adoption Act of 1955 legalised the secrecy surrounding unmarried mothers and adoption. Birth mothers and adoptive parents were not given identifying information about each other. The social shame of pregnancy and childbirth outside marriage continued into the seventies, and adoption was still considered the best solution to the problem by those involved in helping the unmarried pregnant woman make decisions about her baby's future. 'But against the prevailing policy that stranger adoption was the tidiest solution, social attitudes were slowly changing. There was increasing talk of the need for more support for single mothers, but it was finally the oversupply of babies for adoption in the late 1960s which swung government policy. Single parents (and working mothers) were regularly blamed for delinquency. It was not just humanitarianism but a desire for social stability which led to the establishment of a Domestic Purposes Benefit (DPB) for solo parents by the Labour Government in 1973.'[12]

Not all the troubles of single mothers were solved by the DPB. Social disapproval remained and government harassment of solo parents intensified with the election of the Muldoon Government in 1975. The new Minister of Social Welfare, Bert Walker, maintained that the DPB 'facilitates marriage breakdowns, and encourages mothers of children born out of wedlock to keep their children.'

Adoption waiting lists appeared again in the mid-seventies as fewer babies became available. The seventies and eighties saw a gradual opening up of the adoption process and the rights of adopted persons and birth parents, a new openness in interpersonal relationships, improved status and financial support for single mothers, and the stigma of illegitimacy 'officially removed' following the 1969 Status of Children Act which removed all legal disabilities for children born out of wedlock. When the Adult Adoption Information Act was finally passed in 1985, after a seven-year campaign, it allowed adopted adults and their birth parents to have official access to each others identity.

Now, in the 1990s, with the 'abolition' of illegitimacy and the acceptance of adoption by society, the birth mother is able to choose, (one hopes with less coercion), whether she will place her baby for adoption. Social Welfare and other adoption agencies are no longer responsible for matching babies to adoptive parents. The selection process used in the past was based on physical features, educational qualifications and whatever sort of relationship Social Welfare or the agency might have developed with the birth mother and adoptive applicants. Today, birth parents choose the new parents for their babies from files given to them by Social Welfare, but there are no guarantees that adoptive applicants will be selected as adoptive parents.

New Zealanders wanting to increase their families by adoption are increasingly looking overseas. The procedure can be lengthy and expensive - it might cost up to $30,000 dollars for an overseas child to be adopted, and it is easier to find older children than young babies. In the five years from 1993-1998, Social Welfare work time relating to inter-country adoptions has increased from 6 percent to 15 percent.

It is widely believed that it is almost impossible to adopt in New Zealand in the late 1990s. In reality, New Zealand stranger adoption placements are very high in comparison with other countries in the western world. In the fiscal year ending June 1998, the numbers of adoptive applicants in the national waiting pool averaged 280 and there were 124 stranger placements made. One concern is that if there is too small a pool of adoptive applicants, birth parents may have limited choices about the most acceptable parents for them and their babies.

It is more than one hundred years since New Zealand passed its first adoption act. The past century has been one of challenge and change. Adoption in New Zealand today usually means an open placement where the adopted child will grow up being aware of, and possibly part of, two sets of parents and a wide extending family. The thirty years of adoption secrecy, as decreed by law from 1955 to1985, has been well overturned.

A new adoption era has begun.

# References

1. *Rights and Responsibilities.* International Year of the Family Committee, Wellington 1995, p.201. Butterworth's *Family Law Service,* Butterworth 1990

2. Mary

3. World Health Organisation, United Nations Environment Programme, the International Labour Organisation 1994. *Glyphosate.* Environmental Health Criteria No.159, Geneva, Switzerland

4. New Zealand Parliamentary Debates, 1979, p. 3522

5. Ludbrook, Robert. *Adoption - Guide to Law and Practice.* GP Publications, Wellington 1990, p.35

6. Unknown counsellor, USA 1992

7. Dalziel, Raewyn. *Focus on the Family - The Auckland Home and Family Society 1983-1993,* David Ling Publishing Limited for the Home and Family Society, Auckland 1993, p.12

8. Dalziel, Raewyn. Ibid, p.13

9. Else, Anne. *A Question of Adoption,* Bridget Williams Books Limited, Wellington 1991, p.25

10. Else, Anne. Ibid, p.25

11. Dalziel, Raewyn. *Focus on the Family - The Auckland Home and Family Society 1983-1993,* David Ling Publishing Limited for the Home and Family Society, Auckland 1993, p.53

12. Sandra Coney. *Standing in the Sunshine,* Penguin Books (NZ) Ltd, Auckland 1993, p.78

# Bibliography

Andry, Andrew C and Schepp, Steven. *How Babies Are Made.* Illustrated by Blake Hampton. General Learning Corp.1969. Time- Life International (Nederland) B.V.

Beaglehole, Ann. *Benefiting Women: Income Support for Women, 1893-1993.* Social Policy Agency from the Historical Branch of the Department of Internal Affairs, Wellington 1993

Dalziel, Raewyn. *Focus on the Family - The Auckland Home and Family Society 1983-1993*, David Ling Publishing Limited for the Home and Family Society, Auckland 1993

Else, Anne. *A Question of Adoption*, Bridget Williams Books Limited, Wellington 1991

Kornitzer, Margaret. *Mr Fairweather and His Family*, The Bodley Head Limited, London 1960.

Rockel, Jenny and Ryburn, Murray. *Adoption Today - Change and Choice in New Zealand.* Heinemann Reed, Auckland 1988

Rowe, Jane. *Yours By Choice - A Guide for Adoptive Parents*, Mills and Boon, London 1959

Saunders, E. *A Guide to Adoption in New Zealand*, A. H. & A.W. Reed, Wellington 1971